Command in the
Royal Naval Division

A Military Biography of
Brigadier General A. M. Asquith DSO

COMMAND
IN THE
ROYAL NAVAL
DIVISION

A MILITARY BIOGRAPHY OF
BRIGADIER GENERAL
A. M. ASQUITH DSO

by

Christopher Page

Foreword by Correlli Barnett

SPELLMOUNT
Staplehurst

British Library Cataloguing in Publication Data:
A catalogue record for this book is available
from the British Library

Copyright © Christopher Page 1999
Foreword copyright © Correlli Barnett 1999
Maps copyright © AMA papers

ISBN 1-86227-048-1

First published in the UK in 1999 by
Spellmount Limited
The Old Rectory
Staplehurst
Kent TN12 0AZ

1 3 5 7 9 8 6 4 2

Typeset in Palatino by MATS, Southend-on-Sea, Essex
Printed in Great Britain by
Biddles Ltd, Kings Lynn and Guildford

Contents

List of Maps

All maps are from the private collection of Arthur Melland Asquith, referred to as the AMA papers.

List of Plates

Preface

I have been a keen amateur naval historian ever since I can remember, but in 1977 a friend lent me a copy of Martin Middlebrook's book, *The First Day on the Somme*, an act which set me on a journey into the First World War, and in particular the Western Front. I became fascinated by the way the British Expeditionary Force performed: for the first and only time in our history, it fell to the British Army to bear the brunt of engaging the main forces of the enemy in a continental struggle. In this duty they succeeded, after a long and painful learning process, and at a human cost previously unknown to the people of our fortunate island; after all, history indicated that the 'British Way of War' consisted of maintaining a naval blockade and command of the sea, while our continental allies did the majority of the killing and dying on land; these allies were supported, if it suited us, by relatively small and efficient expeditionary land forces. The Great War changed all this: the British Army numbered a handful of divisions in 1914, yet by 1918 had grown to dozens, initially provided by volunteers, then by conscription. In a land not known for militarism, this transformation from relatively untrained amateurs to a citizen force which became master of the field in 1918, was remarkable. The performance of the Army varied from division to division: some, perhaps one third, were always excellent, and could be relied on to undertake the most arduous assignments; most of the others did not quite qualify to be designated 'elite' units, but performed creditably most of the time, and brilliantly occasionally; a very few won, and largely maintained, a less lofty reputation.

One of the crack formations which formed the spearhead of the BEF was the Royal Naval Division, an extraordinary unit, formed by Churchill at the beginning of the war to provide a maritime intervention force under naval control. The RND fought first at Antwerp and then Gallipoli. In 1916 it came to the Western Front where it spent the rest of the war. From the start, the Division attracted an interesting and unusual officer corps, initially many of them acquaintances of Churchill or his secretary, Edward Marsh. Apart from Arthur Asquith, they included: Rupert Brooke; Bernard Freyberg, who won the Victoria Cross in the Division, and went on to be Governor General of New Zealand; A. P. Herbert; F. S. Kelly, a musician who also held the record for the Diamond Sculls at Henley;

Charles Lister, scholar, and son of Lord Ribblesdale; William Denis Browne, musician, and critic for a national newspaper; Patrick Shaw Stewart, scholar and director of Barings at 25, and Vere Harmsworth, son of the newspaper proprietor, Lord Rothermere. The RND succeeded in maintaining its elite standing even after most of these stars had been killed or wounded, so lasting was their legacy. But the price of the RND being a 'stormer' unit is shown in the human cost: more than 11,000 killed and nearly 31,000 wounded. More than forty per cent of all RN casualties in the Great War were suffered, not at sea, but in the trenches, and more RN personnel were killed and wounded in action on land in the RND, than at sea in the Fleet.

While researching the personalities of the RND, the name of Arthur Asquith kept cropping up. The extent of my knowledge of him at that time was that he was the younger brother of Raymond, killed in action in 1916, and the third son of Herbert Henry Asquith, Prime Minister from 1908 until 1916. I quickly discovered that Arthur (nicknamed 'Oc') was an extraordinary character who merited further investigation and I contacted the Hon. Mary Rous, his eldest daughter.The assistance of the members of the family could not have been more willingly, honestly, or charmingly provided, and I was allowed complete access to the huge quantity of family papers. These cover Arthur's life from his time at private school until his untimely death at the age of only 56 in 1939. In particular, a unique find among Asquith's private papers was an officer's tin trunk, with the painted inscription *Commander AM Asquith, Hood Battalion RND*, full of material on his war service, including all his Field Service Notebooks, containing the carbon copies of the notes he had written; contemporary trench maps and other situation charts, some of which he had used in action; many other documents, some annotated in his own hand; personal effects, including his trench whistle and wallet, and previously unpublished photographs. A further priceless discovery was the unpublished diary of Lieutenant Commander F. S. Kelly, a friend and companion killed in action in 1916; the diary had been edited by Asquith, presumably with a view to publication. From these most detailed records I was able to build up a picture of the detailed workings of the Royal Naval Division.

The story which follows, therefore, tries to be a little more than a war biography of a hitherto largely unsung hero, by exploring the relationships between Asquith and his superiors and subordinates, and thereby drawing out some of the elements which contribute to exceptional leadership at platoon, company, battalion, and finally, brigade level, often in the most trying circumstances. In telling this tale I have made every attempt to retain an objective view of my subject, whose own modesty was extraordinary: on his death, reported in a lengthy *Times* obituary, many of the letters of condolence to his wife and daughters, even those from very close family friends, opened in the vein 'we never knew the scale of his wartime achievements, because he never spoke about them, nor allowed others to do so'.

My research has taken a long time, but it has been a true labour of love. The more I have delved into this period of our history, and the RND in particular, the more privileged I feel to have got to know Arthur Asquith, his friends and companions, and appreciate these extraordinary people in these remarkable times.

Christopher Page
Brussels
1999

Acknowledgements

In the six years it has taken me to research and write this book, I have been enormously gratified and delighted by the unstinting kindness of all those whom I have asked for help and advice. In particular, I am most grateful to Arthur Asquith's eldest daughter, Mrs Mary Rous, and her son, John, for their generous hospitality during my frequent visits to Clovelly, and for trusting me with a huge amount of treasured papers, and for permission to use them, without which the work could not even have been started. I have referred to this private collection as 'the AMA papers'. Discussions with Arthur's other three daughters, Mrs Susan Boothby, Mrs Christine Clarke, and Mrs Jean Toynbee, have also been vital in building up a true picture of their father. Others who offered their recollections of Asquith include Lord Oxford and Asquith, the late Lord Mark Bonham Carter, James Hore-Ruthven, Lady Beckett, Mrs Priscilla Hodgson, and Lady Chaplin.

I am also most grateful to the Hons. Mrs Virginia Brand and Ms Jane Bonham Carter for permission to use quotations from the papers and books of their grandmother, Violet Bonham Carter, Arthur's sister. Mark Pottle, who with Mark Bonham Carter edited Violet's diaries, has been of the greatest assistance and freely provided sage advice and encouragement.

Lady Freyberg's permission to look at and quote from the papers of her father-in-law, General Lord Freyberg, and from her husband's book, *Bernard Freyberg VC – Soldier of Two Nations*, as well her hospitality during my researches is greatly appreciated, as is the assistance of Lord Freyberg and Miss Annabel Freyberg.

Among the many others who have kindly granted me permission to use material for which they hold copyright are: Lord Oxford and Asquith, for the letters of Raymond Asquith; Milton Gendel, for the letters of Venetia Stanley; Mrs Juliet Daniel, for the letters of Venetia Stanley; Mrs Denise Boyes, for a letter from General Hubert Gough; the family of General Sir Ian Hamilton, for one of his letters; Sir Houston Shaw Stewart, for the letters of Patrick Shaw Stewart; Messrs Weidenfeld & Nicolson, for *Lantern Slides* and *Champion Redoubtable*; Mrs Elizabeth Davidson, for the letters and papers of Surgeon McCracken; Raymond Bonham Carter, for the letters of Maurice Bonham Carter; Mr Michael Asquith, for letters from Herbert Asquith and Cynthia Asquith; Captain Dougald Malcolm, for a letter from General Malcolm; Mrs A. White and Mr Iain Macmillan, for the papers of Thomas Macmillan; Mrs Priscilla Hodgson, for the letters and papers of Margot Asquith, and Mrs Jane Bonham Carter for the letters to Arthur from his father, Herbert Asquith.

I am indebted to the following for allowing me to examine or to quote from archive material in their possession: Peter Liddle and the Trustees of the Liddle Collection at Leeds, and to Peter himself for his invaluable help; The Trustees of the Liddell Hart Centre for Military Archives, King's College, London, with thanks to Kate O'Brien; the Trustees of the Imperial War Museum, and for the support of Nigel Steel, Peter Hart, Pauline Allwright, and Mark Moody; the Trustees and the Staff of the Bodleian Library; the Librarian and Staff of the Library of the Royal Naval College, Greenwich; the Staff of the Fleet Air Arm Museum, at Yeovilton, especially Mrs Jan Keohane; the Trustees of the Royal Marine Museum, and to Matthew Little; Caroline Dalton, archivist of New College, Oxford; Mr Patrick MacClure of the Friends of Winchester College; The Naval Historian, David Brown, and the Staff at the Naval History Branch, particularly Jock Gardner, John Claro, Mike MacAloon, Alan Francis, and Jenny Wraight.

I would like to thank the Staff at the Public Record Office at Kew for their unending patience during my many visits. The use of Crown Copyright material in the Public Record Office is by permission of The Stationery Office. Tim Padfield's prompt and helpful advice was significant. Every effort has been made to trace and obtain permission from copyright holders of material quoted or illustrations reproduced.

I gladly acknowledge the many other sources of material or advice not already mentioned. In this connection, I would single out John Terraine, with his unparalleled knowledge of the Great War, Colin Clifford for his extensive help, Mark Wight, of the Second Sea Lord's Office, Professor John Grigg, Dr Michael Brock and Mrs Brock, and Max Arthur. Also the assistance of the Royal Naval Division experts, Tony Froom and Trevor Tasker, whose knowledge is equalled only by Len Sellers, who, apart from allowing me permission to quote from his many publications, has been a key source of advice and help.

Other special people to whom I owe a huge debt include those who, out of friendship, acted as unpaid researchers: among these Professor David Syrett of Columbia University, New York, Mark Dembery, Alastair Knight, Anthony Langdon, Michael Day, Matthew Phillips, and Hugh Montgomery. Some of the many others who have offered practical help and sensible advice include Roy Adam, Peter Hamner, Bill Sharp, Ian Vosper, John Hussey, Jamie Adam, Paddy Griffith, Peter Hore, Patrick Cordingley, Kathy Stevenson, Leo Cooper, Professor Brian Bond, who set me off on this road, and Ray Westlake.

Finally, my particular appreciation is due to Correlli Barnett, for agreeing to write the Foreword, Tom Cutts, my publisher, Jamie Wilson, and David Grant, and my eternal gratitude to my wife Maureen, without whose support nothing could have been achieved, on paper, or in life.

Foreword

This biography of Arthur Asquith is rich in fresh and fascinating insights into the realities of front-line combat in the Great War – and no less into the nature of the British ruling class of the time, linked together by friendships and family connections, and sharing a common sense of duty and leadership. The insights are all the fresher because the book is based on a treasure-trove of Arthur Asquith's personal papers discovered by chance in a tin trunk in the office of the family estate in Devon after lying undisturbed for nearly sixty years. The collection comprises twenty-eight field service notebooks as well as diaries and correspondence with family, future wife, fellow officers, immediate superiors – and also persons in high places in government and military command. For the hero of Christopher Page's biography was the son of Herbert Asquith, Prime Minister from 1908 to 1916, and the man who led Britain into war against Imperial Germany in August 1914.

Arthur's elder brother Raymond, killed on the Somme in 1916, was to figure prominently in the later legend of 'the Lost Generation' of public-school subalterns who fell on the Western Front. Arthur himself, a survivor of the war despite being severely wounded four times, no less exemplified their virtues: patriotic faith in Britain's cause, selfless leadership, personal courage under the heaviest fire.

Yet Arthur's wartime service is the more interesting because he served in the trenches not as a soldier, but as a sailor in the Royal Naval Division. Christopher Page's biography therefore serves to cast important new light on this curious military hybrid, which later comprised infantry units and artillery from the Army as well as its core of naval battalions named after famous admirals. Its invention by Winston Churchill as First Lord of the Admiralty as a means of intervening in land operations explains why in October 1914 the newly joined Sub-Lieutenant Asquith found himself taking part in a vain attempt by the Division (lacking artillery and logistic support) to enable the Belgians to hold Antwerp against the advancing German army,

In 1915 the Royal Naval Division fought in the stalemated campaign on Gallipoli that followed the failure of Churchill's grand scheme of forcing the Dardanelles Straits; and Arthur's notebooks and diaries provide vivid new testimony about the futilities and horrors of trench warfare against the Turk on narrow, naked and sun-roasted hillsides. We learn afresh about the lack of such basic equipment as a solid pier at Helles for disembarking troops and stores, deep wells for clean drinking water and, when winter came, adequate winter clothing.

It was while serving with the Royal Naval Division on the Western Front in 1916 and 1917 that Arthur found his metier as a front-line leader: on the Somme in autumn 1916; on the Arras front in spring and summer 1917; in the appalling swamp-bound last phase of the Third Battle of Ypres (Passchendaele) in October and November that year; and on the Cambrai front in December, where a fourth wound (leading to the loss of a lower leg) ended his active service.

Christopher Page skilfully uses Arthur's notebooks and other papers to bring before us an officer cool-headed and tactically resourceful amid the chaos of trench-to-trench fighting; a man unflinchingly brave, caring of his men, quick to protest against orders which he believed could try them too far. As Arthur rises from sub-lieutenant to battalion commander and finally to brigade commander, we watch a civilian in uniform – and an army of civilians – fast becoming proficient at a new and terrible trade, and at the same time remaining staunch despite the steady loss of close comrades.

Christopher Page's fine study based on first-class new documentary evidence must be essential reading for all who are interested in the Great War – and especially for those who persist in representing the British fighting men on the Western Front as victims led by incompetents.

Correlli Barnett
1999

CHAPTER I
Beginnings

This is the story of a modest and moderate man. In some ways, his modesty was the more surprising in view of his antecedents. Arthur Melland Asquith was born on St George's Day, 23 April 1883, the third son of Herbert Henry Asquith, then a barrister starting out on his legal career. With the benefit of hindsight, it is tempting to say that the family was destined for a high position of influence and esteem, but this was by no means apparent in the 1880s. Herbert Asquith was the son of a middle-class Yorkshire businessman in the town of Morley. He was not quite 8 years old when his father, Joseph, died, and his mother, Emily, and her family had to rely on the support of generous relations. In 1863 Emily Asquith moved to the south coast, and her two sons, Herbert Henry and Willans, entered the City of London School, their education being paid for by their uncles. Cyril Asquith records that both of them repaid the monies lent for their schooling.[1]

Herbert rose steadily in the school, becoming school captain in 1869, then at 17 he won a classical scholarship to Balliol College, Oxford, where he shone as a brilliant scholar and developed a great interest in politics, debating with power and oratory, and becoming President of the Union. His first class degree was rewarded by a Fellowship of Balliol in 1874. Asquith had decided at Oxford that he would enter politics, and astutely realised that the profession of law would serve both as a source of income and provide an entrée into his chosen career. He became a student of Lincoln's Inn, being called to the Bar in 1876 aged 24.

In August 1877 he married Helen Melland, the daughter of a Manchester doctor, with whom he had been in love for many years. A devoted wife of self-effacing unworldliness, she bore him five brilliant children. Raymond (born in 1878); Herbert, known as 'Beb' (1881); Arthur, or 'Oc' (1883); Violet (1887), and Cyril, known as 'Cys' (1890). Herbert supplemented his income during the early years of his increasing family by any means open to him, including marking university examination papers, lecturing on the law, and eventually writing for *The Spectator* and *The Economist*.

Helen's small allowance helped tide over the young barrister until he began to win briefs, and then, in 1886 he took a big gamble and stood for the seat of East Fife in the General Election, which he won narrowly. In

1

Parliament in the early years he was an infrequent speaker, but gained a reputation as a formidable debater. In 1890 he took silk, and as a Queen's Counsel his income rose steadily. Jenkins estimates about £5,000 per year, a large salary, almost all absorbed by his family and professional responsibilities.[2] This figure is confirmed some years later in a letter from Arthur to his sister in April 1907, reporting that one of his guests asked whether his father was very rich, to which Arthur replied: '. . . not very. His pay was £5000 per year'.[3] This provides an interesting insight into the lack of any inflationary effect on salaries at the time, and the poor level of remuneration for Cabinet Ministers. In 1892 his talents were recognised by Gladstone, and Asquith became Home Secretary. His income as a barrister started to rise, and the future seemed secure.

Then in 1891 came a terrible blow: Helen Asquith died of typhoid aged only 35, after a family holiday on the Isle of Arran. The suddenness is revealed in the diary entries of her husband[4]: on 22 August she fell ill, and died on 11 September. Raymond was 13, Arthur 8, and Violet only 4. Herbert Asquith Senior bore the tragedy with stoicism. The family was famously, or infamously, austere in emotional matters. In fact, Cyril Asquith remarks on how the family was united by a 'powerful free-masonry' which bound them closely, but resulted in an 'unwritten taboo against emotional demonstration even of the mildest order',[5] at least among the men of the family, which, with the powerful intellects and personalities of those concerned, could lead to cutting invective. The family was described by Asquith's second wife as: 'Shy, critical, self-engaged, and controversial, nothing surprised them and nothing upset them . . . they were modest and emotionless . . . devoted to one another and never quarrelled . . . Perfectly self-contained, truthful and deliberate, I never saw them lose themselves in my life . . . I was stunned by the steadiness of the Asquith temper'.[6] There are many quoted stories on the Asquith dislike of show and what was seen as affectation; Raymond was particularly puritanical in this regard: his engagement to Katharine Horner was a very poorly kept secret among the family and their friends, but before the formal announcement, no one dared to offer con-gratulations to the happy couple. Raymond wanted to 'save Katharine from the coarse felicitations of maiden aunts when they speak of the great happiness that is in store for her'.[7] Later, in April 1907, Raymond wrote to Oc stating that the announcement of his engagement had little effect other than to release 'the pent up floods' of 'a sticky torrent of 5th rate sentiment and arch humour over many pages of writing paper.'[8]

The family were notoriously careless in following the norms of what were considered good manners at the time, although a friend of Herbert Asquith declared that, 'for an Asquith, Oc was good.'[9]

His political career affected Herbert's income from the law adversely, so that he was not financially much worse off when the Liberal Government was routed in the General Election of 1895, and he lost his salary as a Cabinet Minister. He was re-elected in his Scottish constituency with an increased majority against the national trend, but by now his expenditures had increased enormously, with four boys and a daughter to educate. In May 1894 he married the formidable Margot Tennant, whom he met shortly before Helen's death. Their friendship soon turned into love. She was a brilliant woman, the daughter of a partially self-made landowner from the border country. Her character was totally different from his: she could be captivating and inspiring, with a mercurial temperament and a sparkling wit. At first sight they were an incompatible couple: he was intellectual, indifferent to money, and with a strong inner strength; she a socialite, keen on hunting, and with a vivacious and outgoing personality. In a sense, they both took a risk in deciding to wed: Margot found herself with a ready-made family of five children, and Herbert with someone far different from his quiet, gentle, and unambitious first wife.

Margot brought a completely different social dimension to the Asquith family: she, and her sister Laura, were leading lights in the group known as the 'Souls', whose history has been brilliantly recorded.[10] They were an informal gathering of some of the best minds and most vivacious characters of the latter half of the nineteenth century, and included in their number politicians, such as George Curzon and Arthur Balfour among others; socialite hostesses, beautiful women, some decent and honourable men, plus the odd roué.

Meanwhile, school life went on for the Asquith children. For his preparatory education, Arthur went to Lambrook School, near Bracknell in Berkshire. From the start he was not a brilliant scholar. His Fourth Form reports show that he was in the lower half of the class of ten or eleven boys: his best subjects were drawing ('very good, neat') divinity ('very good'), mathematics (varying from 'very good' to 'now and then dull: sometimes good, slow at Euclid'), and English; his worst subjects were Latin and Greek ('weak' and 'industrious, elementary work very inaccurate'), and French ('very weak, more energy needed'). His head-master, Mr Mansfield, also his Classics teacher, found Arthur's work 'disappointing . . . yet I think he tries'. He made no allowance for his pupil's youth, a year younger than the average age of the class, but noted that the young Asquith was never late, and that his general conduct was excellent. His school work improved, and by the time he left Lambrook, Arthur was either second or third in the class.[11]

Arthur wrote every Sunday to his father in a neat, readable hand, as briefly as possible. His letters demonstrate a desire to please, and for parental approbation. He always closed with ' Your loving son, Arthur Asquith'. When he did well in class either at his studies, or, more frequently, on the sports field, he reported the fact: there were constant requests for small sums of money, asked for with great regret, in the realisation that funds were tight, and enquiries after Margot's health (she lost a baby in 1895). In August 1894, he wrote to her reporting a recent school trip abroad, summarising it in true schoolboy fashion: 'I went to Constantinople and enjoyed it awfully. It is very good'.[12]

In September 1896, at the age of 12, Arthur joined his brothers, Herbert and Raymond, now 17, at Winchester. The two younger boys saw Raymond regularly, and Arthur and Beb became quite close. Arthur joined Bramston's (nicknamed Trant's) division, one of the Commoners Houses, where he began to take golf seriously. His academic performance showed further improvement over Lambrook, and he wrote to his father that he was 21st in the scholarship papers, and in October 1896 he was placed 17th in a class of 21. His report indicated that he was doing well in all subjects, and the Headmaster is pleased with his 'capital progress'. By the end of the spring term in 1898, Arthur had improved to 12th of 19, and is being congratulated for his 'excellent Sophocles paper'.[13]

In December he wrote to his father: 'It is splendid Raymond getting senior scholarship at Balliol',[14] in a tone of genuine pleasure. His letters to his father from Winchester indicate that he was busily learning racquets, rowing, fishing, golf, cricket, rugby, fives and football. Notwithstanding, or perhaps because of, this concentration on sporting activities, he became a prefect in January 1900, duties which he judged 'not toilsome or laborious',[15] and for the first time signed himself 'Oc' in a letter, a nickname which would remain with him.

In his last year Arthur was made the Commoners' Head Boy of the College, and in the Michaelmas Term, 1902, he went up to New College Oxford as an Exhibitioner: not quite up to the academic excellence of his three brothers, perhaps, but still an achievement beyond the capability of most young men. As 'the least intellectual' of the five children of Asquith's first marriage (his father's assessment), he did not possess the academic ability of his brothers, all of whom went to Balliol, two of them, Raymond and Cyril, real stars; nevertheless, by the time he left Winchester, Oc had developed a felicitous touch with words, as evidenced in his correspondence, which he retained throughout his life.

As an Exhibitioner, he was exempted from Responsions, the preliminary entrance examinations, and is recorded as passing 'Holy Scripture' in October 1903. This may have been in some degree due to sanctions imposed on him by the College, for at a meeting of the Warden and Tutors on 26 June 1903, Arthur Asquith was one of five students reported to have failed in 'Holy Scripture' (Divinity). The retake was scheduled for September, and if he had failed he would have been 'gated for the first half of it (Michaelmas Term) at 9 pm.'[16] Among his circle of friends at New College was L S Montagu, the son of Baron Swathling, T C Gibson, who became a professional singer, and A B Lloyd-Baker, of Hardwicke Court, who won the DSO and was mentioned in despatches three times in the Great War. Gibson, Lloyd-Baker and Asquith started a club, 'The Puntsmen and Huntsmen', of which Asquith was the President, Gibson the Treasurer, and Lloyd-Baker the only member.[17] It appears that Asquith did not over-exert himself at Oxford: in his letters to Violet there are frequent references to an arduous social programme involving the consumption of champagne at Avon Tyrrell on his birthday,[18] a 'tremendous orgy' at a 'Fresher's Drunk', in which 'everyone was merry, but very few drunk', after many toasts of port.[19]

Back at Oxford, apart from the social side, Asquith seemed to be becoming progressively more disillusioned with university life. He confided to Violet in December 1903 that he had 'suddenly and sadly realised that I have just 3 months in which to make up for a year of idleness. And though I'm afraid I have no ambition to do well in my Exam in March (for it does not interest me), I think Father would probably be rather bored if I did disgracefully badly'.[20] He showed great indecision over a future career, and invited Violet to poll their friends for suggestions.[21] Arthur's need for revision did not prevent him travelling with Violet and his brother, Beb, to Dresden for a holiday in the New Year. It was here that Beb was to meet Cynthia Charteris, in the city as part of her 'finishing', who later became his wife.[22] Arthur's late surge in learning obviously had some effect, and he took a second class honours in Mods in the Lent Term of 1904. He chose not to complete his degree, and went down in April of that year to take up business. It was not unusual for people at this time to leave university before completing their final examinations.

In the summer of 1904 it was decided that Arthur would not follow Raymond and Beb into the Law, but that he should seek a career in the City.

> For this an understanding of French was considered essential, and in October 1914 Oc was sent to Paris to acquire the necessary skills, taking with him at his own request, his younger sister Violet. He was then twenty one, and she just seventeen. They were accompanied by Violet's maid, Janet, who was herself only nineteen. Apart from the condition that Violet must not go out alone, they were free of all parental restriction.[23]

Violet's relationship with her elder brother is well summed up in her diary entry for 17 October 1904. Having left Cavendish Square, her father's home in London, with no regrets, she was looking forward to the 'prospect of Paris and Artie (Oc) with whom Siberia would be Elysium.'[24] The time spent installing themselves in a suitable flat confirmed to her that:

> For sane, sound judgment and levelheadedness Oc surpasses anyone

I've ever met. He has the faculty of cutting himself & his personal prejudices loose & of looking on any question however near it may be to him, however entangled with his wishes his hopes or his fears, with as much coolness & impartiality as if he had been the man in the moon.[25]

They spent a most enjoyable and rewarding six months in Paris at an apartment in the rue Gay Lussac, and the following March visited friends in Italy, spending some time in Florence and Siena.

Arthur decided to take up a career in the Foreign Service, and returned to the University in the Trinity Term (April 1905), and spent some months learning Arabic. On completion, he was appointed to a post in the Egyptian Civil Service.

Following the establishment of an Anglo-Egyptian Condominium over the Sudan under the terms of the Anglo-Egyptian Agreement of 1899, the British adopted their customary role of colonial administrators. The Sudan Political Service established a reputation as an élite corps over the fifty years of its existence. Ninety per cent of its members were recruited from Oxbridge colleges. Kirk-Greene, quoted by Glen Balfour-Paul, reveals that about one quarter of the graduate entrants were College Blues, and half had first or second class degrees. Balfour-Paul also remarks that the group was distinguished by 'a rare degree of enthralment with the things they found themselves doing and with the length of the rope they were given to get on with doing them'.[26]

Towards the end of his time at Winchester, Arthur had become very close to the Manners family of Avon Tyrrell, Christchurch, near Bournemouth. Margot had been friendly with the family for many years on the social circuit in London, and in the hunting season in Rutland. Lord and Lady Manners ('Hoppy and Con') entertained a great deal, and they and their three daughters Molly, and the twins Angela and Elizabeth ('Betty' or 'Bet') were in demand socially. Arthur grew very close to the whole family, initially at least because of a deep friendship, which developed into love, with Molly, who tragically died at the age of 17 while on holiday in India. Molly's death was a particularly painful blow for both Arthur and Violet. He wrote to Violet about the effect that the tragedy was having on his religious convictions, which he was afraid would not be of any help to his grieving sister:

> they have long been very unsatisfactory, and are even more so now. I'm not sure that I really have any at all, as they are in a constant state of flux between my instinct and my reason.[27]

Arthur and Con, Molly's mother, were particularly attached to each other.

In 1907 Arthur noted in his Sudan diary that 'Con had been my mother for six years'.[28] In the autumn of 1905 Arthur spent a week with the Manners at Avon, which he reported to Violet in fulsome terms, 'alone with their ideal family . . . the forest was at its loveliest'. He enthuses about their 'usual delightful life . . . long rides in the forest, treecutting, and reading aloud in the evenings. Yesterday we shot 53 brace of partridges, and 24 hares . . . Katharine [soon to marry his brother Raymond] was in very good form . . . You can't think what it is to come back to civilisation, to a habitable house like Avon, after the hideous squalor and tame scenery of Rothes.'[29] Through the Manners, Arthur got to know the formidable Christine Hamlyn, Con's sister, who owned and administered the estate of Clovelly in Devon. His free time therefore was divided between London, Avon Tyrrell and Clovelly, and the other places where 'The Children of the Souls' gathered.[30]

On leaving for the Sudan, Arthur's farewells were touching, and out of keeping with the normal image of reserved self-control for which the family was noted. He left Rothes, in North Berwick, the holiday home, after saying goodbye to his family, except for Raymond who was staying with a man called Dankwerts, described by Oc as a 'nineteen stone KC who had sat on his razor on his honeymoon, and shot a man who had spiked his motor car tyres'.[31] Arthur recollected:

> The three worst moments were first when Violet gave me a hug in her bedroom on Friday morning and broke down entirely: then shaking hands with my Father in the hall after lunch – we had a little talk in the billiard room before, neither of us venturing beyond money matters and banalities . . . he was nearly crying. Finally, Margot Violet and Eliz. came to see me off and I kissed them – Margot and Eliz. hugged me passionately and tearfully, and I should have choked before I saw their backs huddling away in the sunshine, if Violet hadn't been very brave, and cold and stiff.[32]

After Arthur had left, his father wrote him a short note:

My dear Oc,
    Just a line to tell you how much were are all missing you, and wishing you every kind of luck and happiness in your work and life.
    I have always had and have the most perfect confidence in you.
Ever yr loving
Father.[33]

On the same day Margot wrote, referring to an intimate talk that she and Arthur had had previously, and revealed her apprehension at the forthcoming birth of her child:

7

1. Copy of a letter from Herbert Asquith Snr to Arthur Asquith dated 11 Sep 1906, shortly after Arthur has gone to the Sudan. *Private Papers*

My darling boy,
It was with a very sad heart I left you at the station for what seems such a long time. Partings when one is very young are less severe – human nature is recuperative . . . I rather feel with George Eliot that in each parting there is a shadow of death. Little Elizabeth's eyelashes were clotted with tears tho' she was sound asleep when I got to bed. She feels things very deeply I never saw a small child with so much feeling: that is why I spoke to you in the heavenly motor drive & said if anything happens to me at the end of Dec. or early Jan. I trust to you more than anyone after your father to look after the children. I think that you wd. see that E's many love affairs she is sure to have shall be guarded and watched . . . .

as yr. ever true and loving,
Margot

You have always been most dear and considerate with me and I value yr. love, so don't forget me.[34]

Arthur stopped first in London to pack and to write to friends. 'Never was anyone so laden with love and gifts at his departure I am sure: and I felt and feel humiliated and proud and overwhelmed by so much affection and kindness.'[35]

He then travelled to Avon Tyrell, where some of the Charteris family were also staying. After dinner, Arthur, who was 'panting for an intimate talk with Con, or an educational discourse with Bet,'[36] was 'tactfully left for a starlight walk with C', presumably Cynthia Charteris.[37] The next day Katharine Horner arrived, and at sunset she and Arthur walked for a while and talked of Molly. Arthur reveals that he had 'always been faintly jealous of her [Katharine] as the intimate confidante of all her [Molly's] secrets: whereas for me she was then and is now mainly 'le vague elle de tous les volumes de vers' as Flaubert says.[38]

In the margin, in pencil, dated Jan 07 at Omdurman, Arthur elaborates:

This is only part of the truth. Volumes of verse have never meant very much to me. Her [Molly's] companionship and friendship and the thought of her meant more than any I have ever known before or since. She was real, healthy, human, thoughtful, interested, and introspective.
So when she speaks, the voice of heaven I hear;
So when we walk, nothing impure comes near;
Each field seems Eden, and each calm retreat
Each village seems the haunt of holy feet[39]

On the morning of his departure, Arthur, Betty, Laura Lister, John

9

Manners, and Francis Horner swam at Highcliffe in the spitting rain, before Arthur left for London to catch the 11 pm P & O express from Victoria.

After he had left for the Sudan, Con, Lady Manners, wrote to him that she had

> . . . been so miserable since you left thinking how I wasted those few precious minutes that I had with you . . . when there are such <u>thousands</u> of things like I longed to say and do long [sic]- I knew that both of us were on the verge of breaking down, & somehow it has become so part of our daily life to dread tears that we all of us waste <u>precious</u> opportunities that may <u>never</u> come again by such futility. I am weeping as I write when I think of all the love and tenderness and fun that has gone out of our daily life with you.[40]

Arthur boarded the SS *Arabia* at Marseilles on 14 September 1906, and the passengers were treated to the sight of Stromboli erupting. It was the highlight of the voyage, as Asquith complained to his sister that the itinerary seemed to have been planned to avoid the better sights, passing between Sicily and Corsica in the pitch darkness.[41] He passed six days in Cairo, being subjected to 'interminable interviews at the War Office where the officials seemed to have plenty of time to waste although they only work for half the day',[42] and he spent some time sightseeing. He then moved on and spent 'two delightful days at Luxor, starting before sunrise each morning and making long expeditions on racing donkeys to temples more or less ruined three thousand years old and gorgeous tombs . . . the ruins of Karnak are the most overwhelmingly impressive thing I have ever seen'.[43] He reached Khartoum, after a thirty-hour trip on a Nile steamer from Aswan to Wadi Halfa, the frontier town on the Sudan border, and a nightmarish twenty-eight-hour journey of 'almost intolerable heat and dust by train from Halfa',[44] on 30 September 1906.

Asquith found himself one of eight Oxbridge men, 'the newly joined Deputy Inspectors, regarded individually with tolerance, collectively with disapproval' as a result of their predecessors' independent spirits, and was met by a 'big gun called Slatin . . . a squat common-looking little man with a kindly shifty "mine de fouine" [weasel face]' who lectured them on tact in dealing with natives, which caused a little resentment, his talk being commonplace in content, and delivered in 'Austrian English'.[45] Asquith assessed the other new arrivals 'quite good fellows all of them – nothing subtle, speculative, or very sympathique [sic] about any of them except C.S.M. – Colin Scott-Moncrieff',[46] against a photograph of whom in the diary is the note in Asquith's hand, 'On P&O steamer coming out. Colin Scott-Moncrieff asleep. Murdered by Abdel Kadir at Katfiya May 1908'.[47] The newcomers had to pair off for duties, and Asquith found himself with Thomas Leach, a Wykehamist and 'a very good fellow'[48] with whom he got on well.

Very soon after his arrival in the Sudan, Arthur suffered from depression at the thought of the career he had adopted, the lack of sufficient work, the damp oppressive climate, and the frequent 'huboobs' (sandstorms), made worse by the lack of correspondence from home. He wrote to Violet:

> There should be some quarantine in this sort of place to save one from the contagion of mental flatness and lethargy. I have felt its drowsy numbness creeping over me with stealthy stride from day to day; and can well understand how Anglo Indians and dwellers in hot and distant lands are so hospitable, and how they must welcome the stimulant of every newcomer. The authorities behaved very stupidly in bringing us out here this month. It is absolutely the deadest month of the year as far as work is concerned . . . so we sit and yawn from 9 – 2.45 every morning . . .
>
> Three mornings a week we are drilled by Quarter Master Sergeant Fridlington! This is that we may be able if necessary to take command of police, and may know the native words of command.[49]

As an indication of the general lack of family finances, in his postscript he reminds his sister that letters from England to the Sudan are only a penny rather than twopence halfpenny, the normal rate.[50] By the following day the gloom had departed, and he requested a hair-brush, and informed Violet that he was 'a rich man now; prospective horseowner!'[51]

He and Leach messed with their boss, a Major Phipps, which they found unstimulating;

> Middle-aged soldiers have a conventional sense of humour of no great price, and a narrative style of conversation peculiar to themselves. My host is no exception to this rule. His monologues at meals are like the Khartoum golf-course, long and flat and sandy: and one is often inclined to break one's clubs across one's knee in the bunkers of his self-complacency.[52]

At first, Asquith was attached to the office of the Governor of Khartoum, under the control of the Deputy Governor, who had little work for them, other than to assist at the occasional trial of 'weird creatures' who appeared before Asquith in his capacity as a first-class magistrate. Asquith was also employed in the Mosquito Brigade, where he spent about one and a half hours daily testing the water of wells and stagnant pools. If larvae were found, an attendant servant poured petrol on the water, which prevented them from forcing their trunks through the film thus formed, and suffocating them. He wrote that the malarial mosquito had been practically stamped out in Khartoum by these means. At this time he also requested his father that his overdraft be transferred to the Khartoum Branch of the Bank of Egypt, confiding that he hoped to be able to live on his pay once he had settled in to the job. He recorded that his salary was £420 per year increasing by £60 every two years. At the same time, he was receiving a small allowance from home.[53]

There were social functions, notably a dance at the hotel, attended by ten English women and 'about thirty English officers looking absurdly like the male chorus that comes rollicking on to the musical comedy stage'. Also the new trainees were able to take a few days' leave for hunting and exploring the countryside, although an inability to make camels kneel for mounting and dismounting made life difficult.[54]

From an early stage, Arthur grew to dislike Khartoum, which he perceived as 'hideously European, crammed with Government officials and Greeks'. At the first opportunity in his training programme, therefore, he opted for transfer to Omdurman, described as 'six miles of straggling mud huts, only three European houses', where he arrived in December. He was accommodated in the Mahdi's house, not as grand as it sounds; a photograph in Asquith's private papers reveals that it consists of a very modest building on one floor, with a rickety verandah on one side.

> This house is next door to the Mahdi's tomb: it is one story high, built of mud-bricks; the floor is hard mudcoloured sand, the walls inside sandcoloured mud, and the roof palm-matting. There is a sand compound outside with a few mud huts dotted about where the Mahdi's wives and retainers used to live: no tree nearer than Khartoum, and no attempt at furniture except the beds, tables and chairs without which one never moves here. This is a great come down from the luxurious bungalow of 'Phippsey Bey' in the way of comfort, but the life here is infinitely preferable. At last one sees something of the natives, and almost all one's work is in the open air.[55]

His duties initially consisted mainly of trying petty cases, involving slavery, land, and drink; these he enjoyed, but office administration, which he undertook as a necessary chore, he found less inspiring.[56] The newly arrived Deputy Inspectors, as they were titled, also had the task of assessing the levels of rent for each of the 28,000 houses in the town. Asquith reported ruefully: 'By house you must understand, one story of mud kneaded with the hands into a habitable shape, roofed – usually with matting, and surrounded by a compound inhabited by donkeys, goats and camels. The interiors are more primitive than any Bible illustration.'[57]

While serving in Omdurman, he received news from Margot that she had lost the baby she was expecting. A moving letter is revealing of Arthur's tender feelings for his stepmother: 'It does seem bitterly hard that the central object to which you have devoted months of energy and hope and passionate cares and pain should be perfected only to be shattered. Knowing that there are greater happinesses does not make one discontented with lesser ones: and it is poor comfort when one is smarting to know that worse things might have befallen'.[58] This letter also contains the first reference in correspondence to his family of Betty Manners. Oc tells Margot that the Manners are caught up in Betty's forthcoming debut, a fact which he has learned from Con, Lady Manners, with whom he regularly corresponds. In the same letter he reveals for the first time some feeling for Betty, saying that she 'breathes affection and admiration as a pleasant atmosphere, quite absentmindedly'.[59]

Asquith stayed on in Omdurman after his initial training period, getting on well with his immediate boss, a Captain Young, while complaining of his failure to devolve responsibility, and his secretiveness. Arthur particularly liked the gentle, cooling desert winds and the low humidity. His responsibilities now included the Land Commission, which brought him into touch with interesting people, including Dervish Emirs, sons of the Mahdi, and with others who had been with Gordon during the siege.

While at Omdurman he won the Sirdar's medal for golf and commented to his father, 'What a providential disposition it is that you should have one son to fling nothing but laurels at your feet – pure modest greenery to hide from the public gaze the scarlet police court seedlings with which your other children embarrass your goings!'[60]

In these early months of 1907 Arthur developed an affection for the Sudan which was never to leave him. The colonial authorities had realised that Omdurman was booming, and had granted money for many local improvements to roads, water, and buildings. Because of absences on leave, Arthur found himself the Sub Governor, 'despatching a large number of civil and criminal cases every day with a minimum of knowledge of procedures'.[61] He sent his father a locally made golf bag of such extravagant design that he estimated it would 'lose him [his father]votes if used in Fife'. At about this time Asquith was involved in an exploit which he categorised as 'an ill-timed expenditure of flamboyancy' reported in the local Press:

On Monday at 1000, fire broke out in a house and wood store belonging to some people near the English Girls' School in Omdurman. Flames reached the school. All the furniture and household effects were brought out. Were it not for the zeal of the police and soldiers under the command of Mr Asquith and Ahmad Effendi Darwish and Aziz Effendi Fahmi, the fire would have spread and caused great damage because the wind was blowing strongly.

Onlookers were astonished at Mr Asquith's zeal and energy in fighting the fire. He attacked it several times at the risk of his life and was seen to jump from the highest roof of the school to the ground, a height of not less than twenty feet.[62]

His courage and daring earned him no thanks from his superiors: their one wish was to be rid, without compensation, of some 'scrubby shops and market huts near which the fire occurred',[63] so that they could be rebuilt.

He had bought himself a pony (for £11), and had taken up polo, which he attempted to play twice a week. His other major recreation was shooting, particularly sand grouse, which were plentiful by the river a few miles from Omdurman.

Like most young men, Asquith was occasionally overcome by home-sickness and doubt as to the value of the work he was doing: the first serious time of doubt and depression occurred in March 1907. He confided to his diary:

Health and a clean conscience and open air alone are not enough for my happiness and peace of mind. The transition from theory to practice is painful. Romance at first hand is often prosaic, sometimes squalid. My work is that of a land-agent: my interests and inclinations are at an opposite pole. In my heart of hearts I cannot help feeling that a training of character which involves cramping natural aptitudes to exstinction [sic] in such narrow boots must be a mistake. I have been trying hard to pretend that I am enjoying my profession. I have tired myself out physically day after day in unacknowledged fear of letting myself think. I have written reams of cheerful correspondence to blind others and myself. Is it merely the mill through which I should have to go in any profession? Is it the homesick weakness against which I believed myself to be fully armed?

If I had the courage, after such a fuss had been made at my departure, to go back, to say I had chosen the wrong profession, and try another, should I be able in any other to do as much good to my fellow creatures, keep the flesh under control, and be happier? Or should I always look back wistfully from a miasma of mammon upon my time here and wonder how I could have been discontented with sun and moon, brave free winds, and first-hand dealings with the little cares and tragedies of men?

Shall I have the desire and courage to give it up a year hence? and if so shall I spend all my life falling in love with people far too good for me: and philandering thro' vanity with others, but not letting myself go wholeheartedly with these, because they do not satisfy my ideal, – an ideal which will always plague me without giving me the energy to make myself worthy of those who do satisfy it?

Dieu disposera.[64]

The full entry has been quoted because of its insights into Arthur Asquith's character, and as an example of his literary style. It was not in his nature to remain down for long, and he soon recovered. In May he undertook his first long camel trip. His companion was R G More, a contemporary of Raymond's at Oxford, a cricketer for Middlesex, and five years a civil servant in the Sudan. The gloriously cool weather and difficult camels provided 'just enough discomfort to make one enjoy the many comforts one takes with one.'[65] In this case More brought 'six tins of pheasant with truffles, tinned fruits of all sorts, and a boar's head. These with an extensive cellar which I have provided go far towards making the dry places a standing spring.' The menu for one of the evening meals was lentil soup, minced guinea-fowl, cotelettes d'agneau aux petis pois, stewed pears, champagne, port, & coffee.[66]

During his time in the Sudan, Arthur kept up his correspondence, particularly with Betty and her mother, Con. To the latter he wrote revealing his innermost thoughts, reassuring her that there was nothing between himself and Cynthia Charteris, who later married his brother Beb. In a revealing passage he says, 'It sounds like an insult to say you are not in love with a beautiful woman friend . . . she is a good, loyal, generous creature and I think her very pretty'. Using a quotation from George Eliot, he informed Con that his friendship for Cynthia was, 'I'm afraid a friendship of Chinese lanterns and glass panels, – in crowds on the ice in Dresden: and my most constant and agreeable partner at routs, balls and water parties last July: and in desultory joking dispassionate correspondence since I have been out here'.[67]

His absence confirmed his growing love for Betty. Arthur believed, however, that his feelings were not returned, although he noted that when Bet came to see him off at the station for his final departure, he thought he 'saw for the first time a glimmering of emotion in Betty's lovely passionless eyes as we shook hands for the last time'. His dealings with her up to this point in his life seem to have been restricted to discussion of the finer literary points of classic works of English literature; Betty was 'splendidly keen about educating herself, and . . . utterly indifferent to my "solicitous amiability" '. Arthur maintained to his diary that he was not in love with her, but that her 'coldness and beauty fascinate me'.[69] But by May, having been abroad for over six months, he opened his heart to Con and revealed that 'your Bet attracts me more than any living being', something he did not feel able to say to Betty herself. He also observed that the four people who matter most in his life at this time are Con, his father, Beb, and Violet.[70]

It was the spring of 1909, after he had been in the Sudan for about eighteen months, before Asquith had any home leave. Towards the end of his time in England, Violet opened her heart to him over Hugh Godley, later the second Baron Kilbracken, a long-term admirer. Unfortunately, it was all too late as Arthur had to catch the boat train to return to the Sudan. In a letter written on the SS *Arabia*, he revealed the closeness of his relationship with his sister. He wrote:

> Dearest Violet, It was sad leaving you just when I thought that I might be of some use to you. I ought to have invited your confidence before: but I was blind: the possibility of you regarding Hugh in a new light had not occurred to me. Please don't be put off if I seem to lay down the law in what I am going to say: the intention is only to give you my personal opinions and impressions for what they are worth.
>
> I understood from you that you thought of him as a possible husband because he had been in love with you for four years; and because he was the best companion you knew; and because you had not met anyone who stirred you to any deeper feeling than this. You were sorry for him: you despaired of meeting anyone who might fall in love with yourself . . .

Arthur went on to stress that any such match 'would be only a second-best sort of marriage when you are only twenty two'. He continued:

> But surely you have the same sort of ideals of marriage as me. In it you would like to find a background of quiet and simplicity against which the real values of things would shine clear: and in a husband surely you would like to find a rock to build your house on: someone who would never allow the line of least resistance in important things: a man of broad humanity, not glib, but understanding; one in whose courage and character and sense of honour and of proportion you could have implicit reliance: one who could guide your energies into right channels and help you to see all things clearly and in proportion, if in the glare and turmoil you lost your bearings or your vision became blurred. I can imagine that the man I have described so imperfectly might be superficially unromantic compared to Hugh: and – don't be offended at this – that unless you were thrown with him constantly or in trying circumstances, you might be inclined – at your present age – to sum him up and dismiss him in two or three epithets, bearing possibly on superficial characteristics – not because you are incapable of appreciating qualities of the sort I have described, but because I think your, as everyone else's, <u>every day</u> criterion for judging people must result from your every day atmosphere: and your every day atmosphere is social not domestic: and <u>in practise,</u> [sic] in a social atmosphere, Liberty scarves are bound to have it over homespun, and Wit over Worth.

He concluded by saying that for these, and other reasons, Hugh was not the man for Violet, however worthy he might be.

16

I would not give interfering advice of this sort, if I did not feel I was right: I feel all the surer because I know Father agrees with me. . . . This letter reads shockingly: remember it is well meant.

Your loving Oc.[71]

Violet did not marry Hugh, and in the winter of 1910/11 made the trip to the Sudan to visit her brother for a round of tourist visits to the areas for which Arthur had responsibility, with frequent dinner parties at the homes of the more senior expatriates. Immediately after her return on 22 January, Arthur began to plan a hunting expedition with a friend, Robin Buxton.

They caught the train from Khartoum on 1 February 1911, arriving at Sennar, the southern limit of the railway, to pick up their baggage and transport animals, after eleven hours in the train. To Arthur's slight surprise, they found all the animals waiting: to give some idea of the scale of this expedition, Buxton took a pony, a donkey and six camels; and Asquith a pony, a mule, six baggage camels, and one riding camel. Each was accompanied by native servants: one of Buxton's five, Safil, had only two days before the expedition been in prison for a stabbing offence. This was deemed suitable evidence of his prowess with a knife for him to be appointed 'skinner in chief'. Asquith's team of three included one Farlel Mula, 'at his best on journeys, like this, out of reach of the beer shops'. In addition there were five camel men and three trackers, one of whom was an old man called Ahmed Idris, about whom Arthur noted:

No disciple sent forth to preach the gospel in Judaea could have made less preparations for the way than did Ahmed Idris for a journey which may last a month. His complete outfit is a knife, a pair of shoes, a pair of drawers, a white body wrap: and his donkey.

They were in friendly competition with a rival Italian expedition, which had set out at the same time for the same purpose. They dined together the first night at which Buxton

told the story of an ostrich he had taken home with him to England: how it escaped at midnight at the railway station at Alexandria and led him a chase down the line towards Cairo: how he had caught it, and entered an Alexandria hotel at 2 am pushing it before him to the consternation of the hall porter: and locked it in the bedroom next to his where it ate the sheets and most of the looking glass: and how it finally expired at Tilbury Docks of a surfeit of clinker.

The first few days yielded only game birds, but soon, after a stalk in the blackened cinders of burnt grass, Asquith shot a striped gazelle. A couple of days later, he stalked a large female buffalo and her grown calf. Eventually he managed to bring down the bigger animal, but was reluctantly forced to shoot the smaller as it was about to charge. The next evening Asquith was woken by the sound of a shot, and the impression of a bullet whistling over the foot of his bed. The cook had woken to find a leopard's face within a foot of his own: he had scared the beast off with a shot. The following night the unfortunate animal returned, but this time Asquith and Buxton were waiting: both fired practically simultaneously, and the beautiful creature fell dead, 'like a pail full of water emptied on the ground'. The expedition was not so successful again, and they eventually arrived at Disa, nearly three weeks after setting out from Khartoum, and 'had baths, and slept.'[72]

Arthur retained close links with some of the local administrators with whom he had worked in the Sudan: in 1912 he received a letter in England, in Arabic from El Tahir El Haq Arabi, written in fulsome tones of praise, and offering a gift of five different types of dates.[73] Asquith maintained the links with the effusive El Tahir. In October 1917 he received an even more extraordinary note:

To his Excellency the generous, the son of the generous, the pride of the nation, and the beautiful jewel of history, Mr Asquith the son of the Prime Minister of the Empire of Great Britain, whom God may grant shall continue always to enjoy wearing the robes of honour and glory.

With every respect I have to submit to the exalted honour of your glory the most profound respects, and to count myself highly honoured because you deign to call me one of your acquaintances – I your servant El Tahir El Haq Arabi of the Sudan who had been honoured at the zenith of his luck to know you some years ago when you were our Inspector at Omdurman. I can never forget those happy days which were passed under you. I shall always boast and be proud among all my countrymen of having known one of the most distinguished men of Great Britain, nay rather the most priceless pearl in the crown of a kingdom the flag of which waves over us and allows us to enjoy justice and prosperity. We shall always be indebted to the British nation who have saved us, our sons, and our country from the hands of tyrants, and handed us over to prosperity, justice, liberty and equality, things of which neither we nor our father or forefathers before us ever dreamed that we should enjoy. You have given us to drink of the sweet fountain of knowledge by opening schools to educate our sons, and opened for us the way to go forward. For all this we can give you nothing back in return except what a poor man can give his generous benefactor, ie pray to the Almighty God to grant you continuous victory, and that the glory of your nation shall continue to exist so long as heaven is over Earth and day after night.

I am so grateful to you Excellency because you still remember one of your humble slaves who was so greatly honoured by the receipt of your letter dated at London on 23 March 1917. The greatest pleasure has your letter created in my heart and I was also pleased to know that my humble presents of dates and crocodile skin were received by you. It is a great honour you confer on me by deigning to accept them. It is my worth that I present to you not yours, for if I were to present you with your worth the whole world would be too little.[74]

After this introduction, the main purport of the letter, consisting of a report on the situation in the Sudan, takes up only another twelve lines. Even when allowances are made for the customary Arab hyperbole, it is difficult to escape the conclusion that Arthur made a deep impression on El Tahir.

Having left the Civil Service, Arthur took up employment with a company called Franklin and Herrera, which had extensive interests in South America. In August, therefore, he found himself on the SS *Amazon* en route for Buenos Aires. He much enjoyed the passage: 'a delightful voyage . . . with no obligations of acquaintanceship, but every facility for scraping it where the flower promises honey: and glorious opportunities for book reading, and Spanish lessons'.[75]

Asquith enjoyed his time with the company, and travelled all over the region while learning his trade.

NOTES

1. Spender JA and Asquith, Cyril: *The Life of Herbert Henry Asquith, Lord Oxford and Asquith*, Hutchinson 1932, p3.
2. Roy Jenkins, *Asquith*, William Collins, paperback edition, 1988, p50.
3. Letter from AMA to Violet Asquith dated 19 April 1907. The Violet Bonham Carter Manuscripts, henceforth referred to as the VBC MSS, Archive No 0032/028.
4. Spender and Asquith, p73.
5. ibid, p222.
6. Margot Asquith, *Autobiography*, quoted in Jenkins, p80.
7. Letter from Lady Constance Manners to AMA, inserted into his Sudan diary, dated 11-14 April 1907. AMA papers.
8. Letter from Raymond Asquith to AMA, 29 April 1907. AMA papers.
9. *Asquith's Letters to Venetia Stanley*, edited by Michael and Eleanor Brock, Oxford University Press, 1985, p376.
10. See *The Unquiet Souls* by Angela Lambert, Macmillan,1984.
11. All references to Arthur's reports are drawn from the documents in the AMA private papers.
12. Letter from AMA to Margot Asquith dated 22 September 1894, AMA papers.
13. Winchester School report, Spring Term 1898, AMA papers.
14. Letter from AMA to his father dated 1 December 1896, AMA papers.
15. Letter from AMA to his father dated 28 January 1900, AMA papers.
16. From the 'Minutes of Meeting of the Warden and Tutors, Jan 16th 1902 – Oct

4th 1922'. New College Archives. I am grateful to Dr Mark Pottle for this information.

17. *A Gloucestershire Diarist,* by Lieutenant Colonel A B Lloyd-Baker, Thornhill Press, 1993, p28, entry for 29 April 1903.
18. Letter from AMA to Violet Asquith dated 25 April 1909, some of which bemoans the apparent lack of interest taken by the family in Arthur's 19th birthday. VBC MSS No 0032/007.
19. Letter from AMA to Violet Asquith dated 21 October 1902, VBC MSS No 0032/008.
20. Letter from AMA to Violet Asquith dated 3 December 1903. VBC MSS No 0032/009.
21. Letter from AMA to Violet Asquith dated 21 October 1902. VBC MSS No 0032/008.
22. Cynthia Asquith: *Haply I May Remember,* James Barrie in 1950, p226.
23. Lantern Slides: *The Diaries and Letters of Violet Bonham Carter 1904-1914*, edited by Mark Bonham Carter and Mark Pottle, Weidenfeld and Nicolson, 1996, p1.
24. ibid.
25. ibid, p5.
26. *The End of Empire in the Middle East* by Glen Balfour-Paul, Cambridge University Press, 1991.
27. Letter from AMA to Violet Asquith dated 6 March 1904, VBC MSS No 0032/013.
28. AMA's Sudan diary, entry for 1 May 1907.
29. Letter from AMA to Violet Asquith dated October 1905, from the family house in Cavendish Square. VBC MSS No 0032/014.
30. See *The Children of the Souls* by Jeanne MacKenzie, published by Chatto and Windus in 1986. This account of the fortunes of the offspring of the group known as the 'Souls' is subtitled 'A Tragedy of the First World War'. All were enormously affected by the war: most of the men were either killed or wounded.
31. AMA Sudan diary, entry for 14 September 1906.
32. ibid.
33. Letter from HHA to AMA, dated 11 September 1906 inserted into the Sudan diary.
34. Letter from Margot Asquith to AMA, dated 11 September 1906, and inserted into the Sudan diary.
35. AMA Sudan diary, entry for 14 September 1906.
36. ibid.
37. ibid.
38. ibid.
39. ibid.
40. Extract of a letter from Lady Constance Manners to AMA dated 19 September 1906, inserted into the Sudan diary.
41. Letter from AMA to Violet Asquith on board SS *Arabia* dated 16 September 1906. VBC MSS No 0032/18.
42. AMA Sudan diary, entry for 4 October 1906.
43. Letter from AMA to Violet Asquith dated 28 September 1906, VBC MSS No 0032/019.
44. AMA Sudan diary, entry for 4 October 1906.
45. Letter from AMA to HHA dated 2 November 1906, AMA papers.
46. AMA Sudan diary, entry for 17 September 1906.
47. AMA Sudan diary, entry for 14 September 1906.
48. Letter from AMA to Violet Asquith dated 16 November 1906, VBC MSS No 0032/021.

49. Letter from AMA to Violet Asquith dated 7 October 1906, VBC MSS No 0032/20.
50. ibid.
51. ibid.
52. Letter from AMA to Violet Asquith dated 16 November 1906. VBC MSS No 0032/021.
53. Letter from AMA to his father, 1 January 1907, AMA papers.
54. Letter from AMA to HHA dated 24 November 1906, AMA papers.
55. Letter from AMA to Violet Asquith dated 11 December 1906. VBC MSS No 0032/023.
56. ibid.
57. ibid.
58. Letter from AMA to Margot Asquith dated 22 January 1907, AMA papers.
59. ibid.
60. Letter from AMA to HHA date 9 March 1907, AMA papers.
61. Letter from AMA to HHA dated 16 April 1907, AMA papers.
62. Cutting from *The Sudan* newspaper of 6 June 1907, in Arabic, AMA papers.
63. Letter from AMA to HHA dated 25 July 1907, AMA papers.
64. AMA Sudan diary, 23 March 1907.
65. AMA Sudan diary, 16 May 1907.
66. ibid.
67. Transcript of a letter from AMA to Lady Manners in AMA Sudan diary, entry for 1 May 1907.
68. AMA Sudan diary, 14 September 1906.
69. ibid.
70. AMA Sudan diary, entry for 1 May 1907.
71. Letter from AMA to Violet Asquith dated 18 July 1909, VBC MSS No 0036/006 quoted at length as it shows the closeness of his relationship to his sister, and gives an insight into his standards for judging people. The relationship between Hugh Godley and Violet is well explored in *Lantern Slides: The Diaries and Letters of Violet Bonham Carter*.
72. The whole of this portion is taken from a pencil diary, in AMA's hand, of a shooting expedition in the Sudan, February 1911, in AMA papers.
73. Letter from El Tahir El Haq Arabi, dated December 1912, in AMA papers.
74. Letter from El Tahir El Haq Arabi to AMA, in Arabic, dated 7 October 1917, AMA papers.
75. Letter from AMA to Violet Asquith dated 30 August 1911, VBC MSS No 0036/007.

CHAPTER II

1914: Arthur Asquith Joins Up

In Arthur Asquith's papers is a file containing a little correspondence: the file is headed 'Arthur Asquith', and on the front cover, in disregard of an instruction 'THIS PAGE IS NOT TO BE WRITTEN ON', are two minutes. The first, dated 26 May 1920, reveals that the file had just come to light, but should not be destroyed: the second, dated 29 July 1939, from John Gore, then a former civilian subordinate in the Ministry of Labour, sending the file to Asquith, simply states: 'Gen Arthur Asquith, You may like to see – and file!'

Arthur observes wryly at the bottom of the page that 'There is a certain dilatoriness of movement in connection with these papers which is characteristic of Government departments. The original letter comes to roost after exactly a quarter century.'

From this file it is apparent that Asquith wrote naively to Mr Pease, one of his father's Cabinet colleagues, on Downing Street headed paper on 7 August 1914:

Dear Mr Pease,
     I enclose an application for work, – partly civil and partly military, and I shall be grateful if you will kindly forward it to the proper quarter. I hope we did not keep you up too late last night.
                              sincerely
                              Arthur Asquith

Mr Pease had been a guest the previous evening, and had offered to assist Arthur in his search for gainful war employment. Attached to the letter is a hand-written amplification with a brief CV, including the information that he speaks French, Spanish and Arabic, and that he is currently working in England and the Argentine for an Argentine firm. Arthur stated that he did 'not want to abandon the interests entrusted to me by my firm ... until ... necessary', meaning that he did not wish military work that would take him away from London for long periods. He proposed attendance at 'drill and military riding school between 6 and 8pm (three or four nights a week): occasional afternoons on the range: and a fortnight or so in camp'. He foresaw that it might be necessary in the future to devote himself exclusively to military work, and closed by saying that he might be able to get together from his friends 'some volunteers for such work'.

On 14 August Mr Gordon from the War Office, writes to Mr Fass, at the Board of Education asking him to reply, and opining that he did not 'know how Mr Asquith could get the military training he desires without joining the Territorial Force'.[1]

Arthur's sentiments are even more frankly expressed in the undated draft of a letter to his employers, Franklin and Herrera, in which he gives reasons for wishing to leave the company: 'I have two older brothers, both married, and one younger brother with an ailing colon.' He cites his experience in the Sudan as making it easier for him to become a soldier more quickly than his brothers, observing that, 'It is obviously fitting that one of my father's four sons ought to be prepared to fight . . . I cannot sit quietly by reading the papers'. He reveals that his contract with F. and H. runs until 30 September 1915, at £750 per year or seven and a half per cent of the profits, whichever is the greater, and suggests that his chief clerk could assume his responsibilities. He asks to be allowed to cable Mr Franklin abroad: 'Regret absolutely necessary that I be allowed to volunteer immediately, for the duration of the War'. He concludes this letter, 'By hook or by crook I must arrange to free my hands so that I may enlist at the earliest possible moment'.[2]

The situation was rapidly resolved, for Arthur went with his brothers Herbert and Cyril to a training course at the Public Schools' camp near Salisbury as some of the first recruits for Kitchener's New Army. A further short spell of training followed at Crystal Palace. Temporary Sub Lieutenant Arthur Asquith was commissioned into the Royal Naval Division on 23 September 1914. He had chosen this particular formation because it sounded slightly different from the more run-of-the-mill regiments; also, the Asquiths were very friendly with Churchill, then First Lord of the Admiralty, the creator and champion of the Division. Edward Marsh, Churchill's Private Secretary, who was part of Violet's circle of friends, arranged for several of their other friends to be commissioned into the Division, including Rupert Brooke. Herbert Asquith took a com- mission in the Royal Marine Artillery.[3]

The RND did not exist before 1914. Before the war, Churchill judged that there would be between twenty and thirty thousand naval reservists for whom there would be no jobs at sea, and the Committee for Imperial Defence agreed that they should be formed into a division for emergency deployment. As an ironic result, on mobilisation, the volunteer sailors became the first conscripts for the Army. On 30 August 1914 Churchill signed the mobilisation order for the Royal Navy, but already by then, a mixed bag of naval reservists, approximately two brigades' worth, had descended on Walmer and Betteshanger, near Deal, and were under canvas there. In September Crystal Palace was established as the RND depot to receive the recruits answering Kitchener's call: the first intake consisted of 600 miners from the North East. Many of these first Tyneside recruits were reportedly obtained by being diverted from a line waiting in the rain to enlist in the Durham Light Infantry or Northumberland Fusiliers to a spacious and dry naval recruiting hall.

It should be noted that at this time the BEF itself stood at only six divisions. The RND was formed around cadres of Officers and NCOs from the Royal Navy and Royal Marines, supported by a sprinkling of retired officers of high quality, mostly from the Brigade of Guards. A very large proportion of the reservists who volunteered were from the North of England, or from Scotland and Northern Ireland, and this trend continued with every reinforcement of the Division.

As it was not part of the War Office Establishment, the Admiralty set up a Committee under Winston Churchill for the administration of the RND. Not surprisingly, therefore, the organisation and training did not proceed at what might be termed an ideal rate: one battalion even had both a naval and a military adjutant to start with. There was not even a nominated Divisional Commander. At last common sense prevailed, and on 1 October 1914 it was decided that the Royal Marines should administer the Division, which by now consisted of Royal Marine Brigade, made up of fifty per cent regulars from the RM depots at Chatham, Deal, Portsmouth, and Plymouth. These battalions were to be numbered 9, 10, 11, and 12. There would be two Naval Brigades of four battalions each. Benbow, Collingwood, Drake, and Hawke would form the 1st RN Brigade, and Anson, Howe, Hood, and Nelson the 2nd.

On the evening of 29 September 1914 Temporary Sub Lieutenant Arthur Asquith, RNVR, arrived at Betteshanger to join the 2nd Naval Brigade, under the command of Commodore Backhouse, with whom Arthur was 'most favourably impressed'.[4]

Backhouse told Oc that he had intended him to be his ADC, but as there was no work for an aide at the time, he posted him to Anson Battalion, under the command of George Cornwallis West, an ex-Guardsman. Anson consisted of eighteen officers and about 700 men: apart from Asquith himself, the Battalion officers included Rupert Brooke, already with a reputation as a poet, and Brooke's great friend from Rugby School, W Denis Browne, a brilliant pianist and all-round musician; the other officers were 'mostly under thirty, and Scotch. [sic]' Arthur found himself sharing a tent with the Brigade-Chaplain, a padre called Foster, 'mild, pleasant, young, with [the] voice of a stage curate: snarlingly stertorous by night'.[6] Asquith's assessment of the padre is confirmed by Foster himself who recorded that one morning he found a 'motley collection of boots, slippers, books and tins which had been used as missiles [by Asquith], who had been trying in vain to get to sleep owing to what he termed my "melodious slumbers!" '.[7]

The next morning the Battalion paraded at 0700, and Asquith was given command of a platoon of C Company, of about forty-five men, mostly from the North of Ireland, judged by him to be 'good material, rather ungainly, [and] dressed in sailor's blue clothes'.[8] The men had only received their rifles on 26 September, and much of their equipment was incomplete. He comments on the overall lack of experience in all ranks, and reports that the general opinion was that the Naval Volunteers were better than the Naval Reservists, the latter being largely ex-regular Royal Navy stokers of notorious ill-discipline.

Training started immediately, but consisted almost wholly of drill and marching, and on Saturday 3 October, with rumours flying that they were to be moved to Dunkirk to complete their training, Asquith and Rupert Brooke were inoculated against typhoid, and after they had dined at The Black Horse in Deal with Denis Browne, Asquith retired early, feverish from the jab.

NOTES

1. File in AMA papers.
2. Draft letter from AMA to Mr Pease, dated 7 August 1914, in AMA papers.
3. *Moments of Memory* by Herbert Asquith, Hutchinson, 1937, pp201-204.
4. Antwerp diary by Arthur Asquith, a typed account of his experiences during the Antwerp operations *in the* AMA papers. Backhouse went on to Captain the battleship *Orion* at Jutland, and finished his career as a Vice Admiral, retiring in 1929.
5. West subsequently married the actress Mrs Patrick Campbell. Her son, Alan, had a distinguished career in the RND, and was killed on Welsh Ridge, near Cambrai in December 1917, as second in command of Hood Battalion.
6. AMA Antwerp diary.
7. *At Antwerp and the Dardanelles* by Rev H C Foster, Mills and Boon, 1918, p 13.
8. ibid.

CHAPTER III

The Antwerp Expedition

It was therefore a virtually untrained group of sleepy men woken at 0515 on 4 October. The band were sent through the camp to assist in rousing the men. Some of the officers and men were feverish from their inoculations the previous day, and the men had had their rifles for only a week. By 1015 the frantic packing had been completed, and they knew that they were not just involved in an exercise. The RND marched into Dover about two hours later, where they stood around the streets of the town all afternoon, the officers trying to stop the men from being over-liberally supplied with beer by their admirers. The Commanding Officer, Cornwallis West, joined his battalion in Dover from leave by paying for a special train as he had missed the last scheduled departure.[1]

Eventually, by about 2100, the men and equipment had been loaded on to a transport ship: Arthur spent a cold night in a deck chair on deck. No arrangements had been made to feed the officers on board. They arrived at anchor off Dunkirk early the next day, and then spent a frustrating eight hours on a choppy sea waiting to land and unload their kit. As a further indication of the Division's unpreparedness, Asquith reported in his Antwerp diary that only now were some of the men issued necessities such as water bottles, haversacks, and overcoats. There was general surprise when they were told their destination was Antwerp, as the RND did not think it possible that they would be used in action in such an incomplete state of training and equipment. The Division had no transport wagons, artillery, or engineers. The men mustered at the station for the train to the beleagured city. Each man received 120 rounds of ammunition. Just before the train left, Cornwallis West addressed the Battalion and warned that there was a possibility that the train could be attacked. In conclusion, West said: 'Remember you are British and I am sure you will give a good account of yourselves'. A tremendous cheer is reported to have greeted this remark.[2]

Arthur Asquith expressed constant amusement at the use of nautical terms: in the event of the train being attacked en route, it was decreed that Howe Battalion would get out of the 'Port' side, and Anson the 'Starboard'. When permission was requested to leave camp, it was to 'go ashore'; absentees were 'adrift', rather than absent without leave, and the order for men to be quiet was 'pipe down'.

27

At about 2215, just one hour before departure from Dunkirk station, Anson's medical officer announced that he had no medical stores whatsoever, not one bandage, and no stretchers. Asquith received permission from the CO to try to obtain some and, borrowing a car and chauffeur, drove to a nearby local French Military Hospital, where sleepy, but friendly, officials gave him 350 bandages, and some lint and gauze. He boarded the train as it was due to depart, and in the carriage had his first meal for fifteen hours. All slept fully dressed in case of attack.

The purpose of the expedition was to try to delay the German advance on the Channel ports by shoring up the Belgians in their fortress port. The plan was for the Naval Brigades to reinforce the Royal Marines who had already been sent on 4 October, to hold the line of the River Nethe around Antwerp while the French Army and the British Seventh Division counter-attacked the German flank in order eventually to relieve them. Lyn Macdonald has written, 'It was Winston Churchill's decision to send the RND to Antwerp. There was no one else to send.'[3]

The next day was Tuesday 6 October, and there was a good deal of cheering from the people of the towns through which the RND train passed. By 1000 they were at Antwerp station, and could see in the distance German observation balloons and burning Belgian villages. Arthur's company billeted themselves in the botanical gardens. By lunchtime, just as his men were making themselves comfortable, they were told to assemble and began to march towards the sound of the guns. After two or three hours on the road, passing dejected and exhausted Belgian soldiers coming in the opposite direction, Anson Battalion reached a suburb called Vieux Dieu, and bivouacked in the garden of a villa under the walls of a Belgian fort: it was bitterly cold and damp; no one got much sleep and shells were falling close by.

Asquith had had just over an hour's rest, when at 0330 the order came to assemble and move off to some trenches. They marched west, finishing up in a ready-made trench line outside the suburb of Witryck, which formed part of the innermost defences of Antwerp, as by then the outer fortifications of the city had been breached by the enemy. At the time very few of the junior officers knew where they were, as none had maps. They learned later that the suburb they had just vacated had been completely destroyed by shellfire shortly after their departure. Anson Battalion's share of the defence was to man about one thousand yards of trenches which stretched between redoubts garrisoned by Belgian gunners. In front were barbed wire entanglements, though the flat fields beyond were full of piebald cows. Arthur asked permission to drive them away, as their presence made it difficult to detect attacking enemy troops, who would perhaps stampede them at the wire entanglements. West refused to allow it.

The trenches were elaborate, but too wide to give protection against shrapnel, so the first task was to dig narrow, deep trenches. While the men were undertaking this work, Arthur was sent into Antwerp to procure food for the Officers' mess. Once again, his facility with the French language paid dividends, and he returned with beef and kidneys, bread, vegetables, pots and pans, a revealing comment on the logistics of this operation. By now the RND lines were under sporadic shell fire, but it was the Belgian forts which attracted most of the German attention. This situation lasted for the rest of the day, with the German shelling increasing on the front line troops and in the back areas of Antwerp, where petroleum storage tanks were ablaze, some hit by shellfire, and some destroyed by the Belgians. At about 1800 Asquith saw his first enemy soldiers, 500 yards away. Then, at 1845, shortly after a huge explosion and conflagration at the Arsenal, came the order to retire. Asquith is implicitly critical of the CO, West, who had lost his copy of one of only two maps issued to the Battalion, and greeted every Belgian he met on the march with 'Avez vous un plan d'Anvers?'. Eventually, the CO found a Belgian with a game leg who was pressed into service as a guide: unfortunately he kept falling off his bike, and had repeatedly to be helped back on it.

About 2100 the Battalion reached the Scheldt, across which a bridge of boats had been built, where they were met by the Divisional Commander, General Paris, who seemed to Arthur not to be pleased having learned from Colonel West that one of his four Anson Companies was missing. In his despatch of 11 October printed for the Cabinet, Paris records that 'there were thousands of tons of petroleum flaming within one hundred yards of the bridge of boats, lighting up the bridge as if by day. Had the wind been blowing towards the bridge, no escape would have been possible.'[4] The weary men reached Zwyndrecht in good order by 2215, where Anson's missing Company rejoined them. After a three-quarter hour's rest, the RND again moved out, marching on bad cobbled roads towards Saint Nicholas. In the dark and confusion, battalions became mixed up, and some men discarded what they believed to be unnecessary baggage, such as the 250 rounds of ammunition they were carrying, and some, even their rifles. They halted just outside Saint Nicholas, where it had been intended that they would entrain for the coast, moving off at 0330 on 9 October, arriving at St Gilles-Waes at 0730, having passed a jostling welter of Belgian soldiers, buses, cars and refugees of various descriptions on the way. Most were footsore, all were exhausted, having marched for thirteen hours, with less than two hours rest, a distance of about thirty miles. Every man from Anson Battalion who left the Witryck trenches arrived at St Gilles. There they caught a train to Bruges, where they stayed overnight: Asquith slept in the same bed in the billet as Rupert Brooke. The following day Anson hung about all day, until the train left for Ostend at about 1830, arriving at about midnight. Asquith and his men boarded the SS *Eddystone* for home at about 0200 on 11 October and slept the sleep of the dead on hay on the transport.

On 9 October it was not clear how many of the RND had managed to escape from Antwerp, and HH Asquith wrote to Venetia Stanley, with whom he carried on a frequent, and intimate, even passionate, correspondence for many years, until her marriage to Edwin Montagu in 1915, 'They [the RND] have paid their toll – which I pray does not include Oc, whom (if one must have preferences) I put first in character & nature among my children'.[5] By the next day he had been reassured that Oc, and Rupert Brooke, had survived.

The 2nd Naval Brigade, of which Anson was a part, had been lucky: they received the message to withdraw from their trenches in front of Antwerp in good time. Only Drake Battalion of the 1st Brigade acted on the signal and joined the retreat of the 2nd Brigade: it was over four hours later before Benbow, Collingwood, and Hawke Battalions of the 1st Brigade started to move. After the last train had left from St Gilles-Waes, the Germans cut the railway line, and the greater portion of the 1st Brigade and the 10th Royal Marines were cut off. As a result, most of them either fell into enemy hands, or were forced to march into neutral Holland to avoid capture, where they laid down their arms and were interned for the rest of the war. The 10th Royal Marines, gallantly led by Colonel Luard, fought their way through, although down to an effective strength of only 150 by the time they rejoined the rest of the Division. In all, the Division had suffered severe casualties: fifty-seven men had been killed and 138 wounded, but 936 had been captured by the enemy, and thirty-seven officers and 1,442 ratings were interned in the Netherlands – a total of fifty-two officers and 2,558 ratings.

Opinion is divided on whether the enterprise had any effect: it has been argued that the defence of Antwerp caused the enemy to lose the 'race to the sea'. However, when the Division was back in England, the Conservative press had its knives out for Churchill, its instigator[6]. He had taken the precaution of getting an initial brief from Asquith and Rupert Brooke on the evening of their return. Arthur also briefed his father on the expedition. The PM was shocked: he told Venetia Stanley on 13 October, 'I can't tell you what I feel of the *wicked* folly of it all, three-quarters of the Division were a callow crowd of the rawest tyros, most of whom had never fired a rifle, while none of them had ever handled an entrenching tool. Oc's battalion was commanded by George West – an ex (very-ex) subaltern in the Guards who was incompetent & overbearing & hated impartially by both officers and men . . . It was like sending sheep to the shambles'.[7]

According to a Marine, Arthur was 'as daring as anybody . . . Officers like him make a lot of difference . . . and there isn't one of us who wouldn't go through fire and water for him'.[8] It was the first of many such testimonies that Asquith would earn in his short military career.

The Official History is less critical of the operation: it reports that the

Royal Marines did well in the hottest part of the line (around Lierre), and proved steady under fire. Of the Naval Brigades it says:'Without any training in field fortifications, they entrenched themselves;without training in musketry, they used their rifles to good effect: without any supply service or regimental transport, they lived on such food as could be procured locally from time to time, and one day it was only turnips in the fields. . . . The wonder is not that they failed to accomplish what was hoped, but that they fought so well.'[9]

Shambles or not, and in the face of vitriolic attacks from some sections of the press, Churchill faced down his detractors, and ensured the continued existence of the Royal Naval Division. The first action was to recruit for three new battalions to replace Hawke, Collingwood, and Benbow which had been interned in Holland. Other measures were set in hand to provide for training and reinforcement, and it was proposed that the whole Division would eventually be concentrated at a new camp to be built on the racecourse on the Downs outside Blandford Forum, and to be open early in the New Year. The existing depot at Crystal Palace undertook the new-entry training of recruits, NCOs, and officers, and these camps enabled the RND to establish a unique ethos and esprit.

The first troops started to move into Blandford at the end of November 1914: first was Nelson Battalion followed by the other infantry battalions of the 2nd Brigade plus Drake from the 1st. The Marine Brigade and some of the Divisional troops arrived at the end of January 1915.

On return from Antwerp, Arthur decided to change battalions from Anson to Hood, which had already attracted some interesting people with whom he had made friends. On 7 November he dined with his father and Edward Marsh at 10 Downing Street. The latter's machinations resulted, on 19 November, in his becoming a platoon commander in the latter battalion. Hood was commanded by a highly respected ex-Guardsman, Arnold Quilter, whose officers included Bernard Freyberg, then an unknown New Zealander, who had made his way from Mexico to enlist. There is an apocryphal story of Freyberg accosting Churchill in London requesting a commission; also in this group was Rupert Brooke, who had pulled all possible strings to transfer to the Battalion with his friend Denis Browne, and F S Kelly, known as 'Cleg', a multi-talented man, thrice winner of the Diamond Sculls at Henley; also in Hood were Patrick Shaw Stewart, a brilliant Balliol scholar, Fellow of All Souls, who had risen to become the managing director of Baring Brothers before the age of 25; later, Charles Lister, the only son and heir of Lord Ribblesdale, was to be a further member of this close-knit club: another exceptional scholar, Lister would obtain leave from the Foreign Office to give up his desk in the Embassy in Constantinople for active service. With his knowledge of Turkish, and by using his connections, he managed to be appointed to the Naval Division in time for their deployment in action in the Dardanelles

The early days at Blandford were hard even for the officers: the roads were appalling, the huts (shared by eight men) cold, and supplies erratic. The officers resorted to furnishing their living areas themselves, although the fumes from the coke stoves made life unpleasant. In mid-December Arthur, and many others, had influenza. Life was not too bad otherwise: frequent hampers from friends and relatives alleviated the worst rigours of a naval wartime diet. They were allowed visitors. In December Violet, finding that her brother and Brooke were still both unwell, arranged for them to recover at Lady Wimborne's house in nearby Canford.

Before the Christmas leave was over, Marsh proposed to Brooke that they should hold a farewell dinner at the Moulin d'Or Restaurant. Rupert Brooke, flush with some compensation money just paid to him by the Admiralty as a result of a box full of his personal possessions having been lost on the Antwerp expedition, had grander ideas. The categories for invitation to this occasion were three: that they should be 'People one likes to be with; or that they should be amusing, or that they should be female.' Arthur qualified under the first two rules, and his sister under all three. Brooke treated Denis Browne, Marsh, Arthur and Violet to a meal at the Carlton Grill, followed by the theatre.[10]

Among his many subaltern tasks at Blandford, Asquith was responsible for the musketry training of his platoon. His earliest wartime notebook contains many personal details of his men: among much other information, he records their scores on the range. The average at 100 yards was about twelve out of twenty, although AB Jones in 16th Section managed no points at all in his first shoot, only two in his second, eventually achieving nine. Anybody under ten at the first try had to shoot again, and all those who did so showed significant improvement, but one AB Carroll never did better than eight after four attempts. Other routine entries in Asquith's notebook of this period record the numbers of the rifles issued to his troops: AB Fawcett, a single ex-iron worker, C of E and 20 years old, of the 13th Section, was issued Rifle 726, but is also noted as having flat feet. AB Beauchamp's pre-war trade is given as 'illusionist', while the unfortunate Jones, mentioned above, an ex-miner 36 years of age, still could score only twenty out of a maximum 272 in the more advanced shooting practices.[11]

On 15 January Patrick Shaw Stewart, by now in Hood Battalion, 'where Ock [sic] Asquith, Rupert Brooke, the poet, and other niceish men now are' as he put it,[12] and the rest had settled in to the Blandford routine. His platoon consisted of RNR stokers with a 'standing grievance in the back of their evil old minds that they want to be back in their steel-walled pen . . . instead of forming fours under the orders of an insolent young land-lubber'.[13] Also at Blandford at the time was AP Herbert, commissioned from the ranks into Hawke Battalion. He noted 'In the camp, too, there were the famous, the truly "fabulous", Freyberg, and Ock (Herbert) [sic] Asquith, of the Hood Battalion, generally next to us in battles, Shaw Stewart, and I suppose, Rupert Brooke (but I never met him).'[14]

The training consisted principally of making the camp reasonably habitable, road-building, drill, shooting and marching between fifteen and twenty miles a day. Even though they were still virtually untrained, Churchill's fertile mind was full of plans for landing the RND in Gallipoli, and as no other troops could be spared, two Marine Battalions of the Division were ordered to the Eastern Mediterranean to assist in the naval operations which were intended to force the Dardanelles without the need for a large invading army. Churchill reviewed the Naval Brigades in the pouring rain on 17 February. Margot Asquith is particularly scathing in her diary entry for the day, quoting HHA as saying to her, ' Winston just now is absolutely maddening, how I wish Oc had not joined his beastly Naval Brigade. . . . He [Churchill] inspects the Brigade in a uniform of his own which will cause universal derision among our soldiers!'[15] Having dined with Winston Churchill in early February, Violet was informed that the First Lord's intention was to send the remainder of the Division to Gallipoli, intelligence which she had Churchill's permission to pass on to her brother and Rupert Brooke only. She reported in her diary that Arthur came to London from Blandford, and they spent the afternoon buying maps, compasses, tinder-lighters and Baedeker guides of Constantinople, ironically only available in German.

On 20 February the Commanding Officer of Hood Battalion, Lieutenant Colonel Arnold Quilter, addressed his officers and informed them of their destination: they were to go to the Bosphorus, take Constantinople, and open up the passage to the Black Sea. Fighting was expected to last about six weeks, and they would be home by May. There were also rumours flying around that Hood would lead the landings, and that heavy casualties could be expected.

On Thursday 25 February the remains of the Division in Blandford were inspected by the King: after the parade, Winston and Clementine Churchill and Violet and Margot Asquith lunched with the officers of Hood Battalion, for whom Shaw Stewart had provided a luxurious menu including foie gras and champagne. They all knew that the Division was to be deployed to Gallipoli in a few days. Oc kissed Margot goodbye and sympathised with her 'domestic difficulties'. She cried 'bitter tears' in the car returning from Blandford.[16] Rupert Brooke and Shaw Stewart were excited by the prospect of a place in history resulting from a campaign in the cradle of classical civilization; Freyberg was relieved that at last he would see action, for, as he confided to Violet, 'I'm different from Oc and Rupert. I've got to make my own fortune . . . out of the war'.[17]

The next two days were spent in the most feverish activity preparing to break camp, issuing kit and ammunition. On 26 February 1915 there are notes in Arthur's book on sizes and numbers of pairs of boots and other items of uniform for his men; his platoon consists of two Petty Officers, three Leading Seamen (plus two in hospital), thirty-six Ordinary/Able Seamen, and fourteen Special Duties ratings, four machine gunners, a cycle orderly, pioneer, cobbler, bandsman, stretcher bearer, observer, groom, cook, butcher, and an officer's servant.

In the early evening of 27 February Hood Battalion left the camp and marched the nine miles to Shillingstone where they entrained for Avonmouth, arriving at about seven o'clock the next morning. The next day, Violet drove down to Avonmouth, and managed to stop someone with a Hood cap tally, to ask for Oc. Denis Browne took charge of her, and she accompanied her brother, Browne, and Rupert Brooke to lunch. It was a fairly solemn affair, concluded with a glass of burgundy. They arrived back at the docks to see the ship lying at the harbour mouth. Violet went on board the *Grantully Castle*, 'a not bad Union Castle boat',[18] to say goodbye to Arthur, Rupert, and the others, including Shaw Stewart, who was having one of his recurrent bouts of laryngitis. When she said goodbye to Brooke, she saw something in his eyes that made her believe they would never meet again. Having led her to the gangway, Arthur said, 'I shall come back, I may be wounded, but I shall come back.'[19] *Grantully Castle* sailed at 6pm.[18]

NOTES

1. *Edwardian Hey-Days* by G Cornwallis-West, Putnam, 1930, p273. Cornwallis-West, the former stepfather of Winston Churchill, was CO of Anson Battalion at Antwerp.
2. *At Antwerp and the Dardanelles*, p19.
3. *1914* by Lyn Macdonald, Michael Joseph, p374.
4. Despatch of Major General Paris on the Antwerp Expedition, copy in AMA papers at Clovelly.
5. *Asquith Letters to Venetia Stanley*, p269.
6. As examples, *The Morning Post*, on 13 October 1914, carried the headline 'Antwerp Blunder': *The Times* also joined in. Eventually, a counter-reaction was generated in *The Daily News*, *Star* and *Observer*, among others. Churchill never conceded that the defence of Antwerp was a possibly flawed concept.
7. *Children of the Souls*, p156; Letters to VS 13 October 1914 p276.
8. Interview in the *Evening News* of 26 October, quoted in *Letters to Venetia Stanley*, p276.
9. Official History, Vol 1, p.63.
10. E Marsh, *A Number of People*, Heinemann and Hamilton, 1939, pp 202/3.
11. From a notebook in AMA papers.
12. Ronald Knox, *The Life of Patrick Shaw Stewart*, p108, quoting a letter of 25 November to Lady Desborough.
13. ibid, p110.
14. *A.P.H. His Life and Times*, by Sir Alan Herbert C.H., Heinemann, 1970, p39.
15. Margot Asquith's diary, quoted in *W S Churchill, Martin Gilbert Companion* Vol 11, p525.
16. Margot Asquith's diary, p499.

17. *Winston Churchill as I Knew Him* by Violet Asquith, Eyre and Spottiswoode, 1965, p363.
18. *Champion Redoubtable, The Diaries and Letters of Violet Bonham Carter*, edited by Mark Pottle, Weidenfeld and Nicolson, 1998.
19. *Winston Churchill as I Knew Him*, p365.
20. Miscellaneous Correspondence: Arrangements for Embarkation of Men and Stores of RN Division for the Dardanelles, p63, PRO,Kew, box ADM 137/3088A.

CHAPTER IV

To the Dardanelles

By 5 March the *Grantully Castle* was in the Strait of Gibraltar, and in the unaccustomed confinement of the ship, and with little work to be done other than keep-fit and lectures, enduring friendships were made. After a short stop at Malta, where Asquith, Brooke, Charles Lister, Shaw Stewart and Denis Browne toured Valletta, dined at the Union Club, and saw 'Tosca' at the opera, and eleven days after leaving Avonmouth, the *Grantully Castle* anchored off Mudros, on the island of Lemnos, at 6pm on 11 March 1915. The opportunity was taken for extra training and marching. The island was noted as rocky and treeless, and more than one Hood Battalion officer commented favourably on the cleanliness and pleasing appearance of the local villages and their inhabitants. The Battalion Commander, Quilter, gave a talk after dinner on 14 March at which he told his men that they might not be needed for action for weeks, and that they would need to make strenuous efforts to maintain the battalion's efficiency in the meantime. However, on the 18th, six transports full of troops were suddenly sailed from Mudros for the Dardanelles: extra ammunition was issued, but in the end, after demonstrating off Suvla and the mouth of the Strait, they returned to Lemnos, where rumours circulated that the RND was to be sent to Alexandria. The *Grantully Castle* sailed for Egypt on the evening of 23 March, passing close to the new battleship *Queen Elizabeth*, and with the snow-clad heights of Samothrace as a backdrop. A Greek interpreter was on board, who gave free language lessons to Asquith, Kelly, Brooke, and Browne.

In Britain there was the problem of temperance by example for the duration of the war, prompted by a letter written by the King stating that the Royal Family would abstain from alcohol until the war was over. On hearing of the furore in England, Oc telegraphed his father on behalf of Hood Battalion: 'Reported spread of temperance alarms and amazes us. Stand fast.' Margot Asquith's views on the matter were typically trenchant: she wrote to Asquith on 12 April, 'Father enchanted by your drinks wire! The King's letter to my mind (& to a few more) is idiotic ... he never showed it to father ... Ll George & he did it together ... L George, McKenna & Kitchener have knocked off all wine & alcohol ... Fearful rows going on as Winston [and] Ll. G. (not the latter now) want total prohibition & of course that <u>vile</u> *TIMES* has whipped up the agitation till it has grown grotesquely.' In the same letter, Margot refers even more directly to her detestation of the Northcliffe press, quoting Northcliffe himself as boasting to some of Margot's acquaintances that 'I will do for Asquith and get rid of him . . . he must go. Ll. George must be Prime Minister'.[1]

Anson and Hood Battalions on board *Grantully Castle* arrived at Port Said on 27 March, where Asquith, Kelly, Brooke and Browne dined ashore, and had their hair cut short as an example to the men. The following day the troops disembarked and camped in the sand on the outskirts of the town, purportedly to prepare to repel a Turkish attack, but more likely to enable the cargoes, hastily loaded before the ships left England, to be reloaded to be more readily deployable for the landings on the Gallipoli peninsula which were now inevitable. Brooke, who kept up a regular correspondence with Violet, reported on 9 April: 'Oc is well and patient. Charles I like more as I see him more. I didn't realise what an awareness and subtlety he concealed under that equine madness'.[2] Brooke and Asquith shared a tent with Kelly, Lister, Shaw Stewart, and Denis Browne, and the group had grown close.

Many of the officers took the opportunity for a trip to Cairo to see the pyramids. One group, Asquith, Patrick Shaw Stewart, and Rupert Brooke, took a train and called on some friends of Arthur, Lord and Lady Howard de Walden. Arthur's Arabic came in handy, and they were able to luxuriate in 'almost unforgotten comforts'.[3] They made the usual camel ride around the ancient tombs, toured Cairo on donkeys and finished up at Shepheard's Hotel for scrambled eggs and coffee. On their return to camp, first Shaw Stewart, and then Brooke went down with severe stomach disorders, which they put down to a touch of the sun. Both were unfit to attend the parade on 3 April when Sir Ian Hamilton, Commander of the Dardanelles operation, reviewed the Naval Division, and pronounced himself well satisfied. He had written to the Prime Minister on 25 March that the RND was 'immensely keen . . . [their] present weakness lies in their lack of self confidence'. Now he seemed more sure of their potential value.[4] After the inspection, Sir Ian sat at the foot of Brooke's bed and talked with him and Asquith.[5]

On 9 April the loading of the ships was complete, and orders came for Hood to re-embark on *Grantully Castle*, which sailed at breakfast time on 10 April with a lighter of fresh water in tow. With this encumbrance, the ship could only make about six and a half knots; fortunately, at this time, enemy submarines were rare in the area. Rupert Brooke and Patrick Shaw Stewart protested that they were fit and should not be left behind: both were as weak as kittens, but their dysentery had cleared up, although Brooke had a sore on his upper lip, thought to have been caused by an insect bite, which caused him discomfort. The same groups of officers dined together: by now the coterie had been joined by Johnny Dodge, a 19-year-old American or Canadian, no one discovered which at the time, who had come from the USA in 1914 to fight for the rights of small nations. The group now consisted of Charles Lister, Brooke, Asquith, Denis Browne, Kelly, Shaw Stewart, and Dodge. They were known to the mess stewards as 'the Latin Club', for their wide-ranging conversation which invariably contained discussion of some matter of classical antiquity. Usually Dennis Browne or Kelly would play the ship's piano. The men occupied themselves with getting the sand out of their equipment, physical training, and on the last evening, a fancy dress dance and 'Sod's Opera', an irreverent and traditional naval review. Chief Petty Officer Flynn, the Battalion CPO, came in for special treatment from two men who provided an amusing imitation of him. Kelly and Browne played the piano, and most of the men dressed as negroes. Brooke retired early.[6]

The *Grantully Castle* arrived back at Mudros early on the 16th, and had to anchor in the mouth of the harbour, as farther inshore was crowded with other transports and warships; at about 1030 the ship was ordered to sail to the island of Skyros, where she eventually anchored in the evening. On the following day most of the stokers of A and D companies left the ship to act as boat crews for the landing force. This depressed the remaining battalion officers, who believed that other working parties would be likely to be drawn from a battalion which had already been used as a source of such labour. Freyberg was the Officer Commanding (OC) A Company, and his platoon officers were Dodge, who was sent with the landing party, Lister, Brooke and Shaw Stewart. Arthur remained a platoon commander in D Company.

Violet wrote to Arthur on 6 April in reply to one of his letters and was 'much amused by the futile & <u>imbecile</u> attempt at excision by the censor ... Do in future ... write under cover to Father as they could hardly wish to censor your communications with him.' In the same letter, Violet reveals that the Prime Minister was 'much amused by your telegram, he has not yet given up his own liquor & doesn't I believe intend to do so'.[7] This shows one of the indirect and unofficial channels of communication between the RND and the very centre of political power. As well as the frequent and candid correspondence between Arthur and his sister and step-mother, he wrote directly to the Prime Minister, and his Private Secretary, Maurice Bonham Carter, known as 'Bongie'. Also, Violet had very close links with both Winston Churchill and Eddie Marsh, his Secretary.

At Skyros, on 20 April, as part of their preparations for their part in the landings, the remainder of the RND continued their training among the olive trees with a 'Field Day'. In a small grove during a lull in the exercise, Browne found a tranquil spot, and took Brooke and some of the others there for some peace and quiet. The day finished with a scramble down to the beach. AB Joe Murray tells how, while racing the other platoons back to the ship, his platoon commander, who was Asquith, heard that some of his men had badly injured a tortoise earlier, by cracking its shell: Asquith immediately ordered the responsible section to abandon the race and return and put the creature out of its misery, an act which made an impression on Murray who wrote, 'My section lost the race but it had a new respect for its officer, a gentleman who, even on the eve of battle, had a soft heart and a detestation of suffering'. Murray and the rest of his section eventually arrived at the water's edge to see the finish of a swimming race between Freyberg and Asquith, narrowly won by the former. Both were powerful swimmers, especially Freyberg, who was of Olympic standard. Brooke was going to join the swim, but did not feel up to it.[8]

It was an indication that Rupert Brooke, who had seemed to be recovering satisfactorily from the illness contracted in Egypt, was still not well, and he retired to his bed on Wednesday 21 April. Asquith noted that his upper lip was very swollen. During the night, he suffered a relapse: by the afternoon of the 22nd, it became obvious that he was critically ill with a high temperature and severe swelling of his face and neck, and he was moved to the French hospital ship *Duguay–Trouin* accompanied by Asquith; after consultations with the Fleet Surgeon, Asquith drafted telegrams to be sent to Churchill and Sir Ian Hamilton explaining that Brooke's condition was critical, asking for his parents to be informed, and requesting burial instructions in case he should die. By the following morning the French surgeons had decided to operate to relieve the septicaemia: Asquith and Browne took turns at his bedside, but by midday his condition was desperate. It had become known that the Fleet was due to sail for the Dardanelles at 0600 the following morning, so, leaving Denis Browne with Brooke, Arthur went to make the necessary arrangements for burial should Brooke die before then. At 1646, with Browne at his bedside, Rupert Brooke died. Asquith soon returned, and together they decided to bury him that night on Skyros. The digging party of Brooke's company landed at 1900 under Lister, Freyberg, and Browne; Arthur stayed behind to organise the coffin and its transport. On the French ship, the body was put in the coffin and taken on deck, where, to save time, Asquith borrowed a cauterizing iron from the French, and branded the name and date in the wood. It was about 2300 when the twelve bearers arrived at the grave via a stony path after a two-hour walk. Browne had chosen the place near where the 2nd Naval Brigade had rendezvoused during the recent Divisional Field Day. On seeing the coffin at the graveside, Asquith realised that the grave was too short, so he jumped in and lengthened it. He found it lined already with olive and sage.

Brooke was buried with garlands of laurels, at a service conducted by the Chaplain of the 1st Naval Brigade, the Rev. BJ Failes RN, his resting-place marked by two crosses, a larger at the head, and a smaller one, given by his platoon, at the feet. The Greek interpreter, brought from Lemnos by Asquith, wrote in Greek, in pencil, on the back of the larger cross: 'Here lies the servant of God, Sub Lieutenant in the English Navy, Who died for the deliverance of Constantinople from the Turks'.

When the rest of the party had left, Asquith, Denis Browne, Freyberg, Kelly, Shaw Stewart and Lister piled a small cairn of pink and white marble stones. Patrick Shaw Stewart had commanded the firing party at the service, an experience he considered 'anxious work, as I am not strong on ceremonial drill, but all went well'.[9]

All who were there were moved by the experience: Kelly wrote that 'the scent of wild sage gave a strong classic tone . . . the sense of tragedy gave place to a sense of passionless beauty, engendered by both the poet and the place'.[10] It was not until he was on the boat returning to *Grantully Castle* that Asquith realised that his thirty-second birthday had come and gone. Four hours later the Fleet sailed.

Sir Ian Hamilton had French, British, and Australian troops under his command and had planned for the main landings to be on the tip of the Gallipoli peninsula, by the British 29th Division, while the Australians and New Zealanders were to land a short distance up the west coast. The actual landings would be supported by feint attacks by the French, and by the RND. The Naval Division's part in these diversions was to demonstrate off the coast at the northern end of the peninsula, a narrow neck of land known as the Bulair Lines. And so, in the early hours of 25 April, they were aboard their transports a short distance offshore.

Arthur had written his father a note on 26 April from *Grantully Castle* immediately before he believed he was to be in action, a document which effectively served as his will. Considering that he was the son of a highly successful man, that he had been in business himself for some years, and was a bachelor with no dependants, it reveals how modest his financial circumstances were. He wrote:

My dear Father,
    In case I am killed, which somehow I do not expect:
My life is insured with the Metropolitan Life Assn. for £4000.
I have £1500 in shares of Franklin and Herrera: these may
prove valueless. I have some other odds and ends of Stocks and Shares
with the Union Bank of Scotland: also a loan from them.

He stated that his debts were small, and that he would like Betty Manners, Margot, his half-sister Libby, and a friend from his time at Franklin and Herrera to receive good gifts. Apart from two small donations to clerks in his pre-war office, the remainder was to be split among the other members of the family. He concluded:

I have owed a very large part of my happiness to Con [Betty's mother] and Christine [Con's sister and owner of Clovelly Court near Bideford]: please give them and theirs my love and any little things of mine they may care to have.

Yours,

Oc[11]

While Asquith was taking care of his own affairs, the proposed demonstration off Bulair by the Division had been discussed: it was originally planned that, after steaming close inshore, the RND would attempt to convince the Turks that a night landing would take place at the narrow northern part of the peninsula; boats full of troops would be lowered at dusk and towed towards the land, but as soon as it became dark, they would return to the ships. Once it was fully dark, the second part of the deception plan would be put into effect. This consisted of putting ashore a platoon of Hood Battalion to light flares, and generally make a noise to simulate a real assault. It is well known that Freyberg pointed out that this would probably result in a large number of casualties to the landing platoon, and he volunteered to swim ashore to light the necessary flares, and create the required diversion. What is less well known is that three other strong swimmers from the battalion, Lister, F S Kelly, and Asquith, also volunteered to accompany Freyberg on this dangerous enterprise. It is typical of both Kelly and Asquith that neither revealed later that they had tried to be included in the plan: Kelly's part was reported in a footnote comment in his diary, edited after the war by Asquith, who characteristically omitted his own request to go with Freyberg.[12] Both were refused. It is reported that Colonel Quilter, Commanding Hood Battalion, said that he did not mind risking one officer on a madcap mission, but he was blowed if he was going to be responsible for the drowning of the Prime Minister's son![13] Freyberg went alone, successfully carried out the task, and was picked up half-frozen after a return swim of over two hours. The feint worked: two of the four Turkish divisions on the peninsula were retained around Bulair. Freyberg was awarded the DSO for his actions.

NOTES

1. Letter from Margot Asquith to AMA dated 12 April 1915, in AMA papers.
2. Letter from Rupert Brooke to Violet Asquith, 9 April 1898, quoted in *Champion Redoubtable*, ed by Mark Pottle.
3. *The Life of Patrick Shaw Stewart* by Ronald Knox, p177.
4. Asquith papers Bodleian, Box 14.
5. Green bound book used as a diary for March and some of April 1915 by Asquith, written in pencil in his own hand, entry for 2 April, AMA papers.
6. *Edward Marsh, a Biography* by Christopher Hassall, Longmans, 1959, p319.
7. Letter from Violet Asquith to AMA dated 6 April 1915, AMA papers.

8. *Gallipoli As I Saw It* by Joe Murray, William Kimber, 1965. Recorded in NEL paperback edition, published 1977, p61.
9. Knox, p126; Letter from PSS to Edward Horner, 25 April 1915.
10. Kelly's unpublished diary, entry for 23 April 1915, AMA papers. Asquith was asked by Kelly's sister after the war to edit F S Kelly's diary, with a view to publication. The typed transcripts of the original diaries, and the edited version, with comments by AMA are both in the AMA papers. So far as I can determine, the diaries have not been published.
11. Letter from AMA to HHA dated 26 April 1915, AMA papers.
12. Asquith told Violet of his attempts to join Freyberg in this dangerous enterprise in a letter of 29 April 1915, quoted in *Champion Redoubtable*.
13. *Bernard Freyberg VC, Soldier of Two Nations* by Paul Freyberg, Hodder & Stoughton, 1991, p54.

CHAPTER V
In Action at Gallipoli

On the 25th, the landings around the tip of the peninsula had not gone according to plan. The 29th Division landed in the teeth of desperate opposition and suffered severe casualties, and the ANZACs had been dropped in the wrong location, and were forced to scale rugged and precipitous cliffs before they could come into action with the enemy. Nevertheless, by determination and courage, and at serious cost, footholds were gained. It was now the turn of the reinforcements, to land and add weight to the assault.

The Royal Naval Division were not landed as an entity. As previously mentioned, Anson Battalion and parties from Hood and Howe had been taken for beach parties, and one of the Marine Battalions had landed with part of the 29th Division on Y Beach, on the left flank of the British line. At V Beach, where the SS *River Clyde* had been driven ashore in an attempt to provide protection for the assaulting infantry, there was carnage, as the unsuppressed Turkish machine gunners cut down the troops emerging from the sally ports in the ship's hull. In this maelstrom of fire, Sub Lieutenant Tisdall of Anson Battalion, a member of the beach party, won the first VC for the RND, for his heroic efforts in rescuing the wounded under fire.[1] In addition, on the 28th, the remaining Royal Marine Battalions had been landed to reinforce the ANZACS. For days the transports of the rest of the Division steamed up and down the peninsula, watching events ashore from the comfort and safety of the ships.

There was a general air of depression amongst the officers of the 2nd Naval Brigade still afloat: the RND seemed to have been committed piecemeal, and some believed that the rest of the untested battalions would be used for working parties and beach control, in fact, for anything other than fighting. Hood officers were pleasantly surprised, therefore, when the order came for them to move down to Cape Helles, at the tip of the peninsula, for immediate disembarkation. During the night of 29/30 April, which was clear and cold, under the light of a full moon, Hood Battalion landed at W Beach, at a place known as Lancashire Landing, after the courage of the men who landed there four days earlier, where the RND spent a miserable night in the open on the beach, huddled together for warmth.

The following day they marched about a mile and a half to the north on the road to the village of Krithia, where they were engaged in digging, and experienced Turkish shell fire for the first time. They returned later to their bivouac area on the top of the cliff between Gaba Tepe and Cape Helles, within range, but fortunately out of view of the Turkish artillery. Kelly, Lister and Browne were able to do a little sightseeing in the captured areas. Kelly noted ruefully that the French beaches seemed to be more orderly than those of the British.[2] The next day was spent as the last, preparing support trenches, while the British and Turkish batteries played lethal tennis intermittently over their heads. The countryside impressed the Hood officers as delightful, with trees, small orchards, wild flowers and herbs. They would soon learn to take a less appreciative view of their surroundings.

Throughout the night of 1/2 May, the Turks carried out major night attacks which were repulsed, and Hood Battalion was among the British troops moved up to support the left of the French positions. When daylight came, a counter attack was ordered: Hood Battalion's part in this was to advance and attempt to dig in on a line on an exposed ridge. They had gone forward without artillery support and suffered about ninety casualties in twenty minutes, mostly from enemy shrapnel, among them Charles Lister, who received his first wound. It was later decided that their position was untenable, and the Battalion withdrew. The following day was spent in fatigues and working parties, but any thoughts of a quiet night were shattered by the noise of British and French naval gunfire on Turkish positions, and by the retaliatory shrapnel bombardment, a great deal of which seemed to be directed at the RND encampment. Kelly reports that his servant was 'quite unhinged, . . . and completely out of his senses'[3]. Kelly and Browne comforted the unfortunate man, and after a sleeping draught from the doctor, McCracken, he went to sleep between the two of them. Later in the evening the doctor himself sought refuge in the same area, having found six bullets in his trench bed where a Turkish sniper had marked him down. Late in the afternoon of 4 May, the Battalion moved up to the firing line, relieving some French troops. The 2nd Naval Brigade had been lent as an entity to reinforce the French on the right of the Allied line. They were about to take part in their first set-piece attack, scheduled for 6 May.

The plan was for the French, with the RN Brigade attached, to advance about 2,000 yards, and hold, while the remainder of the British line enveloped the village of Krithia and the hill of Achi Baba in a huge sweeping movement. Arthur has left no record of the battle from his own perspective, but his friend Kelly relates his own experiences in some detail in his diary. Hood Battalion was due to advance on a four-hundred-yard front, led by A Company, followed by the remaining companies at two-hundred-yard intervals; Anson would follow and support. They were to go forward at 1100, reaching the objective by midday. Just before the start, the French changed the plan and decided that they would form the whole of the assault line themselves and use the RN troops as supports for their own advance. As the time for the attack had already passed, however, the naval battalions stuck to the original intentions, and began to leave their trenches. They were under very heavy small-arms fire, and by the third rush Kelly found himself isolated: there were no French visible to his right, and no other British troops to his left. Soon he joined up with some of Anson Battalion, and, although they were some way short of their final objective, they decided to dig in and extend the line to the left where they hoped to find the rest of Hood Battalion. At last, Kelly made contact with Lieutenant Nelson, of A Company, who had earned fame as the marine biologist to Scott's Antarctic expedition. The other Hoods had gone on farther and had held positions several hundred yards in front of the rest of the Allied forces all day under heavy fire. The great sweep of the left flank had failed, so during the night the forward positions withdrew to conform to the gains on their flanks. The Hood survivors clung on for the night and for another full day and night, finally being relieved after daybreak on 8 May.

Of the officers of B Company who had set off on the 6th, only Browne and Kelly were still unwounded, and Denis Browne was wounded in the neck by a sniper on 8 May. The Battalion CO, Quilter, had been killed early on, and was already buried when the rest of the Battalion came back down from the line. He was sadly missed by his Battalion, for his ability to instil morale, and for his solicitude towards his men. Freyberg received a nasty stomach wound, and Asquith had been shot through the knee. He was very lucky: the bullet passed through without touching a bone or injuring the joint; a quarter of an inch difference in the point of impact, and he would probably have lost his leg, or worse. John Churchill, brother of Winston, and a Staff Officer at headquarters reported in his diary that he called in at the hospital in the evening of the 6th and found it 'rapidly filling. Asquith came in looking bad from loss of blood'. His wound was assessed as serious, but not dangerous, although John Churchill believed he would be lame.[4] Sir Ian Hamilton visited Arthur that evening, and telegrammed the PM.

Margot Asquith recalled the effect in the Asquith household when the news came through. In a letter to Arthur she wrote:

> Imagine our feelings when we got 2 wires one Jack Churchill the other Ian Hamilton 'Asquith shot near left knee. Has been seen by dr.wound serious but not dangerous bullet passing through – Jack'.
>
> 'Have seen Oc very cheery no danger of loss of life or limb Ian Hamilton'.
>
> I was dressing at 9 when father held these two wires on one paper in his hand his eyes full of tears. I'm not ashamed to say I said 'He's dead!'

put my arms over my head but he said no he's not & we both cried while we read them I had been waiting & watching & sleepless with longing and apprehension & here it is – we know the worst please God you are safe and I pray no pain and clean surroundings I had been reading this wonderful account of the whole thing wh. I enclose for you and was moved to the core. How <u>thrilling</u> & glorious & pathetic it must have been. <u>What an xperience</u> [sic] for you my dear darling. Puff Elizabeth and I have prayed for you all the time always. I cd. Not think God wd. take you from us. 'Nothing in the History of any war has ever been more wonderful' yr. Father said when he came back from the cabinet – he said every man in the cabinet held his breath they were so moved.[5]

In her diary at the time, relieved that he had been spared, she wrote: 'The reason Oc is the most loved of my step-children is that <u>he</u> is far the most human of them. He has a rich nature and a real sense of responsibility. He is absolutely unselfish. He knows the precise value of brains and puts them in proportion. He can give up, and serve others. He isn't self-enfolded. He has no cruelty, either conscious or unconscious, and is not at all ashamed of simpleness'.[6]

A further vignette on Arthur's first wound is given in a letter, dated 9 June from his father to Sylvia Henley, the sister of Venetia Stanley. A correspondent reported a heated argument between Arthur and the stretcher bearers who were transporting him to safety. 'He wanted them to put him down and carry some poor Tommy who was trying to struggle down in the arms of two pals . . . rather touching, so like our dear Oc'.[7]

Margot had been hoping that Oc's wound would be sufficient for him to be sent home, and on hearing that he was to be treated in Egypt, wrote of her terrible disappointment.[8]

Patrick Shaw Stewart was hit in the same engagement, but was completely unhurt as the bullet had struck a steel mirror purchased from Asprey's in his breast pocket. He drily observed that it was 'almost as good an advertisement for that firm as Ock's [sic] wound for the government'.[9] Shaw Stewart also reveals that the glamour of war had already begun to lose its edge for him. He judges his experience to be 'a thing that a man should not have missed; but now that I have been there and done the dashing, I begin to wonder whether this is any place for a civilized man, and to remember about hot baths and strawberries and my morning *TIMES*'.[10]

Among the expressions of concern for Asquith's well-being was one from the French Minister of Finance to the Prime Minister, who wrote a card in French to HH Asquith on 9 May, with 'cordiale sympathie et mes voeux les plus sincères'.[11] Arthur arrived at the 15th General Hospital at Alexandria on 12 May 1915, from the transport ship HMT *Southland*, with an injury described as 'GSW. Knee sev.' (Gun Shot Wound, Severe).

On hearing of her brother's wound, and after receipt of a telegram from Cardy Montagu reporting that Arthur would probably be in hospital for about six weeks,[12] Violet decided to travel to Alexandria to visit him, with the additional, and secondary, aim of setting up an information service for the next of kin of RN and RND wounded in the theatre. Margot would have liked to accompany her 'if V and I had been partners but alas! as you well know we are not'.[13]

A few days after entering hospital, Arthur wrote to Violet explaining that he was not in any pain, but could not put his left foot to ground, and complaining of

> a black plague of Padres who come in, different ones every day, and ask the same questions. This is hard on a delightful Australian colonel in my ward, who was hit in the spine in a boat before being able to land, and is paralysed from the waist down for life. I hear him daily having to answer these Padres' mechanical questions as to when he will be fit again.[14]

Two days before Violet was due to leave, a crisis arose at home over the sudden resignation of the First Sea Lord, Fisher, and Violet cancelled her plans so that she could provide moral support to her father. It was, therefore, not until 20 May that she left for Alexandria, a sense of urgency having been engendered by a telegram from Arthur saying, 'Wound healing, sands running out, come soon'. After a frustrating journey across France, she at last caught a ship from Marseilles to Alexandria, where she spent four weeks among the wounded of the RND. Oc had telegraphed a meeting place at Sidi Gaber, and when Violet put her head out of the train window, 'there he was – hopping down the platform in the white glare like a lame jackdaw'.[15] She noted that his wound was 'quite healed and the mark tiny . . . he is still very lame but extremely agile'.[16] Despite the joy of the reunion, the major talking point was the recent ousting of Winston Churchill from the Admiralty, and his relegation to the Chancellorship of the Duchy of Lancaster.

As well as touring the hospitals, Violet found time to talk to Schlesinger, a doctor who had treated Rupert Brooke during his last illness. She became friendly with some of the other Hood officers, Kelly, who was wounded in the heel on 4 June and arrived at Alexandria, and 'Cardy' Montagu, the brother of Edwin who was about to marry Venetia Stanley, to the dismay of the Prime Minister. But particularly, Violet came to know, and be very fond of Freyberg, who took her bathing in the Mediterranean surf even though his abdominal wound had still not healed.

The announcement of the forthcoming marriage of Venetia Stanley to Edwin Montagu revealed a less tolerant side of some members at least of the liberal Asquith family. The 'problem' was that Montagu, the Financial

Secretary to the Treasury, later Minister of Munitions and Secretary of State for India, intelligent, cultivated, and rich, if not particularly handsome, was Jewish. There existed in most countries at the time an unlovely anti-Semitic prejudice, although this bias was less pronounced in Britain than in most other Great Powers. Prime Minister Asquith himself, although he disliked Judaism as a religion was, for the era, remarkably free from prejudice against Jews. Nevertheless, he suffered great personal distress and a sense of betrayal at the news of Venetia's marriage. The other Asquiths' objections were not so much against Venetia's marriage to a Jew, as the insistence that, to meet the terms of Montagu's father's will, she would have to change her religion.

The attitudes of the various members of the Asquith family to the match have been covered elsewhere. Of special interest in the family correspondence is the change in attitude when the engagement was announced: on 6 April Violet, in her letter to Arthur, reports a 'nice Wharf Easter with Wu', Montagu's nickname.[17] Once it was clear that the marriage was going ahead, Violet became its most violent opponent. On 19 July she wrote to her brother again saying, 'Venetia's unhallowed union with Wu is alas nearing – I enclose you a cutting from the *Daily Mail*. The whole thing simply <u>revolts</u> me both in its physical & spiritual aspect – & I think it <u>vile</u> of Montagu to drag Venetia thro' the mud of this bogus conversion – the first of its kind since the Crucifixion I verily believe! – to save his income.'[18] On the same day, almost certainly without collusion, Maurice Bonham Carter wrote to Arthur informing him that opinion in the Asquith family was divided on the propriety of Venetia's intention to change her religion, concluding, 'I need not tell you . . . in which camp each individual is to be found'.[19]

Margot's reaction was more moderately expressed, undoubtedly influenced by a degree of relief and satisfaction that the correspondence between her husband and a younger woman was over. When the engagement was announced she had written to Venetia 'a delightful letter'. She reported to Arthur that the announcement had been a '<u>great</u> blow to him [HHA] – a repulsive marriage in many ways, but I love Montagu & think they will be happy – He has what so few have the <u>power to love</u>'.[20] Montagu himself comes out of Margot's letter well. She reveals that he had poured his heart out to her and said, 'I am a Jew & ugly & old. She has nothing to gain by marrying me – I am a ridiculous marriage & all her friends will mind & ridicule it & mock at it – I don't know even how much she loves me but I will do my best to make her happy'.[21] On 15 June Margot expanded: she and Cys, Arthur's younger brother, 'see no reason why they sd. not be happy . . . I think Venetia is marrying a <u>very</u> good fellow & if she chucks him she will certainly never find another man to marry her unless she goes to India or Canada or some new place'.[22] This impression of Margot's liberal view of things did not

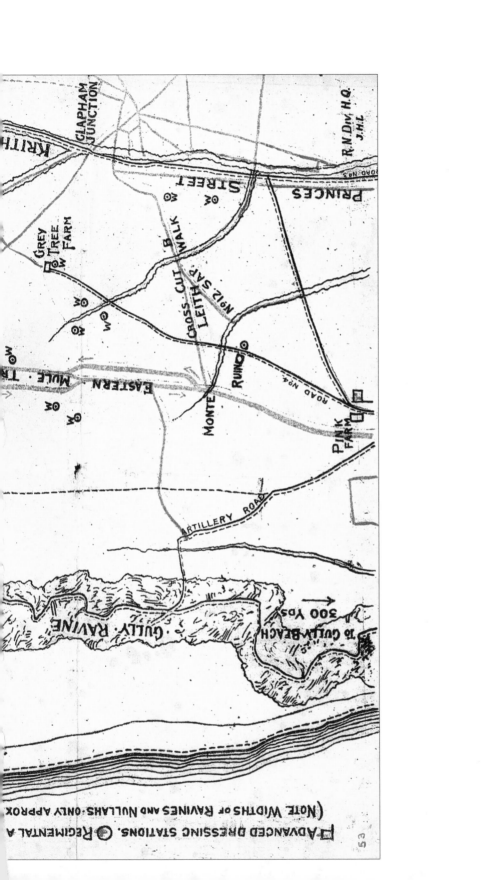

CLAPHAM JUNCTION

R.N.Div. H.Q.
J.H.L.

KRITH

ROAD No.3

PRINCES STREET

4B

4A

GREY
TREE
W FARM

B

CROSS CUT WALK

No.12 SAP

LEITH

4W

4W

4W

W

W

MULE · TR

EASTERN

RUIN

MONTE

ROAD No.4

40

4W

PINK
FARM

ARTILLERY ROAD

GULLY · RAVINE

To GULLY BEACH

½ 300 Yds

(NOTE WIDTHS OF RAVINES AND NULLAHS · ONLY APPROX

▯ ADVANCED DRESSING STATIONS. ◉ REGIMENTAL A

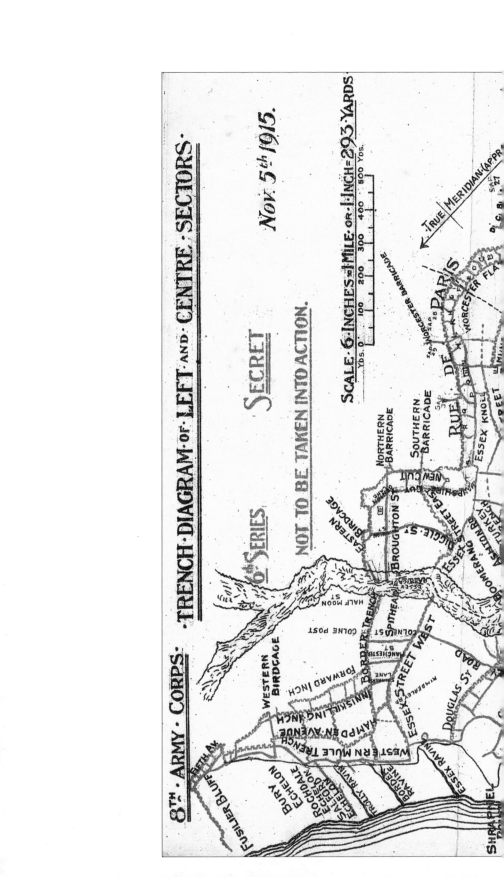

8TH · ARMY · CORPS · · TRENCH · DIAGRAM · OF · LEFT · AND · CENTRE · SECTORS ·

6TH SERIES

SECRET

NOT TO BE TAKEN INTO ACTION.

Nov. 5th 1915.

SCALE · 6 · INCHES = 1 · MILE · OR · 1 · INCH = 293 · YARDS

YDS. 0   100   200   300   400   500 YDS.

TRUE MERIDIAN (APPR

PARIS

RUE · DE ·

WORCESTER FLA

ESSEX KNOLL

NORTHERN BARRICADE

SOUTHERN BARRICADE

NORTHERN BARRICADE

NEW CUT

HAMPSHIRE CUT

BIGGLE ST

EASTERN BIRDCAGE

BROUGHTON ST

ESSEX STREET EAST

HALF MOON ST

SPITHEAD

COLNE POST

MANCHESTER ST

ASHIDAN

BOOMERANG

ROAD

WESTERN BIRDCAGE

FORWARD INCH

BORDER TRENCH

INNISKILLING INCH

ESSEX & STREET WEST

WIMBERLEY LANE

DOUGLAS ST

HAMPDEN AVENUE

WESTERN MULE TRENCH

FUSILIER BLUFF

BETHLAK

BURY

ROCHDALE

ECHELON

ROCHDALE

SALFORD

EGERTON

ROLLY RAVINE

PROLLY RAVINE

ESSEX RAVIN

SHRAP

last very long, for in June 1917 she was furious with Montagu for 'playing with Lloyd George', and concludes with 'Privately. He and Venetia are Jews and base.'[23]

Raymond took the same realistic, initial approach as his step-mother. Writing to his friend Conrad Russell in his typically waspish way, he revealed that he was 'entirely in favour of the Stanley-Montagu match' for several reasons, including the fact that it annoyed her parents, it would shock the 'entire Christian community', and an allusion to the size of Montagu's private means, and private parts, which made him a 'convenience to a woman'.[24]

Arthur's reaction, conditioned mainly by the perspective of his sister, and affected by his friendship with Cardy Montagu and Venetia Stanley, was ambivalent: writing to Violet from the Dardanelles in August, he says, 'I hate the whole business; but my social self-indulgence or natural immorality is such that the crimes of my friends rarely make me wish to forego their society.'[25] The marriage went ahead on 26 July. A few weeks later Arthur wrote to the new Mrs Montagu from Gallipoli. Venetia replied, 'it was very sweet of you to write and you wrote me a delightful letter'. She complained about the loneliness which she ascribed to being 'someone else's property'. Surprisingly, in the same letter, she states that they were 'feeling the pinch of poverty, both of us having lived rather prodigally in our youth', and that her debts had been paid by her brother from a legacy.[26] It seems that the huge riches of Edwin Montagu, believed by some to be the reason for Venetia's attraction, and mentioned in nearly all accounts of the affair, were a little slow in coming.

While Arthur was recovering from his wound, on the peninsula, after the May battles, the 2nd Naval Brigade was returned to the command of General Paris from the French, but the average strength of the battalions was only about 500. Reinforcements were on their way, however: Hawke, Benbow, and Collingwood Battalions, now reconstituted after the original units had been interned during the Antwerp operation, were at sea, and the two Marine battalions lent temporarily to the ANZAC front were being returned. Throughout May, the line was pushed forward towards the main Turkish positions. Trench life was very unpleasant, and many good men were lost to snipers. The arrival of the new battalions at the end of the month brought welcome reinforcements, but even these fresh troops could not replace all of the losses. Nevertheless, it was decided that the Division would be used as a whole, concentrated under its own Commander, for the next major attack, scheduled for 4 June. There was reason to believe that this time the operation would succeed where others had failed: the artillery bombardment would be much greater; the objectives were more limited, and the troops had been able to obtain some rest before the battle.

Once again, the modus operandi was to be a frontal assault along the line: by now, the continuous trenches across the peninsula made any outflanking impossible. 4 June was a fiercely hot day. The bombardment of Turkish strong points began at about 0800. The front-line enemy trenches were then subjected to what passed at the time for an intense artillery barrage from 1050 until 1120; this was followed by the whole British line waving fixed bayonets and cheering lustily to try to deceive the Turks into thinking that the attack was imminent. It was ominous, therefore, that the response provoked by this subterfuge was so violent that it showed the unfortunate waiting troops that the bombardment had not seriously weakened the enemy resistance. From 1130 to 1200 the artillery resumed; conditions for the British troops in the trenches were appalling: besides the heat and millions of persistent flies, the exchange of fire turned up corpses from earlier encounters, all in various stages of noisome putrefaction. Nine Hood officers and about 250 men went over the top at noon on a frontage of about 200 yards. Enemy fire was terrific, and despite some early gains, very little of the captured ground could be retained. In the process, Collingwood Battalion, in action for the first time since arriving from England, was practically wiped out. It was subsequently disbanded and never reconstituted. A simple ceremony of commemoration takes place at a plain memorial on the Blandford-Salisbury road at Blandford Camp every year on the anniversary of this disaster.

Kelly received the wound to his heel already mentioned, and Denis Browne was missing, having been seen to be badly wounded in the Turkish trenches after gallantly leading his men into action. He was sorely missed, not only for his exceptional musical ability, but for his care for his men. Asquith, in his notes to Kelly's unpublished diary, reports that his zeal for the welfare and training of his men was unlimited: at Blandford he had arranged for all his men to be seen by a dentist, and in Malta, concerned that they were suffering from the effects of the sun, he bought all his platoon sun-glasses. He had only just returned to the Battalion after recovering from a wound received in May.[27] Freyberg's brother, Oscar, was killed on the same day. In the general air of gloom, Violet wrote home reporting that: 'Even Oc said to me quite seriously – it is simply a case of being killed and being disabled for life – one or the other must happen in time.'[28]

The remaining personnel of Collingwood and Benbow Battalions were reassigned to other units, and the two Naval Brigades reduced to three battalions each. Further costly and unsuccessful attacks in the next few weeks further reduced the size and fighting efficiency of the Division, so that by the end of July, when the tired troops were withdrawn to rest, numbers totalled just over 5,000, and of these, the majority were affected by health problems brought on by continuous fighting in unsanitary conditions. From now on the RND could be used only for trench duties.

While these momentous events were taking place on Gallipoli, Arthur had been steadily recovering, and by 14 June his wound had healed sufficiently for him to be discharged from the hospital to the base at Mustapha, where he was judged fit enough to return to the peninsula, sailing from Alexandria in HMT *Seeang Bee*, and rejoining his unit on 28 June. Aunt Christine Hamlyn expressed regret that he and Charles Lister were returning to the trenches: 'My dear old Arthur I can't help being a wee bit sorry you and dear Charles are well enough to go back to Gallipoli . . . I think him one of the most delightful people in the world.'[29] Violet sailed home on the P & O SS *Arabia*, and within one week of returning, had become engaged to the Prime Minister's Secretary, Maurice Bonham Carter. It is indicative of the close relationship between Violet and Arthur that their father was relying on Oc to tell his sister that a marriage to Bonham Carter would be viewed favourably. On return home she caught typhoid, which although a 'mild attack', according to the doctors, was 'the most violent and unpleasant disease' she had ever suffered from.[30] Violet left Egypt before Arthur returned to his unit, 'in Rest camp', at the end of the month; being three days senior to Patrick Shaw Stewart, he took over command of D Company in the rank of Lieutenant Commander with effect from 5 July,[31] with the latter as his deputy. Shaw Stewart wrote to his sister, 'Fortunately I have no violent military ambitions and am delighted to have him back.'[32] Charles Lister also rejoined the Battalion at the same time. When Kelly rejoined on 11 July, he remarked that a few days earlier he had seen Sub Lieutenant Asquith in Alexandria, and now he was a Lieutenant Commander. Asquith's reaction was to write to Violet reporting his 'meteoric' naval career. 'I need no longer blush to meet the Sudani night porter'.[33] Asquith's command consisted of about 160 men, none of whom he knew from before.[34] Freyberg took command of Hood Battalion on 12 July when the previous CO, Myburgh, went sick.

On 16 July the Battalion moved up from the base camp to the support trenches, and then the front line, when the 2nd Brigade relieved the 1st. This period was assessed by Asquith as 'among the most trying ordeals to which the troops were subjected at any time. The Turks who had been killed on July 12th [during a gallant attack by the 52nd Division] lay everywhere, unburied and half-buried, in these newly captured trenches. The weather was sweltering, the stench overwhelming, and many of our officers and men were sick again and again. Reluctance to face this nauseating experience was so strong that during the afternoon there were three cases of self-inflicted wounds . . . the only cases . . . I can remember in the Battalion.'[35] Conditions improved as the bodies which could be safely reached were buried, but the general unsanitary conditions, and millions of flies, resulted in very serious health problems among the troops. Most were verminous, nearly all had dysentery to a greater or lesser degree, and jaundice and typhoid were rife. Lister reported to his father that his spell in the trenches consisted of major digging operations within two hundred yards of the Turks, to make the position secure from enemy fire. He commented that 'Oc has been extraordinarily dogged, and is practically responsible for all this corner, which will be known as Asquith triangle. He hadn't a wink of sleep all the four days'.[36]

Asquith had rejoined a weakened Division, and it was quickly apparent that the flow of reinforcements had dried up. Worse, the Admiralty decided to remove 300 stokers from the Naval Battalions for service afloat, which had the effect of withdrawing the core of trained and disciplined veterans. Hood Battalion alone lost 140. This blow came on top of a previous one, when miners had been removed for mining and tunnelling duties. Many of the stokers were pleased to go, as they were far from happy at having been made to serve ashore in the first place, and the rigours and dangers of this most unpleasant campaign had not convinced them otherwise. Their removal precipitated another reorganisation. The Royal Marines were reduced to two battalions from four, and brigaded with Anson and Howe Battalions as the 2nd RN Brigade, and the four other naval battalions, Drake, Nelson, Hawke and Hood formed the 1st RN Brigade. Commodore Backhouse fell out with General Paris over the reorganisation and returned to naval service and was appointed to command the battleship *Orion*. In May 1916 he and his ship were in action at Jutland. Backhouse went on to be the Admiral Superintendent at Devonport, and retired as a full Admiral. When he returned home from the Dardanelles, he wrote to Edward Marsh complaining that decorations had been too few in the RND, especially for the now broken-up 2nd Brigade. He made recommendations for awards, including DSCs for Asquith and Lister, a DSC and bar for Denis Browne, and a VC for John Dodge for his part in the landings. None of these recommendations was adopted.[37]

On taking over D Company, Asquith immediately set about getting to know his men: he recorded their personal details, including the next of kin and their addresses. In the removal of those men from the Royal Fleet Reserve for sea service, he lost eighty-four stokers from his Company, who were replaced by sixty-six recruits, nearly all of whom were from the north of England or Scotland. Asquith also set in hand trying to trace other members of the Battalion who had gone missing for some reason. By a systematic interrogation of his troops, he was able to verify the where-abouts of the missing men: twelve were discovered to have been killed during the last major Battalion attack, while AB Ansell was confirmed by two witnesses as having been killed on 6 May; AB Brookman was reported by AB Hill as coming back wounded on 4 June. He then fell full length as if shot again; AB Quick was found to be wounded on 2 May and was said to have been found by a French field ambulance, his leg was ampu-tated and he was sent home. By means of this painstaking work, Asquith was able to discover what had happened to thirty-nine men. He also noted the next of kin addresses of his five officers, all Sub Lieutenants. By September, his Company was nominally well up to strength, with forty-eight original Hoods, sixty-four from the first draft of reinforcements, fifty-seven from the second, twenty from the third, plus forty-eight from the disbanded Collingwood Battalion, and six bombers. It was during these summer months that the casualties from sickness were at their worst. Asquith observed in early September that seventy-six of his men had gone to hospital and not returned in the short time he had been in command.[38]

For the next four months, the depleted Royal Naval Division would be involved in more or less static trench warfare before, during and after the failure to bring about a successful conclusion to the Dardanelles campaign by landings farther up the west coast of the Gallipoli peninsula at Suvla Bay. During this time the effects of sickness would be far more serious than the number of casualties inflicted by the Turks.

The Royal Naval Division was now down to less than 6,000 men, from an establishment of 16,500; after short spells in the trenches battalions were allowed to rest in turn in the area of the base camp. 'Rest', in this connection, meant the usual amount of back-breaking labour involving digging trenches, strengthening dugouts, and moving ammunition and stores. The officers' lives were not so physically arduous; the RND billets were fairly safe from Turkish bombardment; there were proper baths, and bathing in the Dardanelles and the Aegean; fish began to appear on the menu for the evening meal, sometimes caught by the simple expedient of bombing them with grenades.

In August Freyberg, having recovered from another dangerous wound received during a major trench raid on 20 July, was in command of Hood Battalion with the rank of Commander. The injury had not fully healed. In the same engagement, Charles Lister was also wounded, with a number of shallow wounds in his back; bored with hospital life, he also returned to his battalion with the wounds still not properly mended, and every morning he called for his batman to dress them. Whatever the merits of Lister's batman may have been in civilian life, he was not a good officer's servant, and one morning after calling for him repeatedly with no result, Lister turned to a brother officer and said, 'That man is hopelessly inefficient. What can we do with him?', and then, after a pause, 'I think we shall have to make him an officer!'[39]

At about the time Asquith became a Company Commander, he began to keep his Army Field Message Books, Army Book 153, containing carbon copies of his correspondence. From this time they form a continuous record of his military career.

In the middle of August Hood Battalion moved up to the trenches where they found saps dug out from the front line, used for listening posts and sniping. It was still very dangerous for men to expose themselves, and casualties from Turkish snipers were common. The trenches were equipped with rudimentary trench mortars and elastic-powered catapults for throwing bombs, and by use of these devices, and the occasional raid, Asquith and the other officers in the RND kept continuous pressure on the Turks. The catapults were not liked: the elastic failed too often, putting the operators in peril, the bombs were notoriously unreliable, and the very operation of winding them back in preparation for launching a missile resulted in such creaking and groaning from the apparatus that the nearby Turks had plenty of time to take cover.

On 24 August Charles Lister was hit by shell fragments: the more serious injury was a piece which entered just behind and below his right hip bone into his lower stomach. There was no exit wound. F S Kelly saw him coming back down the trench looking a 'dreadful pale green colour',[40] but he was not thought to be dangerously hit. The event was the culmination of a depressing time for the naturally optimistic Asquith who wrote to his father on 31 August:

> Our present programme is alternate weeks in front trenches and rest camp. We came back from the trenches last night, and are not sorry to have a rest. This last week was fairly uneventful: we were separated from the Turk by about 200 yards of heather – except in two places where their old communication trenches ran into our front at right angles, and these were barricaded and defended by bombing parties. Our casualties for the week were six killed and three wounded – one of the three, alas being Charles Lister. This is the third time he has been hit by shell: he was hit behind, and it is not clear whether his bladder or pelvis-bone was injured . . . We have not been able to get any news of him since . . . Faces grow long at the thought of a winter campaign, the washing-out of the lightly-buried bodies and fouling of wells . . . It is not so amusing for me as it was, now that Patrick [Shaw Stewart] is liaison, [with the French] and Charles away wounded . . . There is a good deal of sickness – chiefly acute diarrhoea: some staleness – among those who have been out here all along: and some lack of confidence as to how our green men would follow if we had to take an offensive'.

He concluded by saying that he was hungrily awaiting the Fortnum and Mason parcel that step-sister Elizabeth had promised.[41]

Even as this letter was being written, Lister had already been dead for days: his condition had deteriorated rapidly after an operation, and he died on board a hospital ship on 28 August 1915. His death greatly affected all who knew him: he was known for his fearlessness and disregard of his own safety, and it was desperately ironic and unlucky that, on the three occasions when he sustained wounds, he had been taking no risks. Kelly notes that his loss was 'as great a blow as Rupert

Brooke's . . . His sense of humour was exquisite. There was something wonderfully fine and refined about him, and he was completely unselfish. As an intellect, too, he was remarkable.'[42] His father was 'shattered'; he had recently written that 'Charles was and is my chief companion'.[43] Being Lord Ribblesdale's only remaining son (his elder son had died in 1904) the peerage died with him.

During these months of trench warfare, Asquith had been making a reputation for himself as an excellent soldier: a letter from Edgar Bonham Carter in the Sudan congratulated him on his rapid promotion and his excellent military reputation, of which he had heard from several sources.[44] A less unbiased commentator, Violet, wrote that she was 'thrilled by your rocket-like career – I long for you to be a Commodore'.[45] A marginally more objective comment from his sister in law, Cynthia, Beb's wife, was that she was hearing 'from all quarters that you are such a wonderful soldier and I observe you striding up the military ladder.'[46]

An example of Asquith's actions during this spell in the trenches can be found in F S Kelly's journal. On the night of 26/27 August a Hood officer carried out a reconnaissance by crawling out alone to the Turkish trenches only forty yards away, where they had heard digging. He first of all came across an enemy soldier who appeared to be sleeping, and who would need to be dealt with if the mission was to continue. Having decided that he could not murder the man in cold blood, he crept very close with the intention of taking him prisoner. On grabbing the Turk, he discovered it to be a corpse in a sitting position; the rest of the trench was full only of enemy dead. Asquith had deleted his own name from this story during the editing of Kelly's journal. On his return to his own lines, Arthur was nearly attacked by his own men wielding pickaxes. Kelly reports that the 'little adventure was strictly against orders, but like other forbidden things, as it was successfully carried out, he got nothing but praise from the authorities'.[47] For this, and the other good work he had done, Asquith was mentioned in despatches on 22 September 1915.[48]

Nearly all the troops on the peninsula suffered from dysentery. Asquith notes that, during the month of August, one company whose average strength was about 130, had 102 men invalided, and practically all of those remaining were weakened by the sickness. F S Kelly remarked in his journal that, in such circumstances, it was not 'the higher ratings who suffer, but the rank and file who are incessantly sent out on working parties both in the trenches and down in the rest camp'.[49]

Turkish trenches, during the spell in the line in early September, were between fifty and one hundred and twenty yards only from the British: on the left, they were less than fifty.

When out of the line Asquith and Kelly were able to spend a few days on the island of Imbros, the nearest friendly place to the peninsula, where they enjoyed bathing and dinner in peaceful surroundings, and riding through the lovely countryside; but by the end of the month, they were back in the trench routine alternating between the Base Camp and the Front Line. Asquith submerged himself in the minutiae of Company life; by 2 October he reported that only sixteen of his men remained from the original Hoods.[50] His friend from the Sudan, Leach, visited him on Gallipoli about this time, and photographed Asquith in the trenches. The various postmarks on the covering letter indicate the excellence of the colonial postal service at the time: Leach wrote to Asquith on 8 October 1915 from Rufaa; by the 9th it had been stamped at Khartoum; on the 14th it passed through both the Alexandria Military Post Office and the Base Post Office. When Asquith actually received it on the peninsula is not known.[51]

On 6 October the strength of D Company was down to ninety-five when it went back to the front line around Worcester Barricade in the old 29th Division positions on the left of the line between Gully Ravine and Krithia Nullah. There was a threat of fog and special orders were issued: patrols were to be sent forward, communicating with the main trenches by strings and a simple system of signals. However, in general, this time in the line was quiet, and the principal alarm was the prospect of a visit to the front line by the Commander in Chief, Sir Ian Hamilton, which resulted in what Kelly called the 'ludicrous orders . . . that the trenches must be fully manned'. As he was holding his part of the support line, of four hundred yards with very few men, he felt like indenting for a 'few hundred men fully equipped'.[52] In the event the visit was postponed until the following day, when the line was filled out with various headquarters troops. The CinC's inspection confirmed his opinions previously expressed in private letters to the Prime Minister: on 2 September he had written that the Division were 'stout fellows, sticking it out well . . . but very tired', and that there was 'a devilish fine spirit about this particular Division, and it would be 10 million pities if it were allowed to peter out'.[53] On the 30th of the month he reported that the 'RND are sticking it out like heroes, but they are very, <u>very</u> tired'.[54]

Meanwhile, in the trenches, the routine of daily infantry life went on, with Asquith asking for stores, usually including sandbags, various grenades, elastic for the catapults and roofing materials. On 10 October he requested a hyposcope rifle sight from the adjutant, for use by AB Hall, his Bisley marksman, on the basis that 'A handsome dusky sniper might be bagged'. His servant, AB Fairburn, had not had a change of tunic and trousers since landing on the peninsula on 29 April, so these were requested from the quartermaster. The routine demanded that each day in the front line Company Commanders rendered a daily report: at this time actions consisted of the occasional raid, and the more frequent exchange of bombs. On the 22nd Asquith reported that 'some of our cricket ball bombs are very feeble'. Rations were always a high priority for the

Company Commander in the front line, particularly if it was believed that his men were not getting their fair share. After the ration run on the 22nd Arthur alerted Freyberg that his men were being sent less than their allocation of beef and biscuit. The battalion quartermaster, Petty Officer Roberts, commented on Asquith's concerns: this reply earned a very swift rebuke, for later that day Asquith again wrote to the battalion commander, 'QM's note returned herewith is no doubt interesting as expression of his personal opinions about what my men ought to want. All I ask is that they should be supplied with what they actually do want in so far as their wants do not exceed the ration allowed'. He then went on to repeat what the rations were, and continued 'I do not care a fig for what P.O. Roberts says or for QM's knowledge of the working classes'. After this somewhat tongue-in-cheek exchange life became more serious. That night Sub Lieutenant Gibson was shot through the right thigh, the bullet fracturing the bone, while assisting in wiring in front of a sap.[55] Gibson, commissioned at the end of 1914, was the son of a doctor and JP from Harrogate. He died of his wounds on a hospital ship two days later.

Asquith also reports that mining continued. During the wiring operation, the body of a man from the 3rd Hampshires was found just outside Worcester Sap, and buried. He was Corporal George Nash, who had been shot through the chest, the bullet shattering a cigarette case which was in his pocket. Asquith's final thought for this entry in his notebook was that his wound was such that 'his friends may safely assume that his death must have been quick and painless'.[56]

Also in this spell in the front line, the men of the Battalion were asked for their preference of rum or cocoa; out of seventy-one questioned in D Company, a surprising twenty-six voted for cocoa! On the same day, 23 October, as Asquith reported this to his CO, Freyberg, an incident occurred in the trenches which was thought worthy of recounting. During that night, D Company fired six double cylinder bombs from a catapult in Worcester Sap; two of them pitched short, the first rolled safely away, but the sixth hit the forward barricade and fell back into the sap.[57] Able Seaman George Ramsay dashed forward and, tearing out the fuse which had already nearly burned for its allotted five seconds, threw it out of the sap. The daily reports in Asquith's notebooks for this time show that trench warfare had developed, at least on this part of the front, into a wary observation of the enemy trenches, and a continual improvement of the RND positions by digging. No one moved above the parapet by day, and the nights were punctuated by regular, relatively harmless exchanges of bombs. Asquith observed in his daily note to headquarters on 26 October that 'Turkish morale probably suffers more from our vocalists' parodies of Turkish melodies', than from any effects of bombing.[58] Kelly was also in the trenches at the same time, feeling under the weather with what was thought to be the early symptoms of jaundice. In order to provide him with a break, Freyberg did him an act of great kindness by pretending that he wanted to spend a couple of nights in the firing line, and instructed Kelly to take his place in the comfortable and safe headquarters.[59]

This period in the front line was followed by a break of about eight days during which the Battalion moved into winter quarters north of X Beach on top of the cliffs overlooking Imbros, and the men were kept busy erecting dug-outs and shelters, although there was no corrugated iron for the roofs.

Kelly took the opportunity to visit Patrick Shaw Stewart, who was serving with the French as a liaison officer. Walking back through the French positions, he was struck by the excellent preparations they had made for the winter. The following day, he inspected the fire trench from which the attack of 4 June had been made, and remarked on 'the absurd distance – some four hundred yards – our men had to cover before they could assault the enemy's trench'.[60] Asquith was given command of Nelson Battalion, when its Commanding Officer went sick. He commented that this battalion was 'the biggest in numbers, the rawest in composition, and the worst in discipline' and that 'it would be interesting to try to pull Nelson together'.[61] In the event, he was only there for two days before a Nelson officer returned unexpectedly to cause him to 'vacate the Nelson throne – which I was beginning to find very comfortable'.[62]

After this short respite, Hood were back at Worcester Barricade for another stint. As well as their own men there were troops from the 2/4th Londons for training. The Turkish trenches were only fifteen yards from the foremost positions, so on 5 November, presumably inspired by the knowledge that it was Guy Fawkes Day, a major strafe of the enemy lines was undertaken. The extent of damage to the Turks was not discovered, but the RND's own lines received some hits from British mortars which fired short. Asquith had taken the precaution of removing all his men from the very forward positions, and hence there were no casualties. Times were evidently not too arduous, for Asquith had time to indulge in correspondence with Freyberg about bandsmen. The latter was always aware of the great morale value of music, and was keen to establish a band. Arthur reported that his company boasted only three musicians, Sub Lieutenant Fish, 'the well-known violinist', Petty Officer Dexter, 'dexterous with the cornet', and another. He added a postscript to the note, 'Have you heard me sing?'[63] There was also a more serious note to the communications with Battalion HQ, with Asquith complaining strongly about the state in which the Marines, whom they relieved, left the latrines. On 11 November, the Battalion came out of the line again, and Asquith and Shaw Stewart obtained permission to spend twenty-four hours in Athens.

While they were away the first real rain fell on the new camp, and predictably, the dug-outs and billets flooded. The rain continued while

Hood were at Worcester Barricade for their next turn in the front line. As an indication of how inured to death and violence even the most sensitive officers had become, Kelly notes in his diary for 20 November that one of his men was shot in sap 30, and how he remembered the 'complete absence of feeling with which I went up to see him and then returned to finish my lunch'.[64]

Asquith had four Platoon Commanders under him in D Company, all Sub Lieutenants, SH Fish, JC Hilton, GH Tamplin, and RV Chapman. Only Tamplin was married. Fish was eventually killed in action in August 1918 as a Lieutenant Commander, having won the MC; Chapman, formerly of the London RNVR, promoted from the ranks, was wounded in the left thigh and ankle in November 1916, and on recovery joined the Indian Army; Tamplin, an excellent officer, was killed at Gavrelle in 1917 as a Company Commander; and Hilton won the MC and Bar.

The junior officers were kept on their toes. Asquith was a fastidious commander who let nothing slip: just after having left the Front Line at the end of November, a typical note calls for the platoons officers to inspect their men and confirm the issue of extra clothing including waterproof capes. Other points to be checked included the marking of all gear (caps on the inside only), identity discs, haircuts, and shoes. In the winter camp, a duty company officer was nominated to attend to the despatch of all working parties, inspect the food of the men at meals, and supervise the rum issue.[65] Throughout this period, Asquith, in common with many of his men, was suffering from continual debilitation from illness. Betty wrote, in typically breathless style, at the end of November, 'I hear you are ill and won't go into hospital oh I am so sorry for you – I suppose you have got a touch of that fearful dysentry . . . '. She also remarked on the excitement engendered by Violet's forthcoming marriage, 'There has been a lot of chat about Miss Violet Asquith marriage [sic] . . . I don't think I have seen Violet for years I don't think she likes me much I think I like her but she frightens me rather as she makes one feel stupid by seemingly being terribly critical. Yours ever Betty'[66]

Following the failure of the Suvla landings in August, it had become apparent that no clear success could be achieved on the Gallipoli peninsula, without massively increased resources which the British government, gradually coming face to face with the enormous problem posed by the German Army on the Western Front, could not spare. In the middle of October Sir Ian Hamilton was relieved by Monro, a confirmed 'Westerner'. By the end of the month he had recommended the evacuation of the peninsula, much to Churchill's disgust. Kitchener himself then visited Gallipoli in the middle of November, and reported in favour of Monro's recommendations. While the Cabinet procrastinated over the final decision, Arthur wrote to his father. His letter is quoted extensively here because, apart from any effect Arthur's opinions may have had on the final decision to evacuate the peninsula, it forms a revealing insight into the conditions of the British Army on Gallipoli at the time. He kept a carbon copy, offering a

cold unexaggerated account of the state of affairs here in so far as they have come under my eyes as a mere Company commander. Winter has found the British forces at Helles utterly unprepared, although it has been obvious since Aug 6th or at the latest Aug 21st that we should have to spend the winter here. Four things were obviously necessary for the winter.

i. a solid pier at which it would be possible to disembark stores and men in all weathers, from a notoriously windy sea.

ii. Deep level wells to replace the shallow pits of liquid sewage which have been giving our men dysentery all through the summer, and which obviously would be and actually have been further fouled by surface water in the rainy months. (Out of my Company varying in numbers between 130 and 190 men, 102 went to hospital with dysentery in August and September: not a dozen of these have returned). So far as I am aware no deep level well is yet available for use of British troops. Certainly the RND have not got one. They started digging one on our sector about three weeks ago: it is now about 30 feet deep and is not producing water.

iii. <u>Winter clothing for the troops</u>. Some good rainproof capes – not enough for every man to have one – have been issued to the troops. 16 pairs of rubber boots <u>per battalion</u> have been issued. Some good vests, drawers, cardigans, winter-caps have been issued. The men have no change of boots. My men carrying up rations in the trenches last week were in places over their knees in mud and water. Their boots have not been dry since.

iv. Roofs and arrangements for washing and drying clothes in the bivouac area. Our programme is a week in the trenches: then a week in bivouacs, in dug-outs 15 by 8 feet and 4 feet deep, on a heathery cliff as bleak as that at Hopeman. We do Cox and Box with the Howe Battalion: next Wed. They return to this bivouac and we replace them in the trenches. Each dug-out 15 by 8 is supposed to house 6 men: so that for a Battn. 500 strong 80 actual living and sleeping places (not counting kitchens, washing places etc) need roofing. Actually, if only some of the men lie down and others sit up, we can squash 12 men into a dug-out and give them shelter. We have so far been given enough corrugated iron to roof 14 dug-outs ie that is all that Hood and Howe Battns have received between them: and other Battns are no better off.

Thus we can shelter, at a pinch, under iron roofing <u>168 men</u>.

We have tarpaulins, begged borrowed or stolen, over 3 officers messes. In these we can give shelter to 32 men.

Each man has a ground sheet 6ft by 3. They try to rig shelters out of these, but there is no timber, and they flap in the wind, and sag down in the middle and gather pools of water which are emptied in a small cataract into the dug-outs by each big gust of wind.

Drying arrangements. There are none

Washing arrangements. Our Battalion has a stove which boils less water than could be contained by two ordinary washing basins. Water is short even for this. There is no cover for it.

Some of my men washed some clothes in it yesterday and hung them out to dry. First came rain, then unintermittently [sic] for the last 20 hours driving snow from the North.

Our Division has at one of the Field Ambulances one Threshers disinfector which does not exactly wash clothes, but puts them through steam enough to kill vermin, and hot air to dry them again.

At the utmost this can deal with the clothes of 100 men a day: and underclothes and blankets are all they can take to it now as obviously this is not weather for standing about stark naked in the open, and the men have no change of uniforms.

To go back to (i) the Pier, the British, who are I suppose the greatest pier-builders in the world, have no pier now at which they can land anything. At W. Beach they sunk several ships as a breakwater and fiddled and fiddled at making a pier. The first storm of any size, ten days ago, washed away the pier and broke the back of the most important of the sunken ships which form the breakwater.

What we land now, we land by courtesy of the French at their pier at V beach when they do not require it for themselves.

I went this afternoon to see Patrick [Shaw Stewart] at French H.Q. The contrast was most painful. All the French have cover, not only from rain, from shrapnel too; built of semicircular sections of iron such as might be used for lining a tube railway. They have stacks and stacks of firewood: and an enormous timberyard of planks: excellent washing-places: carpenters shops with steam-saws: all arranged with perfect orderliness and precision – largely bought in England e.g. the semi-circular iron sections they use for shelters.

If we do not have terrible wastage from rheums, pneumonias etc it will not be the fault of our generals.

You will be told that a ship with 19000 sheets of corrugated iron was sunk. Yes, but that was in November, two months too late: and that one shipload of iron cannot be a defence against all the disgraceful lack of foresight displayed here. When one hears that an answer is given to Hicks in Parliament to the effect that ample provision has been made for the winter shelter and comfort of the troops here, one wishes that those responsible for giving that answer could be made to live here for a week now under the conditions that the troops are suffering from.

It may be that there is material on the sea, but it is too late, and as I have said it can only be landed at the French beach when that is clear'[67]

This letter is not couched in the careful and precise style usually seen in Asquith's letters, which indicates that it was composed in a hurry, or perhaps on impulse. The weather conditions at the time were dreadful: storms battered the area, and torrential rain alternated with snow and freezing conditions, and it is possible that Arthur's frustrations got the better of him. In addition, he was suffering from the common stomach complaint. Nor is the effect of Arthur's reports to the Prime Minister clear. He had been getting an enormous amount of conflicting advice from many sources for a long time, but there is no doubt that the regular, occasionally candidly pessimistic correspondence from his son, whose opinion and judgment he respected highly, must have weighed heavily. The Prime Minister wrote to Sylvia Henley:

> I had a rather depressing letter this morning from Oc – who never grumbles giving a very gloomy account of the winter conditions at Helles – complains Fr. better provided for despite constant pressure from us [on the military authorities].[68]

One more spell in the firing line, largely uneventful except for Freyberg's insistence on making a night reconnaissance on his own of the Turkish trenches against the advice of Kelly and Asquith, merely out of a thirst for adventure, was followed by a return to the uncomfortable camp mentioned above. On 17 December, in a surprise move, the remains of the RND moved to relieve the French in their base camp north-east of Sedd el Bahr, by Morto Bay, on the east of the Peninsula. To confirm what the RND officers already knew, the quarters were excellent: the dug-outs were safe and dry, and the lines reinforced, not by sand bags, but by stones and clay. On the 19th, they learned that Suvla and Anzac had been evacuated, a brilliantly planned operation where more than 83,000 soldiers, 4,695 animals, and 186 guns had been withdrawn without a single casualty,[69] but the official announcement to the remaining troops made it a very clear that no such action was going to be taken on the Helles front.

Christmas Eve 1915 was the occasion for the most ferocious bombardment suffered by the Division on the peninsula. Fortunately, the front line trenches they occupied were lightly held, and the good ex-French dugouts kept casualties down, although Hawke were badly hit. Christmas Day itself passed surprisingly uneventfully when the expected Turkish attack did not materialise: Kelly and Freyberg played a new game which involved finding a large unexploded shell, dragging or lifting it to a safe location, and then sniping at it with rifles until it exploded. A small prize was awarded for the one who caused the detonation. Kelly notes that Asquith 'adopted a croaking attitude as to the silliness of it etc'.[70] Arthur never quite came to terms with Freyberg's eagerness to take unnecessary risks just for the thrill of it.

At the end of December came the news that the VIIIth Army Corps, (those forces already on the peninsula) would be relieved by the IXth Corps. There was great suspicion that an evacuation was planned, despite strenuous denials by all official sources. The men of the RND would not believe that they were at last going, even after they had taken over the rest of the line on their right from the departing French. Even by 2 January there had been no confirmation that an evacuation was going to occur, although the final decision had been taken in the Dardanelles Army Order No 2 of 1 January 1916; nevertheless, it was evident to the troops that some decision had already been made and preparations were in progress. By 4 January measures were well in hand: Kelly noted confidently that 'W.M.E. [Mark Egerton][71] is our Adjutant and I feel confident that the arrangements [for the evacuation] as far as our battalion is concerned will be as good as possible.'[72]

A copy of those orders is in Arthur Asquith's papers: they consist of just over three sheets of indelible pencil on sheets from a Field Message Book (about 7 inches by 5 inches), and are a model of succinctness. The order details the steps to be taken to avoid noise during the withdrawal: feet to be muffled; canteens not to be allowed to clink; no talking, smoking, or lights. Men were permitted one blanket and their waterproof cape, 220 rounds of ammunition, one iron ration, and a full water bottle. All ranks wore a white badge on their right arms to assist in identification. To cover the removal of the four remaining machine guns, sniping was ordered from the few troops in the firing line. Asquith's Company was to be about the last to leave.

Asquith himself was nominated to cover the withdrawal of his Company by sniping from Ravin de la Mort and from the Château. At 2345 Asquith was to leave, using Boyau Nord trench. All the retard parties were then to convene at the eastern side of Caesar's Camp Spur, prior to disembarkation at V Beach.

Asquith's notebook shows that besides himself, only CPO Burnhill, the Quartermaster, and two cooks would remain on 'Z' night, the night of the disembarkation.[73] Kelly's diary records the details of the evacuation in some detail: he himself was stationed in one of the control stations just back from the front line, charged with keeping the evacuation to time. His whole Battalion had to wait for about three-quarters of an hour on V Beach until they were taken off by a destroyer which was 'bumping against a sunken ship from which we embarked in rather an alarming manner. We had quite a roughish passage. The men were packed all over the deck and the officers crammed into the wardroom'.[74] He felt it was 'a mistake not hanging on [on the peninsula] though I was ready enough that the task fell to some other division.'[75]

The remnants of the RND were taken to Lemnos. Freyberg, Asquith and Egerton, who were among the very last to leave the beach, had not arrived at the RND camp, which was pitched near the west shore of Mudros Bay, so Kelly was for the time being CO. So ended the time of the Royal Naval Division on the Gallipoli peninsula. Of the 16,000 men who had passed through the Division during the Dardanelles campaign, over 13,000 had become casualties, or had been sent to hospital because of illness. When they finally left, they had suffered 7,198 killed and wounded, of whom 133 officers and 2,358 ratings are on the peninsula still.

NOTES

1. Tisdall was another brilliant scholar, and a close friend of the Padre of the Second R N Brigade, H C Foster. Tisdall had won the Chancellor's Gold Medal for Classics at Trinity College, Cambridge in 1913, among many other prizes. Foster described him as a 'highly gifted, yet simple and lovable man' [*At Antwerp and the Dardanelles*, p62]. In his few days in action he demonstrated magnificent courage, until being killed in the attack of 6 May.
2. Kelly diary entry for 29 April 1915.
3. Kelly diary entry for 30 April 1915.
4. Quoted in Martin Gilbert, *Winston S. Churchill, Companion Volume II*, p848.
5. Letter from Margot Asquith to AMA, 7 May 1915, AMA papers.
6 From the *Diary of Margot Asquith*, p667.
7. Letter from HHAto Sylvia Henley dated 9 June 1915. Bodleian Manuscripts, Eng letters c 542. I am indebted to Colin Clifford for this source.
8. Letter from Margot Asquith to AMA dated 13 May 1915, AMA papers.
9. R Knox, *The Life of Patrick Shaw Stewart*, p130.
10. ibid.
11. A handwritten note in AMA papers.
12. Telegram from Montagu to Violet Asquith, 12 May 1915, from Alexandria, VBC papers.
13. Letter from Margot Asquith to AMA dated 13 May 1915, AMA papers.
14. Letter from AMA to Violet Asquith, 16 May 1915, VBC papers.
15. Violet Asquith, *Churchill As I Knew Him*, p408.
16. *Champion Redoubtable*, diary entry for 2 June 1915.
17. Letter from Violet Asquith to AMA dated 6 April 1915, AMA papers.
18. Letter from Violet Asquith to AMA dated 19 July 1915, AMA papers.
19. Letter from Maurice Bonham Carter to AMA dated 19 July 1915, AMA papers.
20. Letter from Margot Asquith to AMA dated 19 May 1915, AMA papers.
21. ibid.
22. Letter from Margot Asquith to AMA dated 15 June 1915, AMA papers.
23. Letter of 18 June 1917 from Margot Asquith to AMA, AMA papers.
24. *Raymond Asquith Life and Letters*, edited by John Jolliffe, 1980, Collins, entry for 24 July 1915.
25. Letter from AMA to Violet Asquith, dated 22 August 1915, VBC papers.
26. Letter from Venetia Stanley to AMA dated 6 October 1915, AMA papers.

27. Kelly diary, entry for the day, footnote by AMA.
28. Letter from Violet Asquith to Maurice Bonham Carter dated 13 June 1915, quoted in *Champion Redoubtable*.
29. Letter from Christine Hamlyn to AMA dated 29 June 1915, AMA papers.
30. Letter from Violet Asquith to AMA dated 19 July 1915, AMA papers.
31. Royal Naval Division Divisional Order No. 180 dated 4 July 1915, VBC MSS No. 0035/007.
32. *The Life of Patrick Shaw Stewart*, p141.
33. Letter from AMA to Violet Asquith, 6 July 1915, VBC papers.
34. Letter from AMA to Violet Asquith, 1 July 1915, VBC papers.
35. Kelly diary footnote by AMA pp102/3.
36. Lord Ribblesdale, *Charles Lister*, p211.
37. Asquith papers, Bodleian Library, Box 15 folio 177.
38. All from a blue bound notebook in AMA papers.
39. Kelly diary, footnote by AMA, entry for the day.
40. Kelly diary, entry for 24 August 1915.
41. Letter from AMA to HHA dated 31 August 1915, VBC MSS No 0035/005.
42. Kelly diary, entry for 12 September 1915.
43. Letter from Lucy Graham Smith to AMA dated 9 November 1915, AMA papers. Lucy was one of the elder sisters of Margot Asquith, who had made an early marriage to Thomas Graham Smith of Easton Grey near Malmesbury. Lister's father quotes an Honours Despatch by Sir Ian Hamilton which reads, 'For brilliant deeds of gallantry throughout our operations. On July 16th he was specially brought to notice for heading an assault against an enemy's stronghold. Again, on July 21st, he personally reconnoitred a Turkish communication trench, and, although wounded (for a second time), he returned and led forward a party to the attack.' Quoted in *Charles Lister*, p227. He was killed before he could receive any award.
44. Letter from Edgar Bonham Carter to AMA, 1 September 1915.
45. Letter from Violet Asquith to AMA, 19 July 1915, AMA papers.
46. Letter from Cynthia Asquith to AMA, 13 September 1915, AMA papers.
47. Kelly diary, entry for 27 August 1915.
48. Supplement to the *London Gazette*, No. 29354, dated 5 November 1915.
49. Kelly diary, entry for 3 September.
50. AMA Army Field Note Book No 1, AMA papers, entry for the day.
51. Letter from J Leach to AMA, 8 October 1915, AMA papers.
52. Kelly diary, entry for 9 October 1915.
53. Asquith papers, Bodleian Library, box 15, folio 173.
54. Asquith papers, Bodleian Library, box 15 folio 181.
55. From AMA Army Field Note Book No. 1, AMA papers.
56. ibid.
57. Ramsay, a miner from Bannockburn gave excellent service until his death in action on 13 November on the Ancre, as a Petty Officer. It took Asquith nearly a year to obtain Ramsay's well deserved Distinguished Service Medal for him. He has no known grave, and is commemorated on the Thiepval Memorial.
58. From AMA Army Field Note Book No 1, AMA papers.
59. Kelly diary, entry for 28 October 1915.
60. Kelly diary, entry for 30 October 1915.
61. Letter from AMA to Violet Asquith dated 28 October 1915, VBC MSS 034/011.
62. Letter from AMA to Maurice Bonham Carter dated 14 December 1915, VBC MSS 035/006.

63. AMA Field Message Book No. 2, in use from 31 October to 27 November 1915.
64. Kelly diary, entry for 22 November 1915.
65. AMA Field Message Book No 2, entry for 25 November 1915, AMA papers.
66. Letter from Betty Manners to AMA dated 30 November 1915, AMA papers.
67. Transcript of part of a copy of a letter from AMA to his father, dated 28 November 1915, AMA papers.
68. Letter from Herbert Asquith to Sylvia Henley, dated 24 December 1915, Bodleian Mss.
69. *Defeat at Gallipoli*, Nigel Steel and Peter Hart, Macmillan, 1994, p389.
70. Kelly diary, entry for 25 December 1915.
71. In the assessment of Arthur Asquith, 'none rendered more continuous, efficient and wholehearted service to the Hood Battalion'. Footnote to F S Kelly's diary for 9 June 1915. Egerton, the son of Admiral Sir George Egerton, KCB, who was Commander in Chief Plymouth until 1916, was awarded the DSO in Gallipoli, and was wounded (for the third time) when in command of the Battalion in 1918.
72. Kelly diary, entry for 2 January 1915.
73. Notebook No. 3, undated entry, p35, between 5 and 7 January 1915.
74. Kelly diary, entry for 8 January 1915, written on board HMS *Bulldog* en route from Cape Helles to Mudros.
75. ibid.

CHAPTER VI

Interlude: The Calm Before the Storm

After the evacuation, the Admiralty agreed to garrison the islands of Lemnos, Imbros, and Tenedos on condition that 'the Naval Division (serving with the Dardanelles Army) being placed at their disposal for this purpose and subject to military assistance being provided in details which the Division lacks.'[1] The Admiralty drove a hard bargain, including in their list of requirements: transport, including animals, tents and camp hospitals, and artillery.[2] The Army accepted the terms, and the RND ceased to be part of the Mediterranean Expeditionary Force and was returned to naval command under Vice Admiral Sir John de Robeck, commanding the Eastern Mediterranean Fleet while discussions went on in London about the Division's future. Asquith, Freyberg and Egerton stepped ashore at Lemnos on the morning of 10 January 1916 and joined the rest of Hood Battalion at the South Camp on the West Bay of Mudros Bay, about two and a half miles from the harbour. They threw themselves into the routine of camp life safe from the fear of sudden death. Large new drafts had arrived, seven officers and over two hundred men for Hood.[3] There were rumours about ten days' leave for fifteen per cent of the officers, but nothing for the men. The Hood officers felt so strongly about this that they held a meeting and agreed that they would not apply for leave unless the men received some too.[4] By way of recreation, Kelly, Egerton and Asquith walked the nine miles into the little town of Castro for an excellent dinner and an overnight stop at the Restaurant Français. When they returned to the camp having ploughed through a blizzard, they discovered that it was flooded. The wanderers also learned that the first few officers had been selected, and had left, for leave in England.

On 16 January Asquith learned that he was to be made a Companion of the Légion d'Honneur, and to be awarded the Croix de Guerre.

Major General Paris inspected Hood Battalion on 17 January, and after the parade he announced that leave would be granted: officers could go to England, but the men were only to be allowed to go to Malta. When three cheers were called for the General, the Hoods responded with a raspberry. Paris was furious, and cancelled all leave for the Battalion and confined them to camp for seven days.[5] This may be an apochryphal story, for Kelly, normally a fastidious chronicler of such details, gives it no mention: on the contrary, on the following day he notes that 'there was going to be leave in England for men and we're wondering whether our refusing leave has anything to do with it'.[6]

The Division now began to split: the 2nd Brigade was despatched to the Salonika Front, at the time quiescent, while the 1st RN Brigade was distributed in garrison duties on Lemnos, Imbros and Tenedos. On the 20th, Freyberg took a total of 401 officers and men from Hood Battalion, mostly A and B Companies, to form the Tenedos garrison, leaving Asquith in command of the remainder.[7]

Tenedos proved a delightful place. The French they relieved left them excellent wooden huts, and the pleasant landscape with 'varied cultivation, stretches of heather, a few fir woods, isolated fig trees, and pleasant little valleys running down to white sandy beaches'[8] was benign and restful. The troops were introduced to a strange local food, 'Yaoult, or some such name, a sort of cream cheese one eats with milk'.[9] The British troops had discovered yoghourt! Kelly took a week's break to go to the island of Mytilene to buy a piano.

Back on Lemnos, Asquith was running the rear party and doing his best to ensure that Freyberg was kept supplied with the stores he wanted and the news he craved. He enlisted the help of the GOC 1st Brigade, Brigadier Mercer, to obtain field kitchens, stoves and zinc baths for the detachment,[10] and he nagged the stores organisation for bicycles so that Freyberg's communications within the island could be improved.[11] A great deal of work remained to be done at Mudros: Asquith was making preparations for the rest of the Battalion to join Freyberg on Tenedos, but the latter was suffering himself from a lack of transport, 'not a single mule or waggon'[12] under his charge at Mudros. Spirits were kept up by concerts; the Hood band, beloved by Freyberg, Asquith and Kelly, had become quite proficient, although they still had to borrow seven men from Nelson, and one from Anson Battalions.[13] On Tenedos, Kelly entertained the more thoughtful with Chopin, Mendelssohn, Brahms and his own 'Elegy in Memoriam' to Rupert Brooke, while for others of his Company he lead community singing. A particular favourite of the men was 'Green Grow the Rushes, Oh!'[14]

Meanwhile, interest in leave was occupying the minds of all, and on 18 February, in response to a request from GOC 1st Brigade, asking for names for leave, Asquith wrote to the Divisional AA and QMG:

Commander Freyberg Lieut Commander Asquith Lieut Commander Egerton Lieuts Kelly and Cockey all landed on the Peninsula on April 29th and left on January 8th all were wounded and away at Malta or Alexandria at various times . . . So many as can be spared from above wish to be considered for the next leave home if some of the men are also getting leave home . . . Commander Freyberg did not give me his own name as an applicant for leave. I presume he wants it.[15]

This followed up a previous message to the Brigade Major of the 2nd Brigade RND with a list of officers and the number of days they had spent on the peninsula. The list was headed by:

Sub Lt Battersby	225
Lt Cmdr Asquith	207
Sub Lt Fish	177
Sub Lt Edmondson	177
Lt Morrison	155
Sub Lt Hilton	144

and again repeating the proviso that the men should also have leave.[16]

On the 21st, news came through that leave was to be granted, and that thirty-seven would go from the Battalion. It was hailed 'as a great victory'.[17] The men from Tenedos returned to Mudros to board the troopship for what was planned as ten days' leave. On 26 February, after a parade at which the Hood flag was hoisted, Kelly marched off the lucky men to the strains of the Battalion band, to join Freyberg and Asquith on board HMT *Olympic*. Kelly notes that at night he could hear a shower of rain pattering on the deck above, and remarked on the 'cosy satisfaction' that 'he need have no anxiety as to pools forming and dripping through the joins in the waterproof sheets'.[18] To buoy still further their spirits, Kelly had received a consignment of three dozen bottles of champagne that he had ordered, which he had intended to be drunk at Christmas.[19] The ship, carrying a total of 550 men from the RND docked in Marseilles, and the party went from there overland, arriving home on Saturday 4 March 1916.

The Royal Naval Division was now overstrength for the first time in its history: the *Olympic* had brought 10,000 reinforcements when it docked in Mudros, and the Divisional Commander was chafing at the mis-employment of his men, but also over the uncertainty that surrounded the continued existence of the RND. At home, there was a debate about whether the Division should be disbanded or transferred to the Army: discussions on the latter solution always seemed to founder on the fact that the RND men were legally sailors. In the islands, de Robeck had sufficiently high regard for them to add his weight to the discussions after talking with General Paris. On 13 March he telegrammed the First Lord counselling against any reductions:

'It would be a national misfortune. The men who have fought magnificently have great *esprit de corps* and the units are up to war strength.'[20] He followed it up with another on 17 March, but to no avail. The mind of the Admiralty seemed made up to disband the Division. By the end of the month Paris reported that the 'much-feared blow has fallen',[21] and on 2 April he told Hood Battalion after a parade that 'the

Division would soon be disbanded'.[22] A disappointed Paris left soon after for leave, believing that his command would shortly cease to exist.

Back home in England the RND lobby was working at full pressure to keep the Divison together. Although the Admiralty appeared resolved in its determination to shed its 'problem child', Freyberg, Arthur Asquith and others had different ideas. Despite the fact that Churchill was no longer First Lord, Arthur retained the ear of his father, and the support of his sister, Violet. It is known that Freyberg dined frequently in Downing Street, having been introduced to the Prime Minister by Arthur, and had become well-thought of by all the Asquith family.[23] In March he returned to Mudros where he informed one of his officers that he had seen the Prime Minister during his leave, and had 'got a tentative promise that we should go to France'.[24] Certainly, it would not have been at all in character for Asquith Junior to stand by and allow the RND to be broken up without speaking his mind.

While all these deliberations were going on, Arthur Asquith, home on ten days' leave, was not required to rejoin his Battalion so he, and a few others in the same fortunate position, made the most of their enforced idleness. He saw quite a lot of Kelly, who dined at 10 Downing Street with, among others, apart from the Prime Minister, Margot and Arthur, Maurice Bonham Carter and Violet, Lady Horner (Raymond's mother-in-law), Freyberg and Shaw Stewart. After dinner, Kelly played the piano for the guests, despite being informed by Arthur that his father's two active hatreds 'are music and dogs'.[25] On the following Sunday Kelly joined forces with Jelly Aranji, the famous violinist, to play his violin sonata in G major, and Dvorak's Quintet with others, at the Bonham Carters'. He noted without comment that 'Bongie and Ock [sic] sang "Green Grow the Rushes, Oh!"'[26]

Despite all their efforts to retain the Royal Naval Division, it seemed that they had failed. Then suddenly at the end of April Asquith, Kelly and other RND men on leave were told to rejoin their units in the Middle East. Kelly heard from Freyberg by telephone on 29 April that the RND was being manned to full strength, that Asquith would command one of the newly formed battalions, to be known as 2nd Hood, and that he (Kelly) was to be second in command. Freyberg also revealed that the Division was likely to be in France in a month.[27] Asquith was promoted Temporary Commander RNVR on 4 May 1916, just over eighteen months after joining the RND.

On Friday 5 May 1916 about a dozen RND officers met at Charing Cross to catch the boat train. In addition to Asquith, Freyberg and Kelly, were Lieutenant Commander Nelson and Major Sketchley. Sketchley and Kelly would not see England again. Margot Asquith came to see Arthur off, and brought a bottle of eau de cologne for Freyberg, Kelly and her stepson. After a calm passage, they arrived at Boulogne, and as the train did not leave until 7 pm, Kelly, Asquith and Nelson motored to Wimereux.[28] On 8 May they took passage on the SS *Medina* to Malta from Marseilles. At their destination, they were told that the RND was already in the process of leaving Mudros, and that they were to take the first available boat back to Marseilles. Freyberg and Kelly weighed themselves at the club: the former was the heavier, by half a stone, at fifteen stone seven pounds. Kelly had put on twenty-one pounds in the last couple of months in England.[29] At about 11am on 11 May Asquith, nineteen other officers and eleven men took passage in HMS *Isonzo*, formerly the P&O Steamship *Isis* to Taranto, and thence to Marseilles overland.[30]

On 16 April the RND had been placed under the Army Act, and on 1 May the formal order came through to form the 2nd Hood Battalion. The War Office would assume all responsibility for the administration of the Division from the time of its arrival in France, except for payment and drafting, which would remain with the Admiralty. For the first time the Division was to be complemented as the other Army units in France, with its own artillery, machine gun companies, and divisional train. In May, the elements of the Division in the Middle East began to be transported to France, via Marseilles. By the time Hood Battalion arrived in the Abbeville area from about 24 May, they found that Asquith and Kelly had been there since 17 May and, with Freyberg, were making the necessary arrangements.

NOTES

1. Minute from the Admiralty to the War Office, dated 9 January 1916, pp264-266, PRO, Kew, box ADM 137/3088.
2. ibid.
3. Kelly's diary, entry for 11 January 1916.
4. ibid.
5. From the papers of Thomas Macmillan, Imperial War Museum, Department of Documents. Macmillan was a clerk in the HQ of the Brigade. He was promoted Sub Lieutenant in 1917, and was the co-author of *The Complete History of the Royal Naval Division*, published in 1919.
6. Kelly's diary, entry for 18 January 1916.
7. AMA notebook No. 3, entry for 20 January 1916.
8. Kelly's diary, entry for 21 January 1916.
9. Kelly's diary, entry for 4 February 1916.
10. AMA notebook No. 3, entry for 22 January 1916.
11. AMA notebook No. 3, entry for 1 February 1916.
12. AMA notebook No. 3, note to the Brigade Major, 5 February 1916.
13. AMA notebook No. 3, note to Freyberg, undated, between 1 and 5 February 1916.
14. Kelly's diary, entry for 19 February 1916.
15. Copy of Army form C.2123 'Messages and Signals' dated 18 February 1916, in AMA papers.
16. Copy of Army form C. 2123, Hood No. 3, dated 17 February 1916.
17. Kelly's diary, entry for 21 February 1916.

18. ibid, entry for 26 February 1916.
19. ibid.
20. Public Record Office, Kew, ref ADM116/1411.
21. Imperial War Museum, Dept of Documents, The Papers of Major General Sir Archibald Paris, ref Ds/Misc/57.
22. Joseph Murray, *Call to Arms*, p51.
23. Paul Freyberg, *Freyberg V. C. Soldier of Two Nations*, p77.
24. Sub Lieutenant John Bentham, *A Young Officer's Diary*, Liddle Collection, Leeds University, entry for 24 March 1916.
25. Kelly's diary, entry for 7 March 1916.
26. Kelly's diary, entry for 12 March 1916.
27. Kelly's diary, entry for 29 April 1916.
28. Kelly's diary, entry for 5 May 1916.
29. Kelly's diary, entry for 9 May 1916.
30. Kelly's diary, entry for 11 May 1916.

CHAPTER VII

France: In Command of 2nd Hood Battalion

Asquith and Kelly found their billets, in the small town of Pont Remy, a little crowded, and they moved into 'a small chateau between the bridge and the railway station just south of the river'[Somme].[1] On the following day, they motored into Citernes to discuss the Battalion billeting with the local Mayor. There was insufficient room and fresh water and so Asquith and Kelly went farther afield, to Neuville and Forceville, villages about six miles south of Abbeville.

The next problem was how to divide up the battalion between Freyberg and Asquith. So, after dinner on 25 May, together with their seconds in command, Egerton and Kelly respectively, they sat round a table. Kelly records:

The procedure adopted was the alternate choice of officers (with whom went their platoons), the first choice resting on the toss of a coin. Ock [sic] won the toss, and by this we were able to avoid having one of the obvious undesirables. It was an amusing little symposium – in which either side was much concerned to keep its counsel secret. Ock and I were at an advantage here, as we relapsed into French, which the others did not understand. On the whole the division was a fair one – though, at the end, the intention of giving two platoons of each company to form the new battalion had to be set aside when it was found that owing to the choice of officers A.M. Asquith's and W.M. Egerton's original platoons were separated from their original officers. Freyberg was loth to allow three platoons of two companies to go to one battalion to satisfy these motherly feelings, but these old hens clucked away to such an extent that the original arrangement was amended to allow of their keeping their respective chickens.[2]

Even though the split of talent in the Battalion seemed fair and reasonable, there was still a residual feeling that Asquith and Kelly may have received more than their share of less worthy men.

The following day Asquith was visited by his new Brigadier, Lewis Philips, and both he and Kelly were favourably impressed. Asquith detected that the new general 'might be impulsive in the sense of dealing out a good many orders which, subsequently in the conversational turn of an interview, become modified'.[3]

Asquith was very busy at this time, setting up his battalion organisation. He was hampered to an extent by the need to send men off for courses. Sub Lieutenants Bentham and Chapman were despatched for instruction in bombing and Lewis Guns respectively, while Kelly himself, plus a Petty Officer and three Leading Seamen, joined them at the Infantry Base Depot at Rouen for two weeks to learn about trench warfare;[4] there, as part of the training, he was initiated into the new methods proposed for assaulting enemy trenches, which were 'obviously the result of some careful thinking'.[5] Kelly continued:

A party of some three hundred men were divided up into assaulting party and supports. Each party was then divided up into four equal portions each of whose functions respectively were (from the right) bayonet men, bombers, men carrying horizontal ladders (for subsequent parties to cross trenches gained) and, finally, men with entrenching tools (spades and picks) to consolidate trenches occupied. The chief point of the system is that each party of men is told off for a particular trench, beyond which they're not to go. The first party gains and occupies the first trench, the second the second, etc. Each party of men advanced from the right in double file at a quick march. On arriving at a specified point the bayonet men extended to the left, lay down and opened fire on the trench in front of them, while the next party – the bombers – extended behind them and threw their bombs into the trench. When they had done this the bayonet men charged and occupied the trench in front of them, the bombers following them in.[6]

Kelly made himself unpopular at the base: he insisted on sporting a full beard, something which was not permitted in the Army, and pointed out that the Royal Navy took precedence on parade.[7]

At the camp, besides the normal routine stores demands for stationery and a typewriter, which to his irritation Asquith discovered from the Base Stationery Depot was not standard issue for battalions,[8] he and his adjutant Hilton kept badgering Brigade HQ to hasten the return of officers who had not returned to the Battalion after leave in England, particularly Sub Lt Battersby, a peninsula veteran, who had been away since 26 February,[9] and Lieutenant Farrer. The latter was known to want to join Asquith's Battalion.[10] He also missed no chance to retrieve old 'Hoods' from Gallipoli who had been sent to other RND battalions at Blandford, the base camp, to recover from wounds or sickness.[11]

Discipline appears to have been reasonable, apart from an early court martial for drunkenness of Leading Seaman Sherry.[12] But Asquith was concerned for the morale of his men, and at the end of June he brought up the subject of leave to Brigadier Philips: he pointed out to Brigade HQ that ten percent of his Battalion had not been home for fifteen to sixteen months, and that one third had not been home for between twelve and sixteen months. Asquith reported that he had noticed 'symptoms of a spirit of discontent and lack of keenness among the men . . . directly due to . . . the small amount of leave they have received in comparison with other troops in France.'[13] The minute was returned within two days from Corps HQ with a note refusing 'to allow any increased allotment of leave for the present'.[14] The tone of Asquith's various correspondence with his Brigadier reveals his impatience with the perceived lack of support from his superiors, which would develop into more serious disagreements in the future.

Training continued, as did the inevitable arduous work of the infantryman in the rear lines: there was always more digging, road-building, moving stores and ammunition, to be done. When Kelly completed his trench warfare course on 17 June, he rejoined the Battalion, which during his absence had moved closer towards the front line, and was now in billets around the village of Dieval, a few miles north of Arras, in the Souchez sector.

In late June it had become apparent that there would not be enough recruits to guarantee the continued supply of men to maintain the Royal Naval Division using only sailors and marines: it was decided to form an additional brigade with four Army battalions. The Division was to be known as the 63rd (Royal Naval) Division, with Howe, Anson, and the 1st and 2nd Royal Marines making up the 188th Brigade, and Hood, Hawke, Drake, and Nelson the 189th. The Army Brigade would comprise 1st Honourable Artillery Company, 4th Bedfords, 7th Royal Fusiliers, and 10th Dublin Fusiliers. The result of this reorganisation was that the 2nd Hood, only in existence for a few weeks, was combined back into the 1st Battalion. The 1st and 2nd Battalions met at Verdrel on 5 July 1916 and were amalgamated. Excess ratings were distributed either in the other naval battalions or returned to Blandford. On 7 July Asquith resumed command of D Company, reverting to Lieutenant Commander and three of the four Company Commanders lost promotion and became second in command of companies of the reconstituted Hood Battalion, which now numbered twenty-seven Officers and 1,004 ratings.[15]

Asquith went back to company command with Kelly as his deputy. His only trace of disappointment is revealed in a carbon copy of a letter to an unidentified friend named Bill, who obviously had been trying to be posted to Asquith's battalion:

My Dear Bill, Your letter of 1st only reached me yesterday. Evidently they must have held up my many official applications for you foreseeing what has since occurred, i.e. the reabsorption two days ago of Cleg's [Kelly's nickname] and my Battn. Things are now 'as you were' three months ago. There is much wasted work to be deplored, and, – until we have casualties – it leaves no 'niche' for you in this Battn. as the absorption makes us over establishment for Officers of your rank. This is very sickening and disappointing and how you will be cursing the Division and all its ways at Blandford. If I were you I would be inclined to transfer to the Guards. We expect to go to the trenches this week.

Yours Oc[16]

On 10 July C and D Companies left their billets and headed for Coupigny, from where they went up into the line for attachment to 142nd Brigade. Asquith reported to Freyberg that he was taking five officers, nine Chief and Petty Officers, and 217 men with him to the trenches.[17]

NOTES

1. Kelly's diary, entry for 18 May 1916.
2. Kelly's diary, entry for 25 May 1916.
3. Kelly's diary, entry for 29 May 1916.
4. From AMA notebook No. 4, Army Book 152. Correspondence Book (Field Service), in AMA papers, entry for 4 June 1916.
5. Kelly's diary, entry for 7 June 1916.
6. ibid.
7. Bentham, *A Young Officer's Diary*.
8. Note from AMA to GOC lst RN Brigade No. 1/14, dated 14 June 1916; AMA notebook No. 4.
9. AMA notebook No. 4, entry for 6 June 1916.
10. AMA notebook No. 4, entry for 13 June 1916, with a reminder on 23 June 1916.
11. AMA notebook No. 4, entry for 8 June 1916.
12. AMA notebook No. 4, entry for 10 June 1916.
13. Minute from AMA to GOC 1st RN Brigade dated 24 June 1916, AMA papers.
14. ibid.
15. From Hood Battalion War diaries, entries for 5 and 7 July, Public Record Office, Kew, box ADM 137/3064.
16. AMA notebook No. 5, Army Book 153, Field Message Book, in use from 5 July 1916 to 21 July 1916, AMA papers: entry for 9 July 1916.
17. AMA notebook No. 5, entry for 10 July 1916.

CHAPTER VIII

In the Front Line in France

Asquith left behind at Coupigny four officers and their orderlies, one writer, two as packguard, two cooks, the Quartermaster, eight sick, two on special courses, and AB Boyden, who was under age. His company was attached to, and came under the command of, the 21st Londons of 47th Division, and his notebook reveals the route: via Bully Alley and Corons d'Aix trench.[1] The first stay in the front line was beset with teething problems: the initial concern was over the lack of rations which were not sent up with those of the London Battalion, and rations parties had to be sent from the trenches, on a round trip of two and a half hours on empty stomachs, to transport them.[2] Platoon officers were late with routine reports, and received terse reminders from Asquith in his HQ in Morrow Street Trench.[3] When relief was due, limbers were provided for the officers' gear, and Asquith's horse was requested.[4] Platoons were instructed to proceed independently to Coupigny, to report to the Adjutant.[5] Relationships with the Londons were evidently good, for on relief Asquith wrote to the CO 21st Londons offering his 'best thanks for all the hospitality and help given to us by your Officers and Men'.[6] On the way down the communication trench after relief, Able Seamen Harris, Wild and France were wounded by shrapnel: only Wild, hit in the stomach, was seriously hurt.[7]

A few days after C and D companies went to the trenches, A and B followed them. Kelly led B Company to the lines to the left of where Asquith and his men were posted, known as Souchez II sector. Things were very quiet, but Kelly noted that the trenches, 'both in the firing and support lines were much inferior to those in the Gallipoli peninsula – the firing line except in a few places having no fire step . . . if the Germans had felt disposed to snipe we made excellent targets in a dozen turns of the trench . . . The deep dugouts were a novelty to me but they struck me as being traps . . . The wire was in very poor condition as was also the parapet – sandbags being just heaped up with no apparent consideration as to whether they afforded cover from fire.'[8] Kelly was attached to the 20th Londons, a sister battalion to the one to which C and D Companies were seconded. They suffered considerable strafing from *minenwerfers* and heavy shells.[9]

This short period of training was considered enough for the Royal Naval

Division to be fit to hold a relatively quiet part of the front line, and they were allocated the Souchez sector. The Army battalions which were to make up the Division's third brigade were not ready, and so initially the Naval Brigades alone held the line. After a short rest, Asquith and his company returned to the trenches in Souchez I sector, and took over their defence, relieving their previous mentors of the 47th Division on 17 July. Here, the distance between the British and German front line trenches was on average about one hundred yards, closing in places in Asquith's sector to under twenty-five yards. Hood Battalion's front included a stretch of line from 'M 32 dumbbells [a mark of that shape on the map] to the "S" of S.24', a distance of about 900 yards. His planned dispositions were as follows:

In the front line: 10 bombers on the right of his position
1 Lewis gun by the 'B' of Bois en Hache, Plus 20 men
No work was to be done by day.

In the support line: From Kellet Line to Northumberland Road,
10 HQ bombers at Northumberland Road, 5 Pick and shovel men
with them for storming party in case of a mine at 'S' of S.25.
[Obviously enemy mining had been detected in the area]

Plus 80 Rifles in the Kellet Line.[10]

Also noted are the types and content of the routine reports required from him to Battalion HQ while in the front line:

Daily
1. Situation 2.30 am and pm
2. R.E. Indent 7.30 am
3. Strength 9 am
4. Progress, Intelligence, Patrol, 3.30 pm
5. Casualties 3.30 pm

Weekly
1. SAA in possession (Small Arms Ammunition), Friday Noon
2. Iron Ration Cert. Saturday Noon

Monthly, on 29th inst.
1. No camera cert.
2. Fires in billets
3. Order cert.[11]

In the same notes are the code words in use for their time in the line.

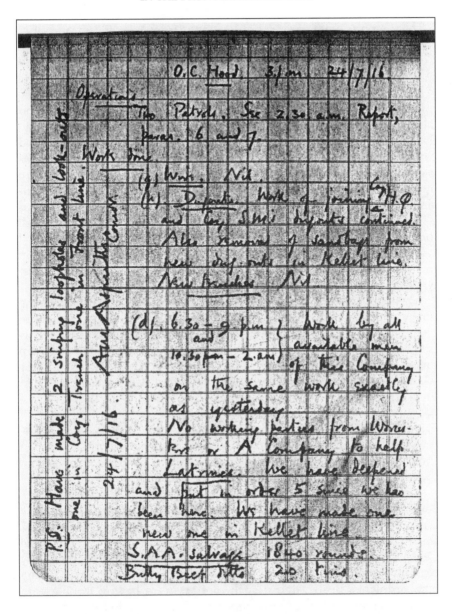

2. A typical Situation Report from Asquith's time as a Company Commander in the Front Line in the Souchez sector north of Arras, dated 24 July 1916, from one of Asquith's Field Service Notebooks.
Private Papers

These reports were an extra burden on the front-line officers, and, after Kelly had been in the front line for a few days, he remarked that 'As a Company Commander in the trenches in France one seems to spend most of one's time writing reports of what one has not had time to observe'.[12]

D Company remained in the front line until 25 July, during which time a great deal of work was done improving the trenches, dug-outs and latrines, the last always a subject dear to Asquith's heart. The trenches in this area had suffered greatly from prolonged bad weather and required considerable work to bring them to a satisfactory standard. There was occasional fire from the enemy: on 21 July German artillery kept up intermittent fire on the HQ trench, and in retaliation 'a few salvoes, well-aimed, between the S and the 2 of S.2.4 on the enemy front line' were fired by British guns.[13] Attacks were always met by a greater response in kind: for 3 'Minnies, 12 trench mortar rounds were returned on 22 July'.[14] Asquith's men also began taking casualties: AB Dickson was wounded in the side by shrapnel, and AB Hesp killed by a sniper, shot in the chest while on sentry duty at night.[15]

Whenever he was in command, Asquith placed great importance on the timely supply of good quality rations for his men. Nothing was more guaranteed to earn a swift rebuke than poor quality food sent to his troops. While in the front line this time it was the practice to bring up rations in sandbags: evidently the Quartermaster's organisation was taking insufficient care with them, for on the 23rd Asquith complained to Freyberg that:

> Rations reach us in the most abominable state. Tea, Sugar, Cheese, Bacon, Bread, and tins of Beef are put without any attempt at separation or covering into one sandbag together, and a mixture of tea, sugar, cheese and blue paint is imbedded in the bacon.

Some sections received incorrect amounts of food, and this also drew censure.[16] The situation reports for the remaining days of D Company's stay in the line were taken up with continuous work on the fabric of the trench system, salvaging of ammunition (several thousand rounds by Asquith's men), and enduring, and retaliating to, occasional enemy bombardments. British light trench mortars were having trouble with fuses at the time, a fact that was reported after a ten-minute strafe of the enemy line on the 25th, when 'At least three-quarters of our L.T.M shells burst high in the air, doing no damage'.[17]

Back in the reserve lines the usual round of administrative tasks continued: Asquith conducted inspections of his troops to ensure their equipment and iron rations were up to scratch, and made sure that the platoon officers had arranged baths at the station in Noulette Wood. Another duty on return from the trenches was to deal with the casualties:

the unfortunate AB Hesp, killed by a sniper, left very few personal effects, including a Bible and a small silk handkerchief. The Orderly Room returned them to Hesp's Platoon Commander, Tamplin, with a message to the effect that they were 'not worth sending home'. Asquith wrote to Freyberg on the matter, concluding

> I need <u>hardly</u> say that Sub Lieut. Tamplin and I hold the contrary opinion strongly: I return the effects herewith for forwarding home.[18]

Even when their troops were in the front-line trenches, the Company Commanders sometimes returned to Battalion HQ for briefings and dinner. At about midnight on 1 August, after dinner with Freyberg, Montagu, Egerton, and the doctor, McCracken, Kelly and Asquith went back to the right of the line by the Souchez river as the latter was the only officer in the Battalion who knew the area well enough to advise on the posting of some of Kelly's men in a listening post. Kelly also noted that :

> Freyberg is like a child with a new toy over his direct control of the Stokes gun batteries at his disposal. Before dinner, at his headquarters, he insisted on my timing how long it took between his telephoning to the trench mortars and their first shot. They were, I thought, remarkably quick in getting off their first shot within a minute and a quarter. Freyberg is delightfully keen on strafing the enemy.[19]

In their next tour in the trenches, it is apparent that the routine organisational problems had been largely resolved. Asquith's notebooks dwell far more on operational matters than logistic difficulties. Work continued to improve the trenches, particularly the latrines, and to make datum measurements from fixed positions in the front line to various places of potential interest between the lines. The area on the extreme right of the line by the river was unheld, as the terrain was too waterlogged, so it offered 'admirable opportunities for scouting'.[20] On the night of 1 and 2 August Asquith with Lieutenant Heald[21] and Leading Seaman Blair, carried out a reconnaissance in no man's land. They returned after four hours; Asquith reported the state of the ground in front of the German front line, but the party heard nothing other than the sounds of working in the Bois en Hache to their left rear. The same party carried out a further patrol the following night; it was Asquith's fourth in as many consecutive nights. This time they reached the enemy wire, which Asquith reported as 'thick, barbed, and rigged on circular iron frameworks. It was about 3ft high'.[22] They remained listening until it began to get light. The Germans were obviously suspicious, for flares were fired near the patrol, and a burst of machine gun fire also came close.

It was a relatively quiet sector: during each spell in the line in the first half of August, there were patrols and exchanges of fire between trench mortars, rifle grenades and machine guns. Sniping was always of the greatest concern in the front line. Asquith reported to battalion HQ that the 'face and cap of an enemy sniper . . . can at times be clearly seen reflected in his box periscope . . . I was not aware before that one could be seen reflected in one's own periscope'.[23] A request followed immediately for a hyposcope, and two periscope rifles.[24] Kelly had an idea that a German could be persuaded to cross no man's land into captivity, and used to crawl to a listening post close to the enemy line and sing 'Siegfried', and the German used to carry on where he left off, but could never be persuaded to come over.[25]

Leave matters continued to preoccupy the men, particularly those who had been a long time away from home. Asquith wrote to the father of AB James sympathising that his son had not been granted leave, concluding that 'Your boy is fit and working well, as he has done throughout'.[26]

Minor administrative matters still had to be dealt with: the steel helmets issued to the troops were finished in shiny paint, and camouflage had to be arranged;[27] a large consignment of candles arrived, prompting Asquith to write to the Adjutant:

> By accepting the whole of your gift of Candles I feel that I may be depleting the Battalion Store unduly.
> Half the candle[sic] you sent will be ample to light all D Company to their little cots: so I return the other half with a thousand thanks.[28]

The routine of trench warfare continued: D Company spent the rest of August either in the front line, or in the support areas around Bois de Noulette, about a mile from the trenches, where the men were kept fit by night route marches in full kit (without packs and waterproof sheets),[29] by foot inspections,[30] and by continual working parties. Kelly remarked that he 'spent the day trying to reconcile the requirements as to working parties, the number of men always to be in the line as garrison, with the order that marching must always be carried out during hours of darkness. I knew it was impossible, but I nevertheless went through the form of tying my head in knots'.[31] Asquith was the President of the court martial of AB Wood. A copy of the instructions for the conduct of such Field General courts martial requested by him is in his war papers. Further examples of minor routine problems in the Army at this time can be detected from Asquith's notes: even by August 1916 the soldiers' identity discs were not stamped, but marked in ink which tended to rub off;[32] D company was still short of gas helmets, goggles, boots, greatcoats and trousers.[33] Nor was the soldier in the trenches free from the long arm of the tax man, for Asquith had been pursued by the Inspector Foreign

Dividends for information on receipts from his old employer, Franklin and Herrera. It was with apparent relief that Asquith was able to reply that he had received no dividends from the company for two years, and that they should contact Franklin's direct for further information.[34]

In the middle of the month there was increased activity in the sector of the RND, with almost nightly exchange of mortar bombs and rifle grenades. The German trench mortars proved disconcertingly accurate, killing one rating, Able Seaman Penny, a bomber of C Company killed by a fragment in the neck. Asquith reported to his Company Commander that he 'walked about 30 yards before losing consciousness'.[35] Gas was used frequently against the enemy positions when the wind was favourable, and the occasional artillery bombardment kept the Germans on their toes, but drew the inevitable retaliation.[36]

An interesting incident occurred on 18 August, when Sub Lieutenant Tamplin, Asquith's temporary second in command, arrested a soldier in the 'uniform of a Lance Corporal of the Scottish Rifles with blue Grenade badge on his shoulder' who had appeared on the extreme right of Hood's positions at 1am unannounced, saying he 'belonged to the Intelligence Dept'. He asked many questions and asked to be shown Sap 6, the most forward position in the line. Tamplin sent him down to the Station Guard, as he had no identification.[37]

By now Asquith apparently felt confident enough of Tamplin's ability as his second in command to leave him in charge of the Company for short periods, and give him his notebook to use. Before D Company left the line this time during the night of 19/20 August, Asquith had called for the names of one Petty Officer, one Leading Seaman, one Able Seaman HG (Higher Grade), and nine men to form a Scouting Platoon. Tamplin wrote the note in Asquith's notebook. Among the qualifications required were:

a. Keenness for the job
b. Intelligence
c. Cunning or craftiness
d. Activity
e. Preferably good shot.

In pencil in Asquith's hand are written the names of PO Purcell, ABHGs Appleton and Daines, and ABs Doherty, J Jackson, Harvey, McCartney, Dorman, Dick, Hay, and J Campbell.[38]

Out of the line again, the emphasis was on routine matters: leave, of course, was the predominant consideration. D company were allowed short leave by platoons to the villages near their Noulette Wood billets only after 7.30pm, and even then lights out was at 10pm. and reveille at 6.15am.[39] More pressing, and a source of discontent among the whole of the Division, was the question of leave to England. Many of the men had come to France direct from the Middle East and had not been home since they had sailed for the Dardanelles eighteen months previously. Asquith's notebooks contain repeated attempts to obtain leave for the most deserving of his men. Some were able to get to the more distant parts of France for a few days, but understandably, the Divisional and Corps Commanders were loth to allow leave to one of their units undergoing training while the Battle of the Somme was at its height farther south, and where those Divisions considered trained were going through the mill. Nevertheless, fifteen of D Company's men, all original Hoods, were sent on leave in mid-September.[40]

Other routine events while the Company was down from the line included the inevitable disciplinary hearings, one of them involving the disrating of two Petty Officers, and arranging that all men had baths. Particularly prominent at this time was the issue and inspection of anti-gas equipment, which was finally tested in an 'unleaky hut', with the cracks stopped up, and filled with lachrymatory fumes produced from, '(i) a hand sprayer mixed with four times the volume of methylated spirits, or (ii) heat lachrymatory liquid over a candle'.[41] In addition Tamplin and two men were sent on the Long Gas Course.[42]

Asquith obviously had known that, following the amalgamation of 2nd Hood Battalion into the parent unit in early July, he would eventually have to revert from Temporary Commander to Lieutenant Commander. Official notification took some time to come through, and until 24 August he was still signing messages as 'Commander'. After 25 August he signs his correspondence as 'Lieutenant Commander', either as 'OC D Company', or as '2 i/c Hood Battalion'. His service record reveals that he reverted in rank with effect from 5 July 1916.[43]

In the middle of September Kelly at last got his wish to conduct the Hood Battalion band in a performance of the '1812 Overture' in Noulette Wood, to the accompaniment of a bombardment by the Battalion guns.[44] Shortly after, the Division received its orders to move to the IV Corps training areas: 'It looks as though we would follow the way of all flesh to the Somme' was Kelly's summary of his feelings on being told that they were to be relieved in the Souchez sector by the 37th Division.[45] Hood Battalion moved off on 18 September in rain and a howling gale for the seven-mile march to the village of Hermin, where they were billeted. Kelly, who was very fond of cats, had arranged for several to be carried on the march in sandbags by his men. Everyone was wet through on arrival. The rest of the month was spent in the peaceful villages away from the front line in the area between Bailleul and Arras. Asquith's company came straight out of the trenches to a most unsatisfactory bath at the facilities at Aix Noulette: the water was cold, and the sprays delivered 'only a grudging trickle'.[46] Asquith understood well the paramount importance of hygiene for his men, and only the provision of poor food to his troops in the front line could be more guaranteed to provoke a serious complaint to the Battalion commander.

Meanwhile, other events were leading inexorably to Asquith being taken away from the front line. In the great attack in the southern sector of the Somme on 15 September, Arthur's elder brother Raymond, serving in the Grenadier Guards, was killed in the first moments of the advance on Lesboeufs. It was his first time over the top. Although hit in the chest, he lit a cigarette so that his men would not realise how badly he had been wounded. He was given morphia, and died without pain before reaching the dressing station.[47] The Prime Minister was shattered by the blow, and at once action was taken to spare him further traumas. Arthur was soon aware that steps were in hand, probably at Margot's instigation, to remove him to a place of greater safety. On 20 September he was given the option of being trained for Staff Duties by General Haking, GOC First Army, which he declined: ' . . . Unless or until the time comes when the shortage of Staff Officers compels Generals to order Officers to go to be trained for Staff duties, I do not think it my duty to leave my present work wh. I understand to some extent and enjoy'.[48]

On the same day the Divisional Commander, Paris, wrote to Arthur:

Dear Asquith,
I am indeed grieved to hear of your gallant brother's death. It is a grievous blow to you and your family & I can only express my deepest sympathy a [sic] that of the whole Division. You have served with us for almost 2 years – & if you now must go elsewhere – I can well understand the advisability of such a course. I would like to tell you how I have always appreciated your good work. The whole Division will keenly feel your departure & you will take with you the good wishes and sympathy of all ranks.[49]

Asquith had no intention of leaving the Royal Naval Division, and carried on as if nothing had happened.

The move to the Forceville area was the first time that the full Division had been moved as a unit: only recently had all the other arms so vital to an infantry division been added. It is often forgotten that at this time there were about forty different units in a Division, of which only twelve were first-line infantry battalions. There were, in addition, artillery and trench mortar batteries, machine gun companies, signals, engineers, the Divisional train, ammunition column, ambulances, veterinary, sanitary, and ordnance sections, and a pioneer battalion (14th Worcesters).

Most of the men had never witnessed nor even taken part in Battalion manoeuvres, including F S Kelly. The Company commanders rode out to the exercise area, south of Ranchicourt and a few miles from their billets in Hermin. After a 'delightful steeple chase' they found a trench system, reputedly laid out to replicate the German trenches on Vimy Ridge, set in the middle of lovely countryside. After the Battalion had practised various assaults, Asquith, Kelly, Egerton and Freyberg rode back together, arriving in time for a test mobilisation at short notice, Freyberg's idea, involving loading all kits on to G S waggons, and route marching. Kelly with understatement recorded that 'Neither Officers or men were in the best of moods'.[50] Many such exercises were repeated in the next few days, increasing in scale and complexity, until by 29 September, they were ready to hold the first ever RND Divisional Field Day, which seemed to be well-planned and carried out.[51] On 2 October Asquith heard that they were definitely to go to the Somme. At the Company Commanders' meeting that evening Freyberg passed on some information that he had received that 'the authorities are confident that the next push forward will be decisive, an absolute ascendancy having been established over the Germans, who are said to be demoralized. I think there is more to this than the customary assurances given before one goes in to have one's head broken – but my memory goes back to the 4th of June and Denis Browne's charming optimism'.[52]

On 4 October, the Division marched the eight or so miles to Ligny St Flochel where they entrained, and after a journey at snail's pace, arrived at their quarters at Forceville No.1 Camp. They could see flashes, but because of the wind direction, there was no sound of the guns.[53] The billets were not good: there were no drying facilities, nor even a place for making a fire: the roofs leaked, and there was no shelter for the kitchens or the Company QM's stores.[54] A few days later Asquith wrote again to Freyberg: 'The filth of ages has been trodden into the earth floors of the men's sleeping huts in this camp. The smell is very foul: and I cannot believe it is healthy. Can representations please be made to have the floor earth dug out and board floors substituted?'[55]

On Saturday the 7th Asquith and Kelly rode the eighteen miles into Amiens, where they dined at the Hôtel du Rhin and toured the cathedral, which was sandbagged against artillery fire and bombs.

Any plans to improve the living conditions in the Forceville camp were curtailed by more pressing needs: on the 14th or 15th orders came to move up to take over the line in front of a small village called Hamel.[56] By now the infantry battalions had been arranged in the usual three brigades, the third being formed by soldiers of the New Army, and it was this Brigade, the 190th, which first moved into the front line extending between Serre, in the north, and the River Ancre in the south. The line was confronted by the German fortified villages of Serre itself, Beaumont Hamel, St Pierre Divion, and Beaucourt, all of which had been in their possession since the first formation of the trench lines in France. The four weeks which were to pass before the Division went into action in the Hamel sector were described by Jerrold as 'the most wearing that the Division had ever experienced'.[57] The weather was appalling with continuous rain and low temperatures. To cap it all, the RND suffered a very serious setback, when, on the afternoon of 14 October General Paris and Major Sketchley, the GSO 2 for the Division, were hit by a shell during a visit to the trenches. Kelly records that Sketchley, an officer of whom he thought highly, 'was killed outright when the shell made a direct hit on his head . . . Freyberg and the doctor [McCracken] came in after dinner and we had part songs and choruses. It was Heald's last night with the Battalion and we made merry.'[58] Paris had been severely wounded in the leg, shoulder, and back, and eventually had his leg amputated. This gave the Army a chance to tighten their control of the RND and they appointed a martinet, Cameron Shute, to replace Paris. Shute could not come to terms with the peculiar ways of the RND, and he resolved to shake them up. In doing so, he alienated his Division. In a memorandum to them on 28 October following an inspection, Shute was particularly critical of the general discipline of the naval units, and in a long and scathing memorandum berated them for, among other things, using small arms boxes full of ammunition to stand on in the trenches, and for paying insufficient attention to the latrine facilities.[59] Shute enlightened the RND at length on their many short-comings, as he perceived them. He tried to prevent the naval units using the RN salute, with the palm down, rather than to the front, as is done in the Army: he thought their naval titles and ranks ridiculous, and even tried to get them to shave off their beards, which led A P Herbert, then the assistant adjutant of Hawke Battalion to write his 'Ballad of Codson's Beard'. 'Codson' was in fact one Sub Lieutenant Codner, who invoked King's Regulations and refused. The poem was finally published in *Punch* in January 1918, suitably modified for anonymity. The need for an enormous amount of back-breaking labour to dig and improve the trench system before the attack, the drenching rain, and the repeated critical inspections of the Division by the Staff did nothing to raise morale.

On 7 November Shute reported unfavourably on the RND to V Corps, his immediate superiors, and in scathing terms stated that the Division was not in a satisfactory state, and that the personnel had a standard of physique and training below that of the Army. He opined that were 'No real sailors' among them, they were all 'practically New Army, . . . but serving under the Admiralty'. There were 'no smart battalions', and while admitting that there was no crime, complained of 'lamentable discipline'. He reached the conclusion that 'They can never come up to or even approach the standards of other Brigades, unless officers of the Army are brought in who have had experience of recent fighting in France'; his final recommendation was that all RN and RM personnel should be trans-ferred to the Army.[60] And yet, on 3 November, only a few days before, the 189th Brigade had been inspected by Shute, who professed himself 'agreeably surprised by its excellence – somewhat of a contrast to his recent memorandum on lack of discipline' noted Kelly dryly.[61]

Some may find it an interesting comment on British generalship during the First World War that, only a few days after so damning an indictment, the Divisional and Corps Commanders were still prepared to allow this unit, assessed as being so far below the standard of Army units, to attack one of the strongest positions then existing on the Western Front, and one which had bloodily repulsed previous assaults.

Meanwhile, the routine of life went on: Asquith was charged with supervising the taking over of Hood's part of the line, helped by the excellent notes and sketches of the trenches provided by the CO of the battalion who had been in previous occupation, the 11th Royal Sussex.[62] Their dispositions formed the basis for Hood's Defence Scheme, signed by Freyberg, containing such items as 'The Front Line . . . should be held at all cots [sic]', and 'In the event of a Coy Commander being annoyed by the enemy rifle grenades T.M.s or Artillery he will immediately retaliate with rifle grenades and Stokes mortars sending back two for one'.[63]

In addition to the difficulties of management, climate and overwork, the RND had never been in such conditions: the trenches 'had been planned by a short-sighted fool and destroyed by a watchful enemy. There were virtually no dug-outs; the communication trenches, which ran across a conspicuous ridge, were under constant and aimed fire;'[64] The men in the front line stood in up to nine inches of water, not regarded as any great inconvenience by Kelly.[65]

The area had been the scene of enormous British casualties, for no gain, during the initial assault on 1 July. Subsequent gains in the southern part of the battlefield meant that further progress would be difficult unless the 'bulge' around Beaumont Hamel were eliminated. Sir Douglas Haig had another reason for wanting one last success before winter came to the Somme: he was due to participate at the Chantilly Conference with the French, at which plans for the following year would be decided. He spoke to General Gough, the Commander of the Fifth Army, to which the RND was attached, on the 12th, when he emphasised that a decision to attack on the Ancre was the responsibility of the Army Commander. Haig's diary entry revealed his true feelings: 'The British position will doubtless be much stronger . . . if I could appear there [Chantilly] on top of the capture of Beaumont Hamel, for instance, and 3000 prisoners'.[66]

Shute may have been unpopular with the Naval Division, but he had had recent experience of the Somme fighting, having commanded a New Army Brigade in front of Guillemont, in the southern area of the battle in September; having looked at the trenches recently taken over by the RND, he was aware of their unsuitability as jumping-off lines for the coming assault, and decided to have extra assembly trenches dug. In order to minimise casualties among the diggers, Shute ordered that the whole system should be dug in one night, that of 20 October 1916, using two

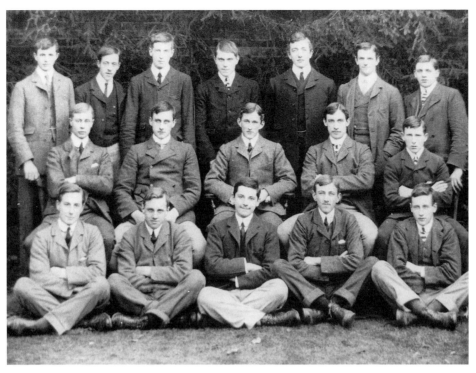

1. Asquith at school at Winchester, seated front row extreme left.

2. His last year at Winchester, seated in the middle to the left of
The Rev Bramston.

Omdurman Battlefield Mr Roosevelt talking to Arthur Asquith.

3. In the Sudan. Asquith (on the right) briefing Theodore Roosevelt.

4. Patrick Shaw Stewart at Clovelly Court before the First World War.

5. Asquith in the trenches on Gallipoli, late September/early October 1915, taken by his friend Thomas Leach.

6. Sub Lt J Bentham: "I am appointed OC Picquet Castro. Cmdr Asquith pays me a visit" Spring 1915.

7. Commander Arthur Asquith listens to Hood Battalion Band, Spring 1915.

8. Asquith as a Brigadier General, 1918. Note the broad Commodore's stripe of rank on his sleeves and the Army cap badge.

9. Asquith on his wedding day, with Betty to his right and his father to his left. Note how much weight he has lost as a result of his severe wound.

10. Another photograph of Asquith's wedding, 30 April 1918. Anthony Asquith, his step-brother, on the left, is the best man.

Puffin   Betty
Arthur   (April 30ᵗʰ 1916)

11. Arthur and Betty by the sea, early 1920's.

12. Arthur, Betty and three of their four daughters early 1930's, probably in Sussex. (left to right) - Susan, French nanny known as 'M'selle', Betty, Dinah the spaniel, Mary, Jane and Arthur.

13. Asquith and his eldest daughter, Mary, swimming in the Salzkammergut, 1935.

14. Asquith towards the end of his life.

15. Asquith's memorial tablet in Clovelly Churchyard. The inscription reads "In memory of Arthur and Betty Asquith who loved and cared for Clovelly".

16. The Royal Naval Division Memorial fountain at the Royal Naval College, Greenwich, designed by Sir Edwin Lutyens.

shifts of 500 men from the reserve battalions. Covering parties were sent out into no man's land to prevent detection of the work by enemy patrols. Divisional arrangements for this complex operation were not good, and it became obvious to Freyberg, when the first working party arrived at Hamel, after a tiring march of four miles followed by 2-3,000 yards of staggering up dark communication trenches, that the men would need proper guidance to ensure that they arrived at their allotted positions. They were formed up and Asquith was given the task of taking them forward. The enemy was alert, however, and the first attempt had to be postponed while a heavy German barrage fell on the communication trenches up which the men had to move. Trying for a second time, the working parties were again subjected to shell and mortar fire. Asquith and a subaltern named Fox, at the head of the party, in a communication trench known as Peche Street, were buried by a *minenwerfer*, a type of large mortar. Both were badly shaken and concussed, and Asquith's eardrums were ruptured by the blast. In the words of Freyberg: 'They carried on in spite of their troubles trying to get the party together again, but the men, who were now badly rattled and under-officered, got completely out of hand and retired to Hamel in spite of all their efforts'.[67] The work was nevertheless completed by daybreak due largely to the abilities of the ex-miners who still formed a large proportion of the Division.

Concerned about the effect of the news on his father, Arthur wrote to Violet four days later:

Four nights ago five others and I were buried at varying depths by a 'Minnie' – or heavy mortar bomb. I realised something odd had happened to my ears, but thought this might pass. Then, two days ago, a cynically unkind order bade me to report for attachment to a Staff. I obeyed, and then – my ears being no better but rather worse – I saw a Doctor who says both my drums are perforated – that they may heal in three or four weeks, and that I may or may not be deafer as a result. I am to be evacuated by tonight's train . . .

I doubt whether anyone, except Fritz. [Freyberg] or Cleg can realise what a very bitter disappointment it is for me not to be with them just now. In case I may appear as a Casualty under the heading Shell Shock, will you please tell Father how things really stand – that I am perfectly well except for my ears, and that I do not mind Shells any less or any more than I did before. If I get to England, I must scheme to be treated at home: I am not in bed.[68]

Asquith was ordered to report to V Corps headquarters on 23 October and was promptly invalided home from the 14th General Hospital at Wimereux, near Boulogne in the Hospital Ship *St Denis*, to King Edward VII Hospital on the 26th. He therefore missed the RND's first major action in France, his place in command of D Company being taken by Cardy Montagu. Freyberg recounted a memory of the time to Arthur's wife, Betty, many years later:

> I can remember quite vividly that I had lost my watch and while I was seeing him off to hospital I asked Arthur to lend me his watch for the coming attack. To my surprise he hesitated . . . and then snatched it from the pocket of his uniform saying with great feeling, 'What a swine I am, of course, take it'. I only learned afterwards that it was a watch you had given him and that it was his most treasured possession.[69]

Worse, from Asquith's point of view, than his temporary incapacitation, was that his injury appeared to have vindicated the concerns of those fearful for his safety, and efforts to prevent him returning to his battalion were redoubled. His suspicions were well founded: the duties he was expected to take on at V Corps headquarters were those of Water Control Officer. Fearing that his protests might be unavailing, he opted for the least bad option, proper Staff training. In a copy of a draft letter, probably sent to his Army Corps Commander, Asquith enclosed a CV and noted that, in his judgment,

> these duties [of Water Control] could be performed equally well or better by a junior officer. In any case I did not feel myself fitted for them either by inclination or by my previous service, which, as shown above, has been regimental, in trenches: and Egyptian.
>
> If I am to do Staff Work, I request that I may be given a regular Staff training; and I should be grateful if you could inform me through whom and in what form I ought to apply in order to do a course of Staff training such as might fit me to become later on a Brigade Major or something of the sort.[70]

Freyberg wrote to him from rest billets in early November expressing frustration at the delay in the attack caused by the 'Pro-German elements', and recounting how, in a recent march, Kelly had taken up Asquith's usual position at the rear of the Hood column, and had prevented other units from overtaking unless they were carrying ammunition or wounded. Freyberg was looking forward to the battle being all over so that they could 'get back to lush pastures and reorganise our band'. The main purpose of his letter was to enlist Asquith's help in getting some Army musicians transferred to the Hood band.

Arthur's enforced absence from the front was a relief to his father, who wrote to Sylvia Henley on 24 October:

> The great news here is the return of Oc – he and six of his men were

buried by a hand bomb [The Prime Minister was mistaken] – ear drums damaged – he was <u>ordered</u> (not offered) to take a place on the staff of V Corps Command.[72]

Violet echoed her father's thoughts in a letter to Freyberg:

Oc arrived here <u>very</u> deaf and looking rather strained and shattered I thought – though he hasn't a trace of shell-shock – and now hears almost perfectly again. He is of course moving heaven and earth to get out again and back to his Battalion and I think he has wired to the Brigadier to apply for him. Whether there will be any Staff hanky panky about it I don't know – it is hard on Oc I do think and was not in <u>anyway</u> prompted or inspired from home though of course it would be a relief to us to know him safe.[73]

In this way, while Asquith was chafing at home, the fateful day drew nearer for his friends in Hood Battalion. The men grew progressively more restive, and casualties and sickness began to take their toll. Raids of the German lines at night were still taking place, something which struck Kelly as being 'a dangerous policy on the eve of a big attack in which all ranks have been instructed in the details and objectives.'[74] The final entry in Kelly's diary is for 11 November 1916, written in reserve lines near Mesnil:

It was a dull, misty, still day and the sun did not appear. I walked to Martinsart for a good hot bath at 1030 am. We had parades at 12 am and 3 pm. Early in the afternoon I tested some fuses of P Bombs.[75] And we set alight to two P Bombs in a trench at the back of our billets on the other side of the road. They emitted a great deal of smoke. There was an Officers' meeting at headquarters at 6 pm. Fish [Lieutenant Sidney Fish of the Battalion] dined with us. It appears to be X day.[76]

On 13 October, while Asquith was recovering in London, the Royal Naval Division kept its appointment with destiny on the Ancre. All the Divisional objectives were finally achieved: Asquith's former battalion, Hood, especially covered itself in glory under the inspired leadership of Freyberg, capturing the fortified village of Beaucourt. Freyberg, wounded three times, received the Victoria Cross for the 'most conspicuous bravery and brilliant leading as a Battalion Commander'.[77] He became a national hero: *The Times* wrote on 23 November 1916, 'The capture of Beaucourt . . . was a brilliant piece of work, and it gave England another hero'.[78] General De Lisle, himself a holder of the Victoria Cross, in an originally anonymous contribution to the history of the 29th Division wrote: 'Probably this was the most distinguished personal act of the war'.[79] Montagu, in command of D Company in Asquith's place, was at Freyberg's side throughout, and eventually escorted him from the line to the dressing station. He was awarded the DSO.

All three brigades of the Naval Division had suffered very serious losses: in the 189th Brigade, of which Hood Battalion was a part, only fifteen officers were unwounded, including Sub Lieutenant A P Herbert, and Lieutenant W Sterndale Bennett, the adjutant and senior survivor of Drake Battalion. Lieutenant Commander Egerton, who had received the DSO for his services in Gallipoli, took temporary command of Hood Battalion. In the month of November the Division had lost a hundred officers and sixteen hundred men killed, and one hundred and sixty officers and 2,377 men wounded.[80]

NOTES

1. AMA Notebook No. 5, undated (between entries for 9 and 10 July 1916): pencil notes, AMA papers.
2 AMA Notebook No. 5, entry for 12 July 1916.
3. AMA Notebook No. 5, separate messages to Sub Lts Milton, Oldridge, and Chapman, all dated 13 July 1916.
4. AMA Notebook No. 5, AMA to OC Hood, dated 13 July 1916.
5. AMA Notebook No. 5, AMA to Platoon Commanders, dated 14 July 1916.
6. AMA Notebook No. 5, 14 July 1916, p89.
7. AMA Notebook No. 5, entry for 14 July 1916, p90.
8. Kelly's diary, entry for 13 July 1916.
9. Kelly's diary, entries for 15 and 16 July 1916.
10. AMA Notebook No. 5, undated (but almost certainly 17 July 1916) pencil notes before going to the trenches pp 101 and 102.
11. AMA Notebook No. 5, undated pencil notes, again almost certainly written on 17 July 1916, p105.
12. Kelly's diary, entry for 5 August 1916.
13. AMA Notebook No. 6, Field Message Book, Army Book 153, in use from 21 July to 4 August 1918, AMA papers, situation report 2.30 pm 21 July 1916, p126.
14. AMA Notebook No. 6, situation report 2.30 am 22 July 1916.
15. ibid.
16. AMA Notebook No. 6, to Battalion HQ, undated, but almost certainly 23 July 1916.
17. AMA Notebook No. 6, situation report, 2.30 pm 25 July 1916.
18. AMA Notebook No. 6, message to OC Hood, 30 July 1916.
19. Kelly's diary, entry for 1 August 1916.
20. Kelly's diary, entry for 6 August 1916.
21. Lieutenant Ivan Heald, poet and soldier, transferred from the RND to the Royal Flying Corps and killed in action on 4 December 1916.
22. AMA Notebook No. 6, entry for 3 August 1916.
23. AMA Notebook No. 7, Intelligence Report, 14 August 1916.
24. AMA Notebook No. 7, AMA to OC Hood, 14 August 1916.
25. Letter from Jeremy Bentham [ex Hood Battalion] to Bernard Freyberg, dated 29 May 1973, Freyberg private papers.
26. AMA Notebook No. 7, Field Message Book, Army Book 153, covering 5

August to 15 August 1916, AMA papers, Clovelly. AMA to Mr James, letter dated 5 August 1916.

27. AMA Notebook No. 6, AMA to OC Hood, entry for 3 August 1916.
28. AMA Notebook No. 7, AMA to Adjutant, Hood Battalion, 6 August 1916.
29. AMA Notebook No. 7, AMA to Sub Lt Carder, 8 August 1916.
30. AMA Notebook No. 7, AMA to Lt Heald, 9 August 1916.
31. Kelly's diary, entry for 8 August 1916.
32. AMA Notebook No. 7, AMA to OC Hood requesting stamps, entry for 7 August 1916.
33. AMA Notebook No. 7, AMA to OC Hood, two further separate requests, both entries dated 7 August 1916.
34. AMA Notebook No. 7, AMA to Inspector Foreign Dividends, 8 July 1916.
35. AMA Notebook No. 7, AMA to OC C Company, 16 August 1916.
36. AMA Notebook No. 8, situation report for 17 August 1916.
37. AMA Notebook No. 8, Intelligence Report, dated 18 August 1916.
38. AMA Notebook No. 8, note from Sub Lieutenant Tamplin to Chief Petty Officer Tobin, Company Sergeant Major for D Company, dated 19 August 1916. Tobin, an excellent man with eight years' service in the RNVR, who was with Asquith in Gallipoli, was recommended for a Commission by Asquith earlier. (AMA Notebook No. 7, AMA to OC Hood dated 8 August 1916.)
39. AMA Notebook No. 8, p81, 'D Company Orders 20/8/16.
40. AMA Notebook No. 10, p80, AMA to OC Hood, dated 15 September 1916.
41. AMA Notebook No. 9, pencil Notes in AMA's hand, undated but between entries for 16 and 17 September 1916.
42. AMA Notebook No. 9, AMA to OC Hood, dated 20 September 1916.
43. 'Record of Service of Naval Officers of the RND', two volumes, held by the Naval Historical Branch of the Ministry of Defence.
44. Footnote in AMA's hand to Kelly diary, entry for 16 September 1916.
45. Kelly diary, entry for 16 September 1916.
46. AMA Notebook No. 10, AMA to OC Hood, entry for 15 September 1916.
47. *Raymond Asquith: Life and Letters*, ed by J Jolliffe, Collins, 1980 (Century Edition, 1987), p296.
48. Draft of a letter from AMA to General Haking, GOC First Army: although undated, the date of despatch of this correspondence is confirmed by other documents in the AMA papers. Copy in AMA papers.
49. Letter from Major General Paris to AMA, dated 20 September 1916, AMA papers.
50. All from Kelly's diary, entry for 22 September 1916.
51. Kelly's diary, entry for 29 September 1916.
52. Kelly's diary, entry for 2 October 1916. He was referring to the fateful day in 1915 when Denis Browne was killed on Gallipoli.
53. Kelly's diary, entry for 4 October 1916.
54. AMA Notebook No. 11, AMA to OC Hood, dated 8 October 1916.
55. AMA Notebook No. 11, entry dated 12 October 1916.
56. Hood Battalion took over from the 11th Royal Sussex on 16 October. PRO box ADM 137/3064.
57. Jerrold, *The Royal Naval Division*, p186.
58. Kelly diary entry for 12 October 1916. Kelly seems to have been mistaken about the date of Paris's wounding. The entry shows how insensitive the men in the front line had already become to casualties, even the wounding of the Divisional General being insufficient cause to change plans for dinner.
59. Divisional Memorandum of 28 October 1916, signed by Major General C D Shute, GOC 63rd(Royal Naval) Division, copy in the scrapbook of Lieutenant

Colonel A R Bare, IWM, Department of Documents.
60. Report by GOC 63rd (Royal Naval) Division to GOC V Corps, dated 7 November 1916. PRO WO 95/3119.
61. Kelly's diary, entry for 3 November 1916.
62. Dispositions of the 11th Royal Sussex Regiment in front of Hamel, hand-drawn sketches and notes in pencil manuscript, AMA papers.
63. Defence Scheme, – Hamel – Secret, Battalion Order by Lt Col Freyberg, dated 16 October 1916, AMA papers.
64. Jerrold, *The Royal Naval Division*, p187.
65. Kelly diary, entry for 19 October 1916.
66. *Goughie* by A Farrar Hockley (Hart Davis & MacGibbon, 1975, p193), quoting Haig's diary.
67. *A Linesman in Picardy*, by Bernard Freyberg, unpublished book, pp5-10, also quoted in *Hood Battalion* by L Sellers, p176.
68. Letter from AMA to Violet Bonham Carter, dated 24 October 1916, from 4th Casualty Clearing Station, V Corps, quoted in *Champion Redoubtable*.
69. Letter from Bernard Freyberg to Betty Asquith dated 26 August 1939, AMA papers.
70. Draft letter in AMA's hand, dated 4 November 1916, containing CV and letter requesting formal Staff Training, AMA papers.
71. Letter from Bernard Freyberg to AMA dated 4 November 1916, AMA papers.
72. Letter from Herbert Asquith to Sylvia Henley, dated 24 October 1916, Bodleian Mss.
73. Letter from Violet Asquith to Bernard Freyberg dated 21 November 1916, Freyberg private papers.
74. Kelly's diary, entry for 26 October 1916. In one such raid Sub Lt Davidson, a Canadian who had joined Hood in January 1916, went on patrol with Petty Officer Colquhoun. The latter returned with his arm almost blown off, and Davidson was never seen again, almost certainly killed by a bomb in the German front line.
75. P Bombs were large smoke-emitting grenades whose aim was to render enemy dugouts untenable.
76. Kelly's diary, final entry, 11 November 1916.
77. Citation quoted in *The Royal Naval Division*, p205.
78. Quoted by P Freyberg in *Bernard Freyberg V.C.* (Hodder & Stoughton, 1991), p94.
79. S. Gillon, *The Story of the 29th Division* (Nelson, 1925) p95.
80. *The Royal Naval Division*, p206.

CHAPTER IX

The Reluctant Staff Officer

Asquith naturally followed affairs in France while he was recuperating, first in King Edward VII's Hospital, and then at 10 Downing Street, and kept in close touch with his friends in the Battalion: he quickly began visiting the wounded who had been evacuated to England. Within a few days of the action on the Ancre he was receiving letters from the front. There was a huge sense of relief that the Division had done so well in spite of the misgivings voiced by their Commander. The doctor of Hood Battalion, later to become one of Asquith's greatest friends, Surgeon McCracken, wrote:

> Words fail me when I try to describe our men . . . They stuck to the barrage like heroes . . . Montagu [commanding Asquith's old company] was splendid and all his men swear he should have had a VC too. Really he was grand. He was slightly wounded in the back and had a lump of stuff through his helmet. He smoked his pipe and cigars all the time and carried his walking stick – a most dignified and imposing fellow . . .
>
> Your little Castle was killed, or rather died of wounds, I found him lying in a shell-hole playing the hero with an H.A.C. [Honourable Artillery Company] fellow who was kicking up Hell with a bullet through his leg.[1] I felt like crying and the next I found was Clegg [Kelly] shot through the back of the head just opposite a dug-out in German 3rd line.[2]

A few days later Montagu, himself recovering, and temporarily second in command to Egerton, elaborated on Kelly's death: 'Poor Cleg was killed right at the beginning. He was so enthusiastic about the whole thing & told me the night before he was really glad to be in it . . . He went to lead an attack on a bombing post . . . and they showed fight.'

Montagu also offered his opinions on the performances of the Battalion officers: everybody did well but he singled out for special mention, in priority order, The Doc [McCracken], Hill, Arblaster, Bolus[3] and Carnall. 'These are the survivors except that Bolus was terribly wounded. Try to go & see him if you can.'

Montagu concluded by making Asquith aware that very few recommendations for medals had been allowed to go forward, and perhaps questions at home, in due course, on the scarcity of medals for such a successful operation 'might be a good thing'. He also enlisted Asquith's aid to improve the regulations on leave in the Division.

Finally he revealed that Hood Battalion were hoping that Asquith would be allowed to return and command while Freyberg's wounds were healing, but 'I think it is doubtful that the CinC will allow it but I know the Brigadier has applied for you.'[4]

Asquith wrote to the relatives of those who had been killed in his former battalion. Particularly moving is the reply from George Ramsay, the father of Petty Officer Ramsay, who had won the Distinguished Service Medal on Gallipoli for bravery. He wrote:'. . . we were looking for a letter from you for George spoke so highly of you in his letters, he told us you were the bravest of the brave, he said he would follow you anywhere'. He tells how George was found by an officer of another Battalion, who had written that he was lying 'beside the railway embankment and he saw he had been a brave lad for he had 3 dead Germans lying beside him. We knew he would do his bit he was an honest and upright boy in all things he had to do . . .'[5]

Asquith wrote to Freyberg at No.1 General Hospital at Etretat, but even ten days after the action, the latter was unable to write in reply, so he enlisted Donaldson, who was less severely wounded, to write to explain his view of the battle. What stands out from all these reports on the action is the magnificent part played by Freyberg, and the unreserved admiration of him felt by the other members of the Battalion. On 23 November Asquith wrote to Freyberg enclosing newspaper cuttings reporting the success of the recent attack, and Freyberg's part in it.

> I'm so glad you got your chance at last and took it so well, and were not killed. And I hope we will meet again reasonably soon. Cleg's death, and Edmondson's are very bitter. Cleg had such a wonderful enjoyment of life and communicated his electricity to those he was with. . . . I was very sad to see that Castle was killed, he was the most devoted brave little fellow . . . I'm anxious to be back and help Mark [Egerton], keep a stiff back against interference by D.H.Q. [Division HQ] with our atmosphere . . .[6]

Asquith had been agitating to return to the battalion, with the intention and expectation of commanding Hood Battalion, at least until Freyberg's return. Meanwhile he wrote in commiseration to Mary Kelly, Cleg's sister, and drafted an article on Kelly's war service, published in the *Eton Chronicle* as part of his obituary. His contribution included:

> As an officer and companion, 'Cleg' will be truly missed and mourned in the Battalion.

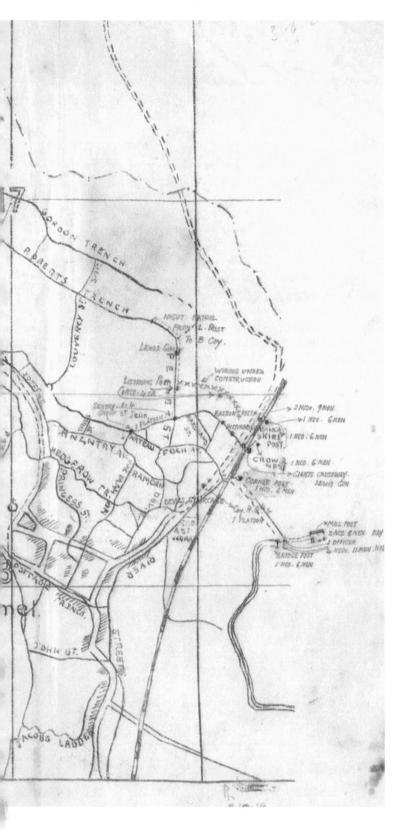

e CO of 11ᵗʰ Royal Sussex. Peche Street, where Asquith was buried

marked with the dispositions of D Company of Hood Battalion, given to Asquith by th
by a minenwerfer on 20 October 1916, can be identified.

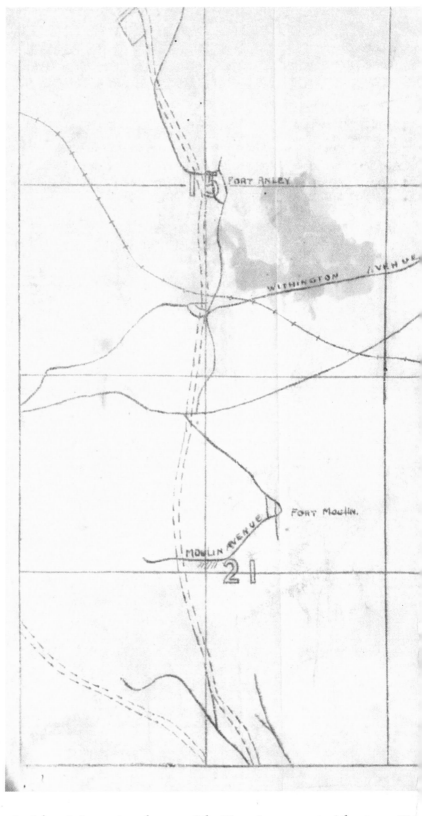

2. A hand-drawn trench map of the Hamel area, west of the Ancre Riv

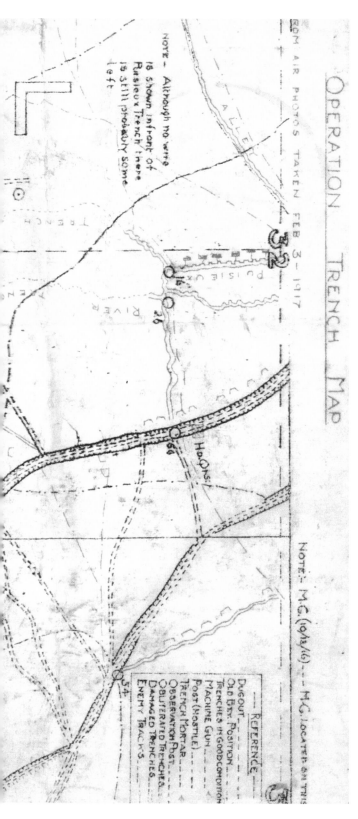

1917. The pencil annotations are Asquith's.

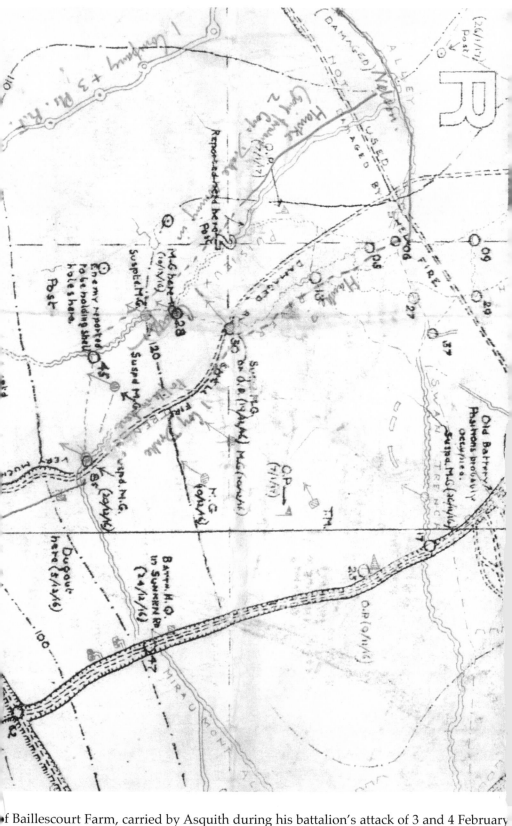

f Baillescourt Farm, carried by Asquith during his battalion's attack of 3 and 4 February
This action resulted in Asquith's first DSO.

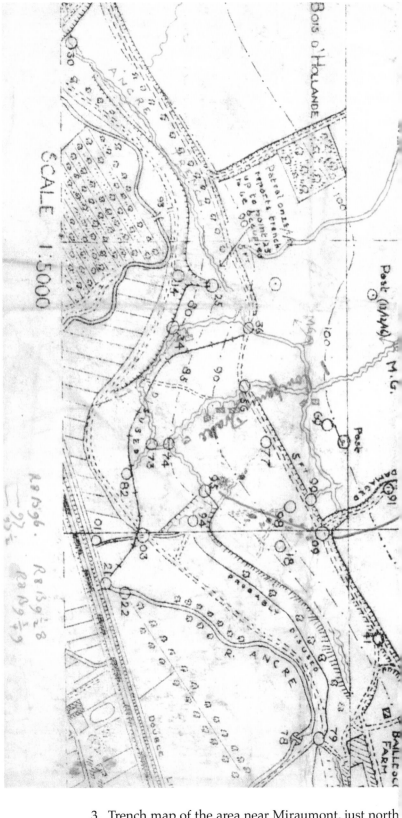

3. Trench map of the area near Miraumont, just north

He was not, and I think never would have made, an enthusiastic soldier. He spent most of his leisure time composing music and reading books, and was not alive to all the aspects of military life around him. But he had all a true artist's desire to perfect his Company. He was an uncompromising disciplinarian, spared neither others nor himself, and rarely turned a blind eye. Highly-strung, and as brave as a lion, aware and utterly contemptuous of all risks, he commanded the confidence and respect of all under his command . . .

He was contentious, always happiest in argument: interested in the psychology of his friends, highly critical of them, and warm-heartedly loyal to them; and violently intolerant of anything that bore the faintest tinge of cheapness, insincerity, pretentiousness or bad manners.'[7]

On 6 December, during the crisis which was eventually to result in his father being supplanted by Lloyd George, Arthur was posted back to France to take command of the Battalion, where he arrived from Boulogne on the 10th. A few days later, he received a signal to the effect that Temporary Lieutenant Colonel H Creagh-Osborne was arriving to take command. This was a severe blow to Asquith, who promptly asked the Divisional Commander to reconsider. According to Asquith, Shute refused saying that he did not consider him suitable to command the Battalion, because, in his view, Asquith had insufficient knowledge of trench warfare in France, and because he could not have an officer in command of one of his battalions who might be ordered to the Staff just before an attack, as had happened before. Shute intended that Asquith should go to Staff training, despite his telling him that he had a strong natural disinclination against such training, and that the course was designed for officers of Captain level, whereas Asquith had been the equivalent of a Major for eighteen months, during which time he had been in command, or second in command, of a battalion throughout. He even offered to serve under Creagh-Osborne as a Company Commander, rather than do Staff work.

At the time, it should be remembered that Shute was still set on transforming his unconventional Division into a 'proper' Army unit. The losses of the November battle had given him the opportunity to replace the missing officers with 'genuine' Army officers, and Creagh-Osborne was only one of several. Asquith bore Osborne no personal resentment and tried to assist him in every way during the change of command, but he was understandably piqued to discover that Creagh-Osborne had less experience of trench warfare than he.[8]

Macmillan reports that, during this period, he caught the tail end of a discussion between General Philips and Major Barnett concerning Asquith: 'The General had expressed his appreciation of Asquith as a soldier. The Major agreed but added: "Why keep him; you can never tell when some woman in London will have him removed to the rear?" I gathered that Commander Asquith had been summoned to the Brigade Office and instructed to join some job on the Corps Staff in order to be out of danger, but that he so hotly resented the interference from London as to require compelling to get him to comply. The General had been considering how the order could be countermanded as I entered.'[9]

All the protestations of Asquith and General Philips were to no avail: Creagh-Osborne arrived on 11 December 1916; Shute requested Asquith's departure on the 23rd, and on the 26th an order was received at HQ 63rd Division for Asquith to 'report to the G. Office, Fifth Army at 10 am Dec 31st.' The file was sent via OC Hood for Asquith to note. On the file, Arthur asked for an interview with the Divisional Commander, and was refused, and curtly told to obey orders, and that there was no time to go through the normal procedure for setting up a formal interview.[10] So, reluctantly, Arthur Asquith arrived at Fifth Army for Staff training on the last day of 1916.

Meanwhile, a battle of a different sort was being fought in the various staffs in the BEF and at home: at stake was the very survival of the Royal Naval Division in its current form. The successful battle in which his Division had recently played so notable a part did not deflect Shute from persisting with his original recommendation that they should become a normal Army unit. On 1 December he wrote to his new Corps Commander, Jacobs, of II Corps that 'the gallantry of the RND on Ancre [sic] only emphasizes the need to re-organise'.[11] This view was supported by Jacobs on 21 February 1917, forwarding the report to Fifth Army: 'having had this Division under my command for over 2 months I do not wish to recommend any modification in proposals made ... proposals put forward by GOC 63rd Division should be carried out without delay'.[12]

At home the War Office was already reacting to Shute's first reports, and on 27 December the Army Council wrote to the Admiralty proposing to transfer the Royal Naval and Royal Marine personnel of the 63rd Division to the Army. Sellers points out that this action by the Army Council 'caused a certain amount of irritation at the Admiralty',[13] which became uncharacteristically protective of its unusual unit. There is no doubt that their fighting performance on the Ancre was a source of pride and satisfaction to the Admiralty, and, despite the fall of Asquith as Prime Minister, there was still a powerful Establishment lobby supporting the retention of the RND. It would have been in character for Arthur to have taken the opportunity to do some canvassing himself during his six-week period of enforced leave at home. On 10 January their Lordships replied to the War Office concluding that either the current arrangements should be left in force, or the Division effectively be broken up and most of the naval personnel returned to RN service. They proposed that the issue be discussed at a meeting, which was held on 5 February at the House of

Commons, chaired by Lord Derby. The Naval delegation was led by the First Lord, Sir Edward Carson, and he brought with him a powerful and comprehensive brief of the practical difficulties involved in the proposed Army measures: the Royal Marines were an integral part of the Royal Naval Service and could not in any circumstances be transferred to the Army; all in the Division would lose financially; many already had a possible grievance at not being allowed to serve at sea, exacerbated by the perception of being 'messed about' by the Army; and there would be problems regarding seniority and pay.

As well as these objections, the Admiralty pointed out that the present GOC, Shute, displayed a lack of tact and sympathy which had been much felt by all ranks. The resentment engendered by his policy of bringing in officers from the Army over the heads of those who had served for a long time in the RND was stressed, and the case of Creagh-Osborne,[14] relatively junior officers promoted to command Hood Battalion (over the head of Asquith), was used as a particular example. The meeting failed to reach a firm conclusion, but the War Office agreed to make new proposals to the Admiralty.

On 7 March the matter was finally resolved when the War Office wrote to the Secretary of the Admiralty:

> As the proposal to recognize the 63rd (Royal Naval) Division on a military basis has, for the present at least, been abandoned . . . there appears to be no advantage in transferring their numbers to Army Vote A.[15]

Another major victory for the RND occurred on 19 February 1917, when Shute was relieved by Major General Lawrie, who turned out to be an altogether more sympathetic character. Shute went on to command a Corps in 1918 and retired as a full General with a knighthood.

While these matters of high politics were under way, Asquith threw himself into Staff training with his customary zeal, although from the notes made in one of his Field Message books it is apparent that certain parts of his instruction were not new to him or necessary: he records without comment the requirements for Bayonet Training, quoting an extract from a GHQ memorandum advising that sacks and straw will need to be procured, and a suitable gallows built.[16] In the same way, it is probable that his attention was not held by the talk on 'Points to be dealt with when writing orders for billets',[17] which included reminders to ensure a satisfactory water supply, and to dispose of manure.

Nevertheless, it is clear that there was much of interest and value during this phase of training. There was instruction on the employment of medium mortars and machine gun companies, and advice on the siting of Lewis guns. Signals procedure was thoroughly covered, and there was comprehensive work dealing with supply, transport, and traffic control. The statistics of logistics seem to have fascinated Asquith, with the realisation that to supply an infantry corps in the field required seventy-two eight-ton lorries per day, while every division needed to be supplied with over thirty tons of coal per day. In this part of his training, Asquith learned about the details of the composition and administration of German Army units.[18]

On 20 January Lieutenant Commander Asquith reported to the Headquarters of 82nd Field Company of the Royal Engineers at Bayencourt where he was to be seconded for the continuation of his training. He spent the next ten days in the company of their CO, Major Godsell, assessed by Asquith as 'a particularly nice fellow . . . doing his best to help the Infantry in every way . . . good wits, considerate, hospitable, cheerful, and a gentleman. A pleasant old Jesuit priest, and a French interpreter, once a Chef, are other members of this variegated mess.'[19] The weather was bitterly cold, so that Asquith's shaving brush froze in his mug while he was having breakfast, and on some nights it was too cold for much sleep. It was one of the hardest winters ever recorded, and Asquith was aware of the terrible conditions for the men in the open when the night time temperatures were dropping to more than twenty degrees of frost. There were many reports of men dying from exposure.

Most days he accompanied Godsell on his visits to the front line east of Hebuterne, to inspect the work being done by the Engineers: in the trenches this consisted typically of digging and drainage work, repairing trenches, and providing flooring. Godsell also instructed him in the construction and siting of strong points, and they had many discussions on the best use of Engineers to support an infantry assault, coming to the conclusion that the Sappers should not accompany the infantry in the initial attack, but be sent up after dusk to build strong points just in the rear of the newly captured front line. They concluded that the infantry were capable of providing themselves with temporary cover and fire positions to repel counter-attacks, without expert assistance. The major consolidation work required fresh, specially trained Engineers.[20] Asquith was initiated into the best ways of providing secure dug-outs, properly revetted and drained. He also records agreement with Godsell that communication trenches needed to be <u>wide</u>, well floor-boarded and dry.[21] After a few days these duties began to pall. Asquith observed that: 'This walking up to the line every day and seeing the same things is good exercise but a waste of time for me.'[22] For the last couple of days with the Royal Engineers, Asquith inspected various subterranean diggings and caverns to see if they could be used for the protection of troops or for storage. They were lowered forty-five feet down a quarry shaft at Sailly to discover '4 large excavated chambers at the bottom – like three fingers and a thumb – one of them about 50 paces long – quite dry in chalk.'[23]

After writing a report to Fifth Army HQ, Asquith left the Engineers and started a secondment to the Royal Artillery. Unfortunately there was no accommodation for him with 168 Royal Field Artillery where he was first told to report, and he was sent to Brigade Headquarters of 155 RFA at Courcelles, part of 32nd Division, although temporarily under the orders of 19th Division. The following day, 31 January, Asquith set off in the snow to walk to D Battery, stationed in front of Colincamps, to begin his instruction. It was equipped with 4.5 inch howitzers, and the Gunners enlightened him on the characteristics of the various propellants, NCT, ballistite and cordite, and on the need for corrections to be made according to meteorological conditions. During the course of the day, Asquith heard that Lieutenant Commander Egerton, second in command of Hood Battalion had been wounded, and that same evening he wrote to the General Staff of the Fifth Army asking to be allowed to return immediately to his Battalion.[24]

After lunch on 2 February, he walked to the scene of the RND's battle in November, via Beaumont Hamel, 'an uncomfortable number of 77 shells falling on the road'.[25] He was looking for the village of Beaucourt for some time before realising that he was standing in it. 'It is one mass of shell holes and broken timber with a brick here and there'.[26] He returned to Hamel via the road alongside the railway and bumped into Hawke Battalion going up to the Front Line. From Lieutenant Commander Lockwood,[27] he learned that Hawke and Hood Battalions were to assault the German lines on the following evening, with the aim of capturing Puisieux and River Trenches. He decided to visit the Battalion 'before the stunt'. Farther back from the line, he ran into Basset, Hood's signalling officer, who was starting his leave. The latter was

> pessimistic about the state of the Battn: everyone longing for Freyberg's return. Egerton and Carnall wounded . . . About 30 casualties and 4 officers in our first tour in these trenches at Beaucourt. Much dysentery and sickness. Anxiety about our men being seen assembling for tomorrow's attack – snow and bright moonlight*. I must go and try and buck them up tomorrow evening and see if I cannot join the battle.

The plan consisted of a surprise night attack, a simple trench-to-trench assault, scheduled to last for eight minutes. The first enemy trench, Puisieux, was 300 yards away, and the second line, River Trench, a further 100 yards behind. Hood Battalion was now under the command of Lieutenant Colonel Munro, who had relieved Creagh-Osborne on 16

---

* Water freezes within 2 hours in men's water bottles. They are to dig in a new line after taking their objective: ground is like iron.[28]

January when the latter became sick. The attack started at 11pm on 3 February with Hawke on the left and Hood on the right. On the extreme left, Hawke Battalion did well, securing the junction between River Trench and Artillery Lane; farther to the right things were not so good: Hood had moved to the right, taking the two right-hand companies of Hawke with them, so that their orientation was now parallel with the Ancre, rather than at right angles to it. A dangerous gap therefore developed in the centre. Asquith obtained permission to go along with the attackers with a view to seeing how effective the barrage was, and he had accompanied Munro. At about 1.30am Munro was wounded,[29] and to the surprise of everyone Lieutenant Commander Asquith appeared 'from nowhere' to take command of Hood, who had 'gone forward on the heels of his old Battalion in the slender disguise of a learner studying the effects of the artillery barrage'.[30] The niceties of the legalities of this situation do not seem to have been closely examined. Munro's deputy, Captain Cardy Montagu, was next in line for military command, which he assumed for the period 'from 5 am until 8 am, when Lieutenant Commander Asquith, who had been present the whole time and as senior officer conducting operations, took command.'[31] There is a letter in Asquith's papers, from HQ Fifth Army to 63rd Division, dated 3 February 1917, which reads thus:

> Lieutenant Commander A.M.ASQUITH now attached to 155th Brigade, RFA, will rejoin his Battalion forthwith.
> This is necessitated by casualties which have occurred in the Battalion since Lieut-Commander ASQUITH's attachment for a course at Army Headquarters.[32]

It is inconceivable that this could have been written during the frantic confusion of what had turned into a major battle, and seems to have been a retrospective action to legitimise a doubtful situation. This is borne out by Macmillan, at the time clerk in 189th Brigade HQ, who reports that, when the Brigade Major, Barnett, heard that Asquith was in the thick of it, turned sharply to his clerk and asked, 'Where the hell did he spring from?'[33] Macmillan went on:

> The favoured ones in London who did not reckon my life as precious as that of Arthur Melland Asquith were far out when they thought that by transferring him to the corps they might sleep at nights without dreading his being killed.
> Asquith had conspired and secured the job of observation officer to the corps heavy artillery which supported us. Being on the spot, he could see how the fight was progressing and, observing the situation getting out of hand, he assumed the role of battalion commander.[34]

Well before 8am on the 4th Asquith had managed to get the direction of the attack in its correct alignment, and the defenders ready to meet the inevitable German counter-attacks, but there was still a gap between Hawke on the left and Hood on the right. Asquith returned to Brigade HQ to report, returning about 11am with Sub Lieutenant Arblaster. He then carried out a complete reconnaissance of the RND positions, and reported again. Brigadier General Philips, OC of the 189th Brigade sent up Drake Battalion to help secure the objectives during the coming night, so at about 8pm on the 4th B Company of that Battalion, commanded by Lieutenant Hugh Kingsmill Lunn, was met by Asquith, who, knowing the lie of the land, was to lead them to a junction with the right of Hawke Battalion. Asquith made an immediate impression on Lunn: he appeared as

> . . . An active and imperious figure, strongly contrasted with the tired troops who had been working hard with little rest during the last 24 hours . . .
>
> In my short experience of the front, I never saw anyone, officer, NCO, or man, except Arthur Asquith and one young Tommy, who did not look like an illustration of the refrain, 'We're here because we're here, because we're here, because we're here'. But Arthur Asquith embodied free will. He was there because he liked being there. Our progress over the torn ground was slow. The men kept falling in and out of shell holes, and Asquith's impatience increased. He seemed to feel as a champion sprinter would who should find himself, on turning out to lower the world's record for the hundred yards, unaccountably compelled to do the course leading a tortoise on a string.[35]

After arriving at River Trench, Asquith led off, under small arms fire, to complete the reunification of the RND Battalions, but was soon hit in the left arm by a bullet. He left Lunn in command of the sector and returned to the rear. Lunn unfortunately became disorientated and was captured by the Germans. Montagu returned and resumed command,[36] and, by dawn on the 5th, the final objectives were taken and consolidated against very heavy counter-attacks, and by the night of 5/6 February the 189th Brigade was relieved by the 190th. So ended, after over fifty hours of stubborn fighting, an attack scheduled for eight minutes. Hood had suffered nine Officers and 144 men as casualties, about twenty-five per cent of those who went into action. Asquith was immediately recommended for the DSO, which was announced in BEF DO 14 of 7 March 1917, and confirmed in the *London Gazette* in April.[37] His friend and protégé, Lieutenant Hilton, was awarded the Military Cross.

Macmillan was in Brigade HQ when Asquith returned to brief General Philips. His assessment was that:

His [Asquith's] personality and indomitable courage gave new life to all around him, and although badly wounded, he carried on until victory was assured. Looking as white as a winding sheet from loss of blood, he hobbled to the rear without assistance to give a lucid and most helpful report to the Brigade before being evacuated to hospital . . .

Lieutenant Commander Asquith received the DSO . . . more substantial recognition would have been forthcoming had there been someone on the spot to witness and appraise the valour and understanding [he] displayed.[38]

Macmillan's superior, General Philips, may have had his differences with Asquith, and would continue to do so, but he pushed through the recommendation for Asquith's decoration, and wrote in generous terms from his London house to Arthur during his recuperation: 'Hearty congratulations on getting the D.S.O., which you thoroughly deserved – I am awfully glad you got it all right, though I never had much doubt'.[39]

Asquith, after preliminary treatment, was admitted to 14th General Hospital at Boulogne, his second stay in under four months, with an injury classed as 'GSW. lt. arm severe'.[40] By the 7th he was well enough to be considered for evacuation home, and his wound was now diagnosed as 'Slight': he had been lucky again, and no major bones had been damaged. On 10 February he was transferred to the Duchess of Rutland's Hospital, in Arlington Street, London, in the Hospital Ship *Princess Elizabeth*. His father visited him and revealed to Sylvia Henley his disappointment that the wound was not bad enough to keep him at home for an extended period:

He is up & dressed & carries his arm in a sling. It is only a slight wound, and I fear he will very soon be fit to take himself again to the front. Meanwhile he is in good quarters, apparently under the sisterhood of Diana Manners[41]

During his recuperation, Asquith was borne on the books of the 3rd Reserve Battalion of the RND at Blandford, and he was awarded sick leave initially to run from 10 February to 5 March 1917. It seems as though the wound to his arm took longer to heal than was at first expected, for he remained on sick leave, and did not finally appear before a Medical Board at Adastral House, Blackfriars, until 23 March.[42]

Whilst in London he renewed his acquaintance with Betty and his other friends. He lunched twice with Lieutenant General Mercer, formerly a Brigade Commander with the RND in Gallipoli, and now Adjutant General of the Royal Marines, when he certainly would have taken the opportunity to express his views of the situation in the Division. He still retained a position of influence, as shown by the fact that Hankey, who lunched with him and the Prime Minister at 10 Downing Street at the end of October, noted that 'Arthur Asquith, invalided from the front with broken ear drums after being buried by a *Minenwerfer* [minethrower], absolutely scorns the idea of breaking the German lines, as a few machine guns with barbed wire can stop anything but the Tanks.'[43]

He and Freyberg dined and went to the theatre, and among his other friends from the RND, he met Montagu and Patrick Shaw Stewart. The latter had been posted to a Staff position at Salonica since being evacuated with the other RND personnel from Gallipoli over twelve months previously, and was home on leave. He and Arthur lunched at the Ritz on 22 February, where they discussed the next step, as Shaw Stewart had just received a refusal from the War Office to a request for a transfer. He decide to make a further attempt, requesting a Medical Board, on the grounds that the climate in Macedonia was injurious to his health. He wrote: 'After I got the Salonica answer from the War Office, refusing to release me, I thought I was finished. But after talking to the RND people, I thought I might play my inside'.[44] He was successful at the Board, and eventually rejoined the Battalion.

During his time at home, Arthur evidently became more and more convinced of the depth of his feeling for Betty Manners. His diary indicates that they met several times while he was recovering: the last time was on 2 April, just before he was due to rejoin his Battalion. They had apparently talked seriously of marriage, and before he left to travel to Boulogne on 5 April he wrote to her. The reply, dated 9 April, caught up with him after he had rejoined Hood where he was delighted to meet Freyberg, McCracken and Hilton again.[45] Betty, revealing the uncertainty in her mind, wrote:

> I feel in a bad dream wondering if I should ever wake up, not daring to and not much wanting to. When for a moment I stop to think I feel heavy with memories and gloom and indecision and selfish bitterness with the perverseness of the world and the life which I have created for myself. I know as you tell me I am old and ought to marry and its [sic] quite true and a future as a spinster is all that is struggling and lonely, but my spirit is still fighting and ungoverned by material facts – I shall never stoop. I trust one day my heart and soul will perhaps find a place and a refuge – a strange change will come. This is a sort of answer to your letter – it really is what you know, just a call from the bottom of a true heart which cannot answer.[46]

Arthur said his goodbyes to his father, Margot, Violet, and Elizabeth, at 20 Cavendish Square, where they were living after leaving Downing Street: he was met by Cardy Montagu at Charing Cross who pressed some fine cigars on him. On the crossing in the packed Transport Ship *London*, was

'Major' Orpen [Asquith's quotes] with many canvasses.[47] After much queueing in Boulogne, Asquith was told that there was no train to take him to Bethune until 3.45 the following afternoon. The next day was Good Friday, and it snowed in the afternoon when he caught the train to St Omer, travelling with French and British officers. They told him of rumours of heavy fighting at Vimy Ridge and around Arras: Arthur recorded: 'Hope I shall not find a smashed Battalion'.[48]

He need not have worried, for the RND had not yet been in action. It took nearly five hours for the train to travel less than thirty miles to Bethune, and then a two-mile walk, before Asquith was reunited with Freyberg and the Hood Battalion. Hilton was temporary Adjutant. He was told that the Division had made a great name for itself, and that it would shortly be moved nearer to the battle zone. In the afternoon Asquith, Freyberg, the Doctor, and Hilton rode into Bethune for a photograph with the Band, now nineteen strong, and, despite Kelly's death, playing better than ever. Morale was high, although the men had had no chance of a bath since the February fighting, neither had it been possible for their blankets to be disinfected, resulting in over 100 reporting to the Sick Bay with septic sores and scabies on Easter Saturday.

On Easter Day Hood followed Drake to Houchin, seven miles away. The men 'look well weathered and are full of spirit, and sang on the march.'[49] Their destination was new billets with plenty of good tents, baths, and a recreation room for the men. Steps were immediately put in hand for all the Battalion to have a bath, 350 at a time, over two days.

Arthur had been with his Battalion for just two days, sufficient to see Hood Battalion beat 24th DAC, unbeaten for over two years, at football, in an exciting match watched by a large crowd, when a message came for him to join the Staff of XVII Corps at Aubigny on the 12th. This was the last straw for Asquith:

> I am sick and tired of this conspiracy . . . to make a Staff Officer of me. It is spoiling my War. There can be no question that my sphere of greatest usefulness – and enjoyment – is in this Battn. and Brigade where I am known to and know everyone. Wrote to Philip Sassoon [who although an MP was on Haig's staff as a political aide and contact man] and my Father to try and get the conspiracy squashed once and for all and immediately. This is not a moment to be away from the Battalion, and too late to learn office work.[50]

He and Freyberg rode to Barlin to speak to Philips, GOC 189th Brigade, and as a result, Asquith forwarded an official letter through Freyberg asking for his Staff Training to be cancelled permanently. During this time, the Battalion was at two hours' readiness to move, and it was this that provided Freyberg with the excuse not to make available a cart to take

Asquith's gear to XVIIth Corps HQ; nor could Corps or the Division spare a car for him. And so, on the following day, Asquith accompanied the Battalion on its next move south to Caucourt, a further seven miles via Hermin through pretty country, although it snowed heavily all afternoon. The next day a blind eye could no longer be turned to his orders, and Arthur rode the four or five miles to Aubigny, where the headquarters of XVIIth Corps were stationed. On arrival, he reported to the Staff Brigadier (BGGS), and told him of his desire to return to Hood at the earliest opportunity. The Brigadier agreed to speak to the Corps Commander. Asquith was extremely irritated to learn that no particular duties had been allocated to him, and wrote in his diary:

> I detest this position in which I have been put so often now, of being sent to a Staff which does not want me just before my Battn. is going into action ie at a time when I might be most useful to it. It is not as though I could be spared easily by the Battn . . . Nor as though my being with the Battn. and so perhaps running more risks would put Father off his work. [a reason frequently given before, when Asquith senior was in office] Those responsible for sending me here or intriguing to have me sent here have acted in a conscienceless and criminal way.[51]

Asquith's good humour had returned by the following day: he was sent to assist the Corps GSO2, Major Thorp, who had nothing for him to do, so Arthur attached himself to one of the Pioneer Battalions, in order to visit the German lines recently taken around Arras. While he was thus chafing at the bit, 189th Brigade marched through Aubigny on its way to relieve 34th Division in the newly captured ground around Bailleul. The next day Asquith and an Intelligence Officer called Williams went up to the old front line: they were able to motor as far as St Nicholas, a suburb of Arras, but then had to proceed on foot. Asquith was impressed that the first three lines of the German defences had been badly battered and the wire well cut, although, ominously, he observed that concrete machine gun emplacements were little damaged. Amid occasional shell fire, they reached Point du Jour where there was a German pill box disguised as a haystack. Thence to Bailleul, where they met 189th Brigade going up to the line. Arthur learned from Freyberg that Hood were the reserve Battalion, which was a source of disappointment as: 'they are the only Battn. in our Brigade who I would trust to make a good job of an attack'.[52]

Returning to Aubigny, he met Commander Nelson, who had been relieved of his command of Nelson Battalion on their way up to the trenches. He had been with the Division from the earliest days, and while Asquith's assessment was that 'he lacks many qualities which a C.O. should have: but he knows his Officers and had reconnoitred this position; and there is no clearer case of the truth about not swapping horses when crossing a stream. I recommended him to apply to teach the Yanks'.[53]

The next day, the BGGS, Charles, a Wykehamist who had made a good impression on Asquith as a man of ability and considerable character, sent him forward to the Headquarters of the 4th and 9th Divisions, and the South African, 26th, 10th and 11th Brigades, all of which were in the line. He noted that the South Africans had suffered 700 casualties 'in the mad 2nd effort to take Roeux, by daylight, with poor barrage, enemy M. guns on 3 sides with a long and perfect field of fire. This Bde. comes out of the line 700 strong. They are naturally embittered.'[54] There was further bad news on return to Corps HQ, from an officer on the staff of Third Army, that GHQ had stated that there was

not an earthly chance of my being allowed to return to my Hood: no reason given. He proposes applying for me as GSO3 to 3rd Army. He says I shall see this battle that way. I told him that I had no job here, and had no objection to being GSO3 to 3rd Army on condition that it is understood I do not desist from my intention of returning to my Battn. I hate being put in these false positions.[55]

To further his education, Asquith visited the Corps Squadron of the Royal Flying Corps, whose CO, Powell, was described by Arthur as 'an Eton don, and a very agreeable fellow'. He commanded three flights between four and six F.E biplanes: two flights flew spotter flights for the artillery, while the third was used for contact work with the infantry, reporting positions of flares shown by them to plot the limits of their advance. The pilots complained a great deal to Asquith about the slow speed of their aircraft, which made them easy prey for any enemy fighters which escaped their own. The Squadron had lost twenty-three aircrew in the last three months. Back at Corps HQ, Asquith received orders to report to HQ Third Army at St Pol 'forthwith', which he did the next morning, calling on General Allenby on arrival. There was much grumbling among the Staff that they were about to leave their comfortable billets for less commodious accommodation in a village nearer the line. The feeling was that the recent advance of only two miles hardly warranted the upheaval. At the same time, while Arthur was enjoying the civilized comforts of the Mayor's House in St Pol, his old Battalion was moving into the line in front of the small fortified village of Gavrelle, a few miles east of Arras on the Douai road: it was alternately hailing and sunny, and there was a bitter wind blowing. The battalion spent the next week either in the line or in reserve trenches, digging assembly trenches for the coming attack, and under periodic heavy shellfire.

For the next three days, Arthur kept himself busy visiting, among other organisations, the Map Section under Colonel Winterbottom, which had in hand the total resurvey of all of the battle area of northern France and Belgium, with signals teams listening to enemy wireless transmissions and using direction-finding gear to detect German transmitters, and with a group of observers, locating enemy guns by their flash. He also spent time with the Counter-Espionage section, where he learned that the British had agents behind the enemy lines, reporting by carrier pigeon. Then, at about noon on the 20th, came the news that Asquith had been waiting and hoping for: a signal was received that Freyberg had been promoted to command 173rd Brigade in another Division. Arthur at once wrote a new application to be allowed to return to Hood to command. At the same time, Brigadier Philips had realised that it made little sense for the Battalion to go into action under an officer not well known to them, and had wired for Asquith's return, and as a temporary relief, appointed Lieutenant Commander Bernard Ellis from Anson, a fine officer, in command of Hood.[56] Freyberg reluctantly left the Battalion: his last Special Order to them concluded: 'I always trusted you and knew you would do well. It is, however, a fine thing to feel that we have proved to others our value as a fighting unit . . . My thoughts will often be with you.'[57] Freyberg, always one to wear his heart on his sleeve, confessed to Arthur much later that he had cried all night because he was leaving his beloved Battalion.[58] Approval for his release from the Staff was received next morning. Even then, he was not sure that he was to resume command of the Battalion. He wrote to his father:

This is just a hurried word to say that Freyberg has been promoted, and I am being allowed, at an interesting moment to rejoin my Battn. – in command of it I think.[59]

A delighted Asquith motored that evening to Arras, via the Divisional HQ at Maroeuil.

From there he went by foot to Brigade HQ, arriving at about 11pm.[60] He was promoted by Divisional Order to the rank of Temporary Commander RNVR, to date from 22 April 1917, although the BEF Order enabling him to wear the appropriate badges of rank, and call himself 'Commander', was only published on 18 May 1917.

NOTES

1. Castle, 19, a former butcher from Wimbledon, had been Asquith's runner and batman for some time. He had accompanied Asquith to V Corps HQ, but rejoined Hood Battalion on 28 October. He was very short and thin (his chest was only thirty-four inches inflated). His death was severely felt by Asquith. He is buried in the Ancre Cemetery, which stands practically on the RND front line.

2. Letter from Surgeon W McCracken to AMA dated 17 November 1916, AMA papers.

3. Sub Lt PH Bolus, of Wimbledon, did very well on the Ancre and was awarded the MC. He paid a heavy price, being wounded in the foot. His right leg was amputated, and he was eventually invalided in October 1918.

4. Letter from Captain Lionel Montagu to AMA dated 26 November 1916, AMA papers.

5. Letter from George Ramsay to AMA dated 12 March 1917, AMA papers.

6. Letter from Bernard Freyberg to AMA dated 23 November 1916, Freyberg papers.

7. Extract from a letter from Margot Asquith to Bernard Freyberg dated 15 January 1917, Freyberg private papers.

8. The above two paragraphs are based on an undated (soon after 30 December 1916) draft of a letter to his Corps Commander, in AMA papers.

9. From the unpublished diary, page 3, of Able Seaman, later Sub Lieutenant Thomas Macmillan, clerk to 189th Brigade Headquarters, part of the Macmillan Papers held at the IWM.

10. II Corps G571/22/23 of 26 December 1916, HQ Infantry Brigade's 1603/a dated 27 December 1916 and No 2728 of 30 December 1916, copies in AMA papers.

11. Report from GOC 63rd Division to GOC II Corps, dated 1 December 1916 PRO WO 95/3117.

12. Report from GOC II Corps to GOC Fifth Army dated 21 February 1917 PRO WO 95/3117.

13. *Hood Battalion* by L Sellers, Leo Cooper, 1995, p203. In Chapter 19 of this work Sellers provides an excellent detailed account of the various machinations between the Army and Navy over the future of the Division.

14. The unfortunate Creagh-Osborne went sick on 3 January 1917 and had to go to hospital. Lieutenant Commander Egerton took over command of the battalion temporarily until relieved by Lieutenant Colonel DC Munro, PRO, box ADM 137/3064, ppl 11 and 112.

15. The material on this subject comes from PRO ADM 1/ 8477-309. I am indebted to Len Sellers for pointing this source out to me.

16. Army Field Message Book No. 12, covering the period 30 December 1916 onwards; Notes on 'Bayonet Training', quoting extract from GHQ memo OB/121 1 dated 16/6/16, AMA papers.

17. Notebook No. 12, AMA papers.

18. All from notes in Notebook No. 12, AMA papers.

19. Army Book 136, marked 'AM. Asquith 1917', a record of his Staff training from 20 January to 3 February 1917, kept as a diary, Notebook No. 13, AMA papers, entry for 21 January 1917.

20. Notebook No. 13, entry for 22 January 1917, AMA papers.

21. Notebook No. 13, entry for 25 January 1917, AMA papers.

22. Notebook No. 13, entry for 26 January 1917, AMA papers.

23. Notebook No. 13, entry for 29 January 1917, AMA papers.

24. Notebook No. 13, entry for 31 January 1917, AMA papers. Egerton was wounded by shrapnel in the right thigh on 21 January 1917, which kept him out of action for some time.

25. Notebook No. 13, entry for 2 February 1917, AMA papers.

26. ibid.

27. Lockwood, E, Lt Cdr, a Londoner, had a distinguished career: gassed in February 1917, he remained on duty. He was awarded the DSO in September

1917. Shortly after he was very seriously wounded in the head in October 1918.

28. Notebook No. 13, entry for 2 February 1917, AMA papers.
29. The time of Munro's wounding is difficult to determine: the Divisional History gives it as 11.30pm, while Macmillan records it as happening at 1.30am. The likeliest explanation is that it was about 1.30 before 189th Brigade HQ, where Macmillan was working, became aware of the situation. This is borne out by the Battalion War Diary, entry for 4 February 1917, p120, which gives the time as 1.30am, PRO, Kew, box ADM 137/3064.
30. Jerrold, *The Royal Naval Division*, p214.
31. Hood Battalion War Diary: note in the hand of Acting Lieutenant William Arblaster, Adjutant, p123. PRO Kew, box ADM 137/3064.
32. Letter GA 388, from Fifth Army to 63rd Division, copy to II Corps and to Asquith himself, dated 3 February 1917, signed for Major General, GS, AMA papers.
33. Macmillan papers, p178, IWM.
34. Macmillan papers, p179, IWM.
35. Hugh Kingsmill, the pseudonym of Hugh Kingsmill Lunn: *I Was Captured at Beaucourt*, from *The Great War: I Was There* pp 1009/1010, The World's Work (1913) Ltd. Also quoted in Sellers: *Hood Battalion* p216. Lunn was repatriated on 30 November 1918.
36. Macmillan papers, p179, IWM.
37. The citation reads: 'For conspicuous gallantry and devotion to duty. He obtained leave to go up to the front when a fight was imminent. Later, although wounded, he returned to Brigade Headquarters and gave a clear account of the situation and of the fighting which had been going on during the night. He has previously done fine work.' *London Gazette* dated 17 April 1917, p 3675.
38. Macmillan papers, pp179 and 181, IWM.
39. Letter from Brigadier General Philips, from 65 South Audley Street to AMA dated 5 March 1917, AMA papers.
40. Record of Service of Officers of the Royal Naval Division, Naval Historical Branch.
41. Letter from Herbert Asquith to Sylvia Henley dated 2 February 1917, Bodleian Mss. Diana Manners, daughter of the Duke of Rutland, married Duff Cooper after the war.
42. Pocket diary, 1917, AMA papers.
43. *Hankey: Man of Secrets*, by S Roskill, Collins, 1970, p312.
44. Letter from Patrick Shaw Stewart, quoted in Sellers, *Hood Battalion*, p247.
45. Pocket diary, entry for 7 April 1917, AMA papers.
46. Letter from Betty Manners to AMA, dated 9 April 1917.
47. From diary, in green bound soft cover, covering the period 5 April to 22 April 1917, henceforth referred to as Green diary, entry for 5 April 1917, AMA papers. William, later Sir William, Orpen had been commissioned as an official war artist, and was given the rank of Major.
48. Green diary, entry for 6 April 1917.
49. Green diary, entry for 7 April 1917.
50. Green diary, entry for 8 April 1917.
51. Green diary, entry for 12 April 1917.
52. Green diary, entry for 14 April 1917.
53. ibid. Nelson, famous for his participation in Scott's fatal expedition to the Antarctic in 1912, joined the Division early in the War.
54. Green diary, entry for 15 April 1917.

55. ibid.
56. Commander B Ellis DSO RNVR.
57. Special Order by OC Hood Battalion, dated 20 April 1917. PRO ADM 137/3064, quoted in Sellers, p230/1.
58. Conversation with Mrs Susan Boothby (one of Arthur Asquith's four daughters), 2 March 1994.
59. Letter from AMA to HHA dated 21 April 1917, AMA papers.
60. Asquith's diary conflicts with the account by Macmillan (Macmillan papers IWM, p 191), who has him returning to the Battalion on the morning of 21 April, and that by that afternoon Brigade was in possession of his orders for the attack. Hood's War Diary, PRO WO/95/3 115, records the battalion CO going forward to reconnoitre on the early morning of the 22nd, which agrees with Asquith's diary entry. Besides, it is inconceivable that Arthur would have produced his attack orders before such a reconnaissance. Final confirmation is available in the Hood War Diary that the battalion attack order is dated 22 April 1917.

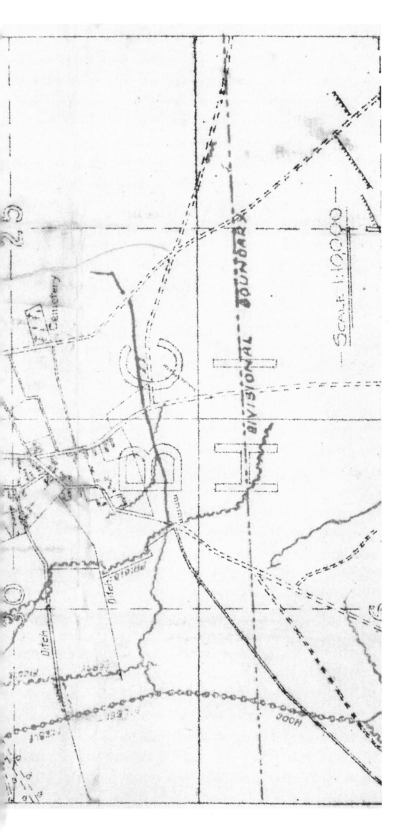

he position of the Front Line during the forenoon of that day,
d the DSO for this action.

attack of 23 April 1917. The faint pencil markings are in Asquith's hand, showing
ants Morrison and Tamplin, and Sub Lieutenant Cooke were killed. Asquith receiv

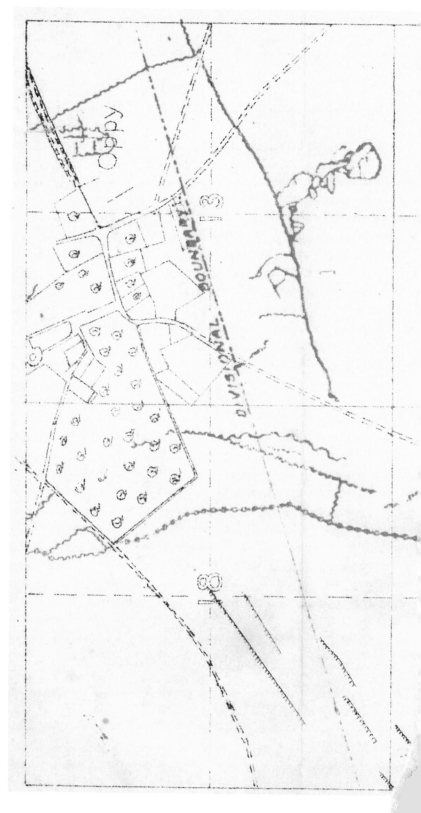

4. Trench map of the Gavrelle area of operations, carried by As
and recording the places w

CHAPTER X
The Battle for Gavrelle

Gavrelle is a very small town to the east of Arras, on the Arras-Douai road, now by-passed by a new carriageway which runs past the site on which stood the notorious Windmill on the high ground to the north. The town was devastated in the war, and afterwards rebuilt, as were nearly all French towns in the battle zone. It was in German hands from 1914 until April 1917, and stands on a slight eminence overlooking a gently undulating plain to the west. It had been fortified with the usual German diligence and efficiency. The new main British lines were situated in newly captured German positions on a low ridge about two miles to the west of the outskirts, and included the former enemy fortress known as Point du Jour, visited by Asquith during his time on the Staff. The British front lines and assembly trenches were constructed on the lower ground, on the slopes facing their watchful opponents. The omens for the battle were not good: the troops had been shelled regularly when in the line; the weather was bitterly cold, snow alternating with sleet.

It was decided by the new Divisional Commander, Lawrie, that the attack would be made by 189th Brigade on the right, and 190th on the Divisional left: from right to left the order of battle would be Drake and Nelson Battalions, with Hood in close support, and 7th Royal Fusiliers and 4th Bedfords, supported by the Honourable Artillery Company. The three objectives were the enemy trenches in front of the town: the road, the 'Yellow Line', which runs virtually north/south through it; and a line between three and six hundred yards the other side of Gavrelle (the 'Red' Line). On the Division's right, the 37th Division would attack and take Greenland Hill. Further operations would be taking place simultaneously around Roeux and Monchy to the south.

During the night of 21 April Philips explained the plan to Asquith at his Brigade HQ, and at 1am the latter received the sixteen pages of typed foolscap which constituted the Brigade order. Asquith was immediately concerned that his Battalion was not due to go forward until twenty minutes after the initial advance, passing through the Nelsons to take the final objective while the left flank was covered by the Army Battalions of 190th Brigade: he believed this delay to be a major mistake, as the German barrage would by then be directed on to the British front line with precisely the intention of catching support troops packed in the assembly

115

lines and ready to move. He noted that he would 'feel more comfortable if we were protecting our own left flank, and taking Nelson's place with no Battn to come through us.'[1] Philips stuck by his decision: he reasoned that, if Nelson were held up on the wire, they and the Hoods would be easy prey to German fire, and that a catastrophe could result.

After a few hours' sleep in a dug-out, Asquith set out at about 7am to have a look at the scene of the forthcoming attack. On completion he consulted with Colonel Lewis, who had relieved Commander Nelson as OC Nelson, and 'carefully went through the orders with him'.[2] He then went through the orders with his four Company Commanders, Asbury – A, Matcham – B, Morrison – C, and Tamplin – D. He then issued his own instructions: in front B on the left, D on the right, supported respectively by C and A Companies. After briefing his officers from the long and detailed orders, which included maps and the intricacies of the barrage timetable, Asquith sent his second in command, Ellis, to have another try to dissuade Philips from insisting that Hood wait the full twenty minutes after the opening of the British creeping barrage before starting out. He was unsuccessful. Asquith tried yet again on the way up to the jumping off point, but Philips remained adamant.

At 9pm the men had hot dinners; Asquith noted that they were 'rather weary after nine days discomfort in front line and support under rather heavy shelling'.[3] At 11pm the Battalion moved off by companies: all reported that they were in position by 2.30am on the 23rd, Asquith's 34th birthday. Hilton, the Adjutant, sent the message to HQ by runner.[4] Rum was also issued at this time. Asquith had still not calmed his fears about lingering for twenty minutes after the Nelsons went forward, so he ordered Sub Lieutenant Hill, a Lewis Gun Officer, to go forward with Nelson Battalion, and to report when they had captured their first objective, 'so that I might be able to judge whether to wait till zero plus 20' before advancing'.[5] At 4.30am Asquith took position in the centre of the leading waves of his Battalion. It was going to be a clear and warm day, in contrast to the cold weather of the past weeks, and dawn was already breaking.

At zero hour, 4.45am, the British barrage opened, and Nelson and Drake Battalions became quickly invisible in the smoke and dust. After ten minutes Sub Lieutenant Hill had not returned to report that Nelson had achieved their first objective, and, as the enemy barrage was already falling heavily on his assembly position, Asquith led on and sent word for the rear companies to follow. Ahead Drake and Nelson had done well. Drake had the very good fortune to be commanded by a brilliant young soldier, Commander Walter Sterndale Bennett, an officer of the highest calibre, the youngest commanding a battalion in France until his untimely death at Passchendaele. Before the war he had determined to be a painter, but joined the Artists Rifles in the early days of the war and was commissioned in the RND in the spring of 1915. Promoted to Lieutenant in Gallipoli, and mentioned in despatches there, he became the Adjutant of Drake Battalion. During the Ancre battle, he took command after all other senior officers had become casualties; for his courage and leadership he was awarded the DSO. 'His men would have gone anywhere with him and done anything for him', is a comment used typically to describe his leadership qualities.[6] It was a very serious blow when he died of wounds in early November 1917.

While Drake were forming up for the attack, it was discovered that the enemy wire was still partly intact on their front. Sterndale Bennett reported this to Brigade and asked 'Is the attack cancelled?'.[7] The message was relayed to Corps HQ, who ordered the attack to go ahead. It was therefore decided that Drake would attack only on the left of their front, where it was believed that the wire had been cut, protecting their right flank from enfilade fire by a combination of fire from Stokes mortars and Lewis guns.[8]

By 5am Asquith was in the enemy trenches. While the front line wire had been well cut, that in the second was virtually intact: fortunately it did not form a serious obstacle, as by now the defenders had abandoned their positions. He halted in the enemy second line to reorganise, and to disperse his men who had been tending to bunch. After sending back about twenty prisoners, Hood then advanced through the village to the remains of the road that marked the Yellow Line, which was reached after some hard fighting, including hand-to-hand exchanges in some of the buildings which had not been destroyed. The pause on the Yellow Line was unavoidable because the barrage was not scheduled to lift until 6.01am, assessed by Asquith as being 'a great mistake, giving the enemy a breathing space just when we have them on the run'.[9] The road was crowded with Nelsons and Hoods, and even a hundred Bedfords who should have been to the north protecting the flank. Asquith collected three of their officers and sent them and their men back over the main road.

At one minute past six Asquith led the remainder of the Naval Battalions through the village. On emerging on the eastern side, the attackers were held up by machine gun fire from several unsilenced positions, particularly one in a trench about 150 yards east of the Mayor's house, which was almost the last in the village on the main Arras-Fresnes road. It is now a hotel. Asquith took Lieutenant Asbury and two men up a shallow ditch to see if the position could be outflanked. Asbury, a very tall officer, provided an easy target for the close-range German snipers, and was shot through the head. One of the two men was also killed. Bearing a charmed life, Arthur retreated and took stock. It was apparent that the key to the situation was the Mayor's house which had to be taken so that suppressive fire could be brought to bear on the enemy in the trenches east of the village. He led a party up the main road and into the house, capturing ten German prisoners, including some NCOs, sleeping or shamming sleep in the two cellars. He then installed snipers and a Lewis gun in positions commanding the German trenches, and left Sub Lieutenant Cooke, the Battalion Intelligence Officer, in command. A shaky hold had been obtained on Gavrelle, but the British positions were under heavy sniper fire, and suffering from their own bombardment falling short. Nevertheless, by 7.23, Asquith reported:

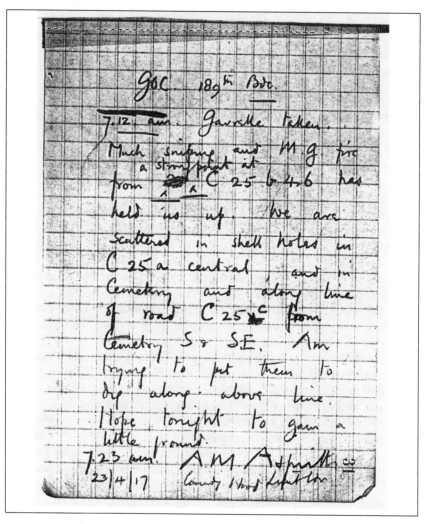

3. The message from Asquith to GOC 189th Brigade reporting the successful capture of Gavrelle village, timed at 7.23 am on 23 April 1917, Asquith's 34th birthday, from one of Asquith's Field Service Notebooks.
Private Papers

7.12am Gavrelle taken. Much sniping and M.G. fire from a strongpoint at C 25 b 4 6 has held us up. We are scattered in shell holes in C 25 a central, and in Cemetery and along line of road C 25 c from Cemetery S & S.E. Am trying to get them to dig along above line. Hope tonight to gain a little ground.[10]

Asquith then carried out a further reconnaissance of his positions: between 9 and 11am he came to the conclusion that it would definitely not be possible to advance until darkness. He continued:

I found about 200 Nelsons and Hoods crowding about behind the buildings of the street in C25a [a map reference] that leads to the Cemetery. I therefore sent 50 Hoods back to the Blue Line [the old German front line trenches] with Sub Lieut Matcham [A Company Commander]: and set all the remaining vagrant Hoods and Nelsons to dig themselves in N & S connecting up the ditches in A1 . . . , an empty piece of sandy ground with many convenient shellholes in it, and not too much bricks and mortar at hand. Before this I had set Hoods to dig in along E side of the Cemetery Road. I also placed a Lewis gun and some rifles at the E. end of the Cemetery. I then went by the much-sniped Cemetery Road to see Lieut. Comdr Bennett, O.C. Drake, but saw his trench was so congested that it would take me too long to reach him: so returned, past two blazing enemy dug-outs. Found Col Lewis O.C. Nelson at West end of ditch A.[11]

Philips was keen to press on to the final objective, and sent a signal, timed at about 9am, to Colonel Lewis for Hood and Nelson to advance at 10.30. Unfortunately, this message was not received by Lewis and Asquith until just before 11am, and Asquith decided that there was insufficient time left in the barrage for another attack to be made. By now the sun was shining fiercely from a cloudless sky, and the men, after weeks, even months, of very cold weather were drowsy and apathetic. Asquith reported to Philips:

OC Nelson has sent you map showing our present positions.
    Enemy gradually mustering 800-1000 yards East of Village, N & S of road.
    Am going to reconnoitre position N of Village.
    Troops very tired and sluggish. Hope we may possibly be able to further out [sic] from village tonight. Send water, rations and ammunition.[12]

The position was precarious: the famous Gavrelle Windmill, north of the Arras-Fresnes road was still in German hands, and from this high commanding position a constant fire was maintained on the British positions. It was because of the weakness of his position that Asquith had despatched Matcham and his men to the former enemy second line in case the advanced positions were overrun. The enemy were massing for a counter-attack, and British heavy guns were dropping shells on the buildings of the Mayor's house, the key to the defence of the captured ground.

Concern for his left flank led Asquith to carry out his reconnaissance north of the main Arras road, where he eventually met Colonel Collins Wells of the Bedfords, who knew the whereabouts of only two platoons of his Battalion, and had not seen any other troops from the other Battalions of 190th Brigade, which was supposed to be assisting him to guard this vulnerable flank. Returning to his main position at about noon, Asquith was dismayed to learn that two of his best Company Commanders, Morrison and Tamplin, had been hit by a shell. Tamplin was killed and Morrison died in his arms. Some time later Asquith received a touching letter from Morrison's father, thanking him for sending a photograph of himself [Asquith]. Morrison senior continued:

> I value it as that of one under whom my son served during practically all the time he was in the Army: one for whom, as he told me in letters and also when on his only leave, he entertained the highest respect and in whom he had unbounded confidence, of whom he wrote 'he'll likely get the DSO, but no honour he will get will be equal to what he deserves'; and the one who tended him as a brother and in whose arms he passed away.
>
> You cannot understand how it touched his mother's heart and mine when we heard of your kindness to our boy, it made us fell that he had died in the arms of a friend.[13]

A small sketch map of Gavrelle in Asquith's papers is marked in pencil 'M&T', where they were killed. Just to the east of the Mayor's house is marked 'C', almost certainly where Sub Lieutenant Cooke of his Battalion died when leading his Lewis gun team from the relative shelter of the building better to disperse the Germans in the nearby trenches.

During the forenoon, Surgeon McCracken left his position in the rear of the action and pushed into the village with one orderly. Here he pressed into his service a German doctor, 2 NCOs, and twelve German Red Cross men whom he found being led to rear under escort. After finding a safe cellar, formerly a German Regimental Aid Post, he set about recovering wounded. During the course of the rest of the day, he brought in and treated over 150 wounded who otherwise would have been left in the open where they lay, and would probably have been blown to pieces or buried by falling houses.[14]

During the afternoon the enemy continued to return to their abandoned trenches in front of Gavrelle, and attacked, principally on the right of the Divisional front, where they were dealt with by Drake Battalion, by now well dug-in, with the invaluable assistance of artillery. Fortunately no major attack was made on the weakly defended northern flank. At about 4.30pm orders reached the three front line Battalion Commanders, Asquith, Lewis, and Sterndale Bennett, to name their time for a barrage, with the intention of pushing the line forward another three or four hundred yards east and north east. As an indication of the poor state of communications, the order had taken about three hours to reach them. They decided that no further offensive action was possible until after dark.

Asquith's communications to Brigade HQ at this time begin to show signs of tiredness, with a hint of despair, in sharp contrast to the generally optimistic note of the Battalion War Diary, written, of course, after the action. This personal pessimism was not communicated in any way to his men still in action. To them he appeared his normal energetic and confident self. Following the decision not to attempt a further advance, Asquith sent a message to Brigade:

> . . . Sniping and shellfire, enemy's and at times our own Heavy's on Mayor's House, have made it difficult to move about or to dig where we wanted to. Also men are dog-tired and apathetic. Bedfords position on our left is weak: they are out-sniped and there seem to be very few of them. I have only two officers left so far as I know . . . Germans have been gathering all day for a big attack. I fancy it will be most serious at NNE and NE corner of the village as nothing can be seen, ground rising steeply on that side, and all movement subject to severe sniping. I have been unable to trace the arrival of any rations or water. This is badly wanted.[15]

Immediately after, he sent a note to his Adjutant, Hilton, stationed in the captured German trenches:

> Position is rotten, especially on the left flank NE of village. Men very tired. No rations or water have arrived. There is a shortage of stretchers. Could you please send me up food and drink from my saddlebag? Bosches have been gathering in large numbers . . . We shall do our best but I feel very tired.[16]

Despite his fatigue Asquith carried out another check of his defensive lines and the enemy positions. He was able to find only about 120 of his Battalion, which confirmed his belief that they would probably be overrun by a dusk attack, so he sent a final message to Hilton:

In case of successful enemy attack on Gavrelle you and your men will put yourself under O.C. Hawke, if there: if he is not there, you will defend enemy old front line in default of your being given different orders by Bde.[17]

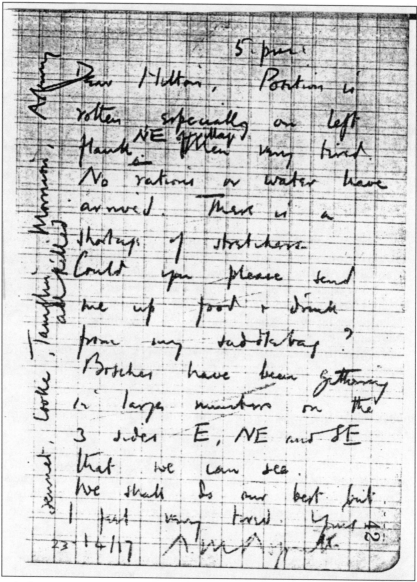

4. A pessimistic message from Asquith to his Adjutant, Hilton, on the chances of holding on to Gavrelle, timed at 5 pm on 23 April 1917, from one of Asquith's Field Service Notebooks. *Private Papers*

The expected enemy attack developed at the predicted time, but was dispersed by Lewis guns and an accurate artillery bombardment. The rest of the evening passed relatively quietly, and at about 10 pm Hood Battalion were relieved by Howe, and, having handed over, Asquith led his men back under heavy shell fire to the trenches near Point du Jour. Their casualties were thirteen officers and 179 men, but an astounding success had been achieved. Gavrelle was a heavily fortified village, manned by high quality troops: the attack formed part of a major offensive and therefore the element of surprise was absent. The key factor in its capture and retention was the outstanding cooperation between the artillery and the infantry. But the prime reason for the success was almost entirely due to the leadership and cooperation of the Battalion Commanders on the spot, who, at the critical time in the battle, organised defences for the newly taken ground which, in the event, proved just adequate to repulse very heavy German counter-attacks. Asquith had long realised that in the ultimate confusion of a major infantry battle, the secret of success was in the commander on the spot knowing where the enemy were, and of even more importance, the positions of your own troops. In order to obtain the necessary information, personal reconnaissance was vital. However, it is hard to exaggerate the danger to which this exposed the officer undertaking the task, who was required to move around, much of the time in the open, under small arms and artillery fire.

The next day the Germans made further massive attempts to dislodge the intruders, but to no avail: at about 3pm a series of attacks developed all along the line. Sterndale Bennett, who was still in the line with his Battalion, witnessed each enemy advance being cut down by shell and small-arms fire:

> I feel that I am not exaggerating when I estimate the enemy's casualties at two thousand. We were firing at them continually all the time we were up there – the fire was well controlled and splendid effects were seen – the artillery was magnificent. The enemy was thoroughly butchered and we enjoyed every moment of it.[18]

In the next few days, further strenuous attempts were made to consolidate the line to the north of the village: the Royal Marines brilliantly captured the notorious Windmill, and the Honourable Artillery Company succeeded in taking, and holding against counter-attacks by the Prussian Guard, key sections of trenches which provided ultimate security for Gavrelle. In this operation Lieutenants Haine and Pollard of the 1st Battalion HAC earned the Victoria Cross.

Later on the 24th, Asquith moved from the trenches through St Catherine's, a part of the city of Arras, to billets at Ecouvres.

Macmillan, the clerk of 189th Brigade wrote in his diary:

> The rejoicings over our victory were confined to Army, Corps and Divisional Headquarters, for the men who had accomplished the job were so overcome by fatigue and so depressed at the loss of old comrades that they could not enthuse.
>
> The Corps and Divisional Commanders visited each battalion in turn to thank them for their great work, but when it came to the tangible recognition of the many acts of gallantry which were reported to the bestowers of awards, the honours conferred were disappointing in the extreme.
>
> Sterndale Bennett deserved the Victoria Cross, for which he was recommended, but what shall I say of Commander Asquith? Viewed from any angle he was the outstanding personality in the fight, the one man who, more than any other, carried our arms to victory, and yet he was recommended only for a bar to his DSO. No Victoria Crosses came our way.[19]

On the evening of the 25th Asquith dined with General Congreve at XIII Corps Headquarters, when he briefed the Corps Commander on the recent action.[20]

After this, Asquith busied himself on trying to reconstruct his damaged Battalion, and with the inevitable after-effects of a major battle. His first action was to provide recommendations for the awards so disappointedly referred to by Macmillan: he was particularly anxious that his three Chief Petty Officers, Kirkbride, Tobin, and Harrison, should be decorated for their performance at Gavrelle,[21] and he very quickly drafted the citation for McCracken's well deserved DSO, concluding with the statement, that after the previous engagement on the Ancre in November, 'this officer was strongly recommended for a DSO and was awarded the MC'[22] as if to ensure that a similar mistake was not repeated. McCracken received the DSO. In addition, in slower time, he instructed Hilton to collect the reports for two of his men to receive the Victoria Cross, Able Seaman William Condie, and Able Seaman William Charlton. The latter was the sole survivor of the original Lewis gun crew, whose fire from the Mayor's house immediately after its capture probably saved the day for the attackers. He received the Distinguished Conduct Medal.

Having had his original quota of medal recommendations severely cut, Asquith had one more try on 2 May, resubmitting four officers, and twenty-one ratings.[23]

To replace his casualties, he wrote to Brigade requesting the return of six officers, including Lieutenant Patrick Shaw Stewart, serving at the RND Base Camp; Lieutenant Farrer, believed to be at Blandford; Sub Lieutenant Arblaster, another fine officer, and Lieutenant Commander

Mark Egerton, wounded in January, 'as 2nd in Command. He is I believe recovered and desirous of returning'.[24] Shaw Stewart had been agitating for some time to leave his job as a Staff Officer on the Salonika front, where he had been since leaving Gallipoli. As early as August 1916, Arthur had written asking him to return to Hood. At the time things had just started to hot up at Salonika, and Shaw Stewart replied that in view of the increased activity, and the chance of 'eating my Michaelmas goose in Sofia', he had decided to wait and see. He continued:[25]

> You certainly paint an attractive picture of regimental life to draw me back! trench-mortars for rifles however I consider a welcome exchange: the rifle always bored me, either on my own back or with a Fleet Reserveman's grimy thumb reflecting so-called light down the barrel at me. (So long as I'm not expected to <u>work</u> a trench-mortar, but only give lectures on it and abuse others for not working it with sufficient devotion.)[25]

Shaw Stewart rejoined the Battalion on 9 May 1917 as the senior Company Commander. Farrer never did rejoin Hood: he was transferred to the Army on 20 April 1917, having been at Blandford Camp since June 1916.

Shortly after coming out of the line, the Army Commander wished to be informed about the amount of war material captured during the Gavrelle operation. Macmillan sent a special message to Battalion Commanders. Asquith, in a rare instance of ill-considered exasperation with Army bureaucracy, replied immediately: 'The half of Gavrelle village'! Needless to say, Philips was infuriated and sent for Asquith. Macmillan wrote:

> The Commander duly arrived, but as the Brigade office did not offer sufficient privacy he was taken outside for his telling-off. I dropped my work and observed both men closely. The General was laying down the law as he paced backwards and forwards, while Asquith followed at his heels looking pale but unrepentant. How the matter ended I cannot say, but neither seemed at all pleased on parting.[26]

Philips was well aware of Asquith's abilities as a soldier, but their personalities occasionally clashed. Reading between the lines of all their correspondence, it is apparent that Philips was wary of his talented subordinate and his influential connections; in addition, the former was always concerned that Asquith would be taken away from front line duties to keep him from danger. It was fairly well known that Margot Asquith had been trying for some time to keep him away from the front. In fact she had informed Cynthia Charteris of her latest attempt to have Arthur permanently staff-bound as late as 21 April, the very day that he was on his way to take command of the Battalion![27] Asquith and Philips had clashed in the previous year over leave for the Battalion, and more recently over the recent orders for the Gavrelle attack, and they would do so again.

Knowing his father was concerned for his safety, Arthur wrote a hasty note on pages torn from his field service message book:

> I have had a most strenuous and satisfactory three days . . . I reached the Battn midnight 21st–22nd and took part with them in the successful attack on the village of Gavrelle at 4.45am on the 23rd. We were relieved early this morning. We badly needed a rest, as the men had been in the line, or close support in trenches, for eight days of foul weather before the attack: then two days and nights without sleep, and with much digging, and not much food and water: also heavy enemy shelling.
>
> I lost three of my four Company Commanders killed, and had three officers left for the consolidation and defence of the village after the attack. Our officer casualties were very unlucky and out of all proportion to the men casualties but with a little rest and training, and some few officers we left out of the attack I think we shall be able to make the Battn. as good as ever again.
>
> I have had only five hours sleep since 24th [he almost certainly meant the 21st], so am looking forward to getting billeted and to bed tonight.[28]

His father wrote back in a tone of congratulation, tinged with relief, enclosing a recent newspaper cutting reporting Arthur's DSO won in February, but only published in the Supplement to the *London Gazette* on 17 April. In the same letter, Asquith Senior revealed that he had recently dined with General Smuts, 'who is not very optimistic about the situation', and a lady called Sybil Rocksavage, who admitted that she was one who had been urging for Arthur to be kept on the Staff.[29]

Hood Battalion's rest after its exertions around Gavrelle was very short-lived: on 3 May they were back to the area just north-west of Gavrelle, digging and wiring at night in the Red Line east of Willerval. They were still very short of men: only 267 were reported as deepening sixty-five bays in the line from four to five feet, while a further fourteen were started and half-dug. This work was not without cost. Asquith laconically records that one man was killed and one wounded during the night of 5/6 May.[30] He also enquired whether any action had been taken on his request of 25 April for officers to be returned to the Battalion.[31]

Immediately after the battle, Asquith set in hand a memorial for those of his Battalion who had died in the capture of Gavrelle: he commissioned the local carpenter at the village of Hermin to manufacture a large wooden cross, which was collected by a routine GS waggon from the workshop and left in the Battalion Quartermaster's Store. Asquith paid sixty francs for it.[32] He also devised the inscription for the cross which reads 'In memory of the Officers and Men of the Hood Battalion killed in the capture of Gavrelle, April 1917'. The cross, with the names of those killed inscribed, is now in the church in the village.[33]

In the aftermath of the battle, attempts were made to try to determine the fate of those who had simply disappeared. One of these was Sub Lieutenant Bailey: he was seen by a leading seaman shortly after the attack began heading towards the village from the captured German front line. Later that evening he was seen by a stretcher bearer emerging from the dug-out which was being used as the Regimental Aid Post 'looking very pale and tired'.[34] He had been wounded at some time during the day, and after leaving the RAP, no trace of him was ever found.

Asquith's reputation was high with his men, as we have seen before, and this was reinforced by his leadership at Gavrelle: in his papers is a letter from one of his sailors in D Company, WP Bryan, to an unidentified friend reporting the recent battle. Bryan was lucky enough to come through 'with nothing worse than being buried twice in the trenches, and being hit with a peice [sic] of spent shrapnel about four inches long.' He added, 'We have an excelent [sic] commander in Mr Asquiths son he is as cool and calm under great shell fire and amid the whizzing of the snipers bullets, as though he was walking down the Strand. The boys think the world of him.'[35]

There was talk of the Brigade conducting a further push to capture those trenches just east of Gavrelle which had not been taken at the end of April, and preliminary orders were issued. Hood and Hawke Battalions were nominated as the front line assault troops behind a rolling barrage: the guns would lift to their final objective sixteen minutes after Zero Hour. In other words, what was planned was another trench-to-trench attack behind a barrage. Fortunately for the battalions, still reconstituting themselves after their earlier exertions, the attack did not materialise.[36]

By early June Hood Battalion was moved back into the line to take over the Windmill position, north of Gavrelle, whose defences at the time resembled a finger pointing north east towards the German lines. To the west of the Windmill there was a pronounced indented curve, or re-entrant, in the British front line. The importance of holding the high ground around the Windmill was well understood, and further consolidation was an obvious necessity. Asquith's notebook covering this period in the trenches refers repeatedly to 'offensive defence', the need for listening posts and active patrolling, the importance of Lewis guns being active, and SOS messages being ready written.[37] His draft orders, 'in case of any part of the Front Line held by Hood Battalion is taken by the enemy', conclude: '. . . the <u>WINDMILL and the ridge on which it stands must be held at all costs</u>, and is of greater importance than the positions of the flanking Battalions.'[38]

127

The site was vital enough to warrant a daily visit by the Brigade Major, Barnett. It could have been no surprise, therefore, that on the evening of 3 June Asquith received a memorandum from Brigade ordering his Battalion to step up the defensive work by starting to dig a chord trench cutting off the bight of the re-entrant which followed the line of Railway Trench. The distance was about two hundred yards. The trench was to be dug in two nights using explosives: on the first night Hood Battalion were told to excavate five large ditches 12ft by 6ft by 6ft deep at equal intervals along the proposed trench line. The next evening explosive charges would remove the soil and rock between the diggings. Asquith passed the order down to Shaw Stewart, telling him to use D Company men for the task, each party to be led by a man from A Company, which was in the line in Railway Trench at the time, and who would know the way back to it. Each hole was to be dug by a party of one NCO and four men, two of whom were to dig while the other two kept watch.[39] This was a dangerous task, and came on top of the many other jobs which Hood Battalion were expected to undertake while in the line. The scheme to form the trench using explosives appears to have been almost immediately abandoned, for Asquith's orders for the night of 4 June instruct Shaw Stewart to continue to dig the Chord Trench, as it was named, from both ends towards the middle.[40]

The following day, having received reports that the digging had not proceeded sufficiently far, Brigadier General Philips wrote a furious confidential note to Asquith, signed as usual by the Brigade Major, but initialled by Philips himself. This extraordinary memorandum, copied to the Commanding Officer of Drake Battalion, read:

> The Brigadier is so extremely dissatisfied with the amount of work done ... that he has decided that the Company of Hood Battalion holding the WINDMILL sector shall remain in that sector without relief ... [until the work was complete].
>
> An Officer of the Divisional staff who was round that portion of the line yesterday morning reports that no work appears to have been done since the Battalion went into the line; and another Officer who was there last night reports that the posts holding the line were making no attempt to work whatever.
>
> The Brigadier wishes to be informed of the name of the Platoon Commander of that section ...
>
> He considers that this unsatisfactory position is entirely due to lack of proper supervision by the Battalion and Company Commander concerned.

The memorandum concluded by repeating that Drake would not relieve Hood until the work was complete.[41]

Asquith took unkindly to this semi-public rebuke and replied immediately in manuscript on pages torn from his field message book:

> Respectfully submitted that your Confidential No BM 676 is based upon a misunderstanding of local conditions, and would never have been written had these been appreciated.
>
> The digging of the line mentioned has in the past been . . . the work of the three Platoons of the left rear Company – the 31 O.R. of the three posts concerned also sapping as opportunity offered.
>
> I am prepared to account for the activity of my Company Commander Capt. SHAW STEWART, and of these men and of myself, and if your order is persisted in I shall request that I may be allowed to do so to the Divisional Commander as I am clearly of opinion that an injustice is being done to all concerned.
>
> I request an immediate reply as it will be difficult to ration these posts without casualties.
>
> I would point out that this letter has been written without my being given any opportunity of explaining the position, in the same way that your BM 643 [the original memorandum ordering the work] was written without my being consulted as to whether I had sufficient labour available without stopping other work.
>
> I would further point out that at the Brigade Conference I drew your attention to the great urgency of deepening and digging the line round the WINDMILL, and requested that I might be allowed to use one or more Companies from the Reserve Battn. for this purpose; but was refused permission to do so.
>
> Three different Platoon Commanders took watches at various times in the part of the line concerned.
>
> In so far as I am personally criticized I am prepared to clear myself of any lack of proper supervision before any tribunal which may be appointed.[42]

At Headquarters, Macmillan was handed the file with the correspondence, with an instruction to

> guard it carefully and allow no curious eye to look upon it. There was a covert hint that the matter need not concern me overmuch.
>
> As I folded the correspondence before stowing it away on my person, my eye caught the last communication, which was from Asquith. It was characteristically brief and bold, the purport being that he was prepared to defend his action before any court the General cared to convene. This troubled me, and the opinion I previously held that there was a 'set' against Asquith, grew stronger.[43]

Philips seems to have realised that he had overstepped the mark. The matter was resolved later that same day with a further communication to the Commanders of both Drake and Hood Battalions:

> This office B.M 676 having been cancelled by Brigade telegram . . . the following arrangements will be made for work by the Officers Commanding Drake and Hood Battalions this evening.
>
> The Hood Battalion will work on the new chord trench . . . both before and after relief and will continue working on this trench when they are in Reserve until it is completed.

The same memorandum instructed Drake to continue the work while in the line.[44]

The business continued to rumble on. Macmillan went on:

> Not many days afterwards Winston Churchill arrived at Divisional Headquarters. Asquith sent a polite note asking to be relieved for two days in order that he might proceed to Division to meet him. This was agreed to without demur; but before he returned to his battalion I was instructed to hand back the correspondence entrusted to me as the matter was now considered closed.[45]

By 8 June Philips wrote a personal note to Asquith in conciliatory tones saying that he was 'anxious to complete the new Chord Trench and Support Trench to the Mill before we go out of the line . . . and if you finish those two jobs, it will be a real feather in your cap.' Also, in this personal letter, Philips stated that he 'was particularly anxious to do away with the impression that the Hood Battalion are not good workers'.[46] Even this retraction was not enough for Asquith who requested Philips to confirm that such an impression was not still held either at Brigade or Divisional Headquarters With ruthless logic, Asquith contended that 'If, however, this impression no longer remains either with the Division or with yourself, I submit that so far as I can see an unfounded impression which has already been allayed, cannot be used as a reason – if any reason were required – to urge us to work our hardest'.[47]

What can be made of this storm in a teacup? It seems that the amount of work to be done was far in excess of the resources available to Asquith: the task was still not complete by the 8th, three days and much labour after the originally intended date. The General's intemperate criticism and the irrational tone of his original correspondence indicates that he was under considerable strain. In normal circumstances, it would have been expected that the Brigade Major, Barnett, would have moderated the communications, if only to protect his Brigadier from going too far. It is apparent,

ing some of the key features of the defences.

by Sub Lieutenant Wyall of Asquith's battalion, showing battalion boundaries and detai
The Mayor's House and the ditch just to the south of it can be clearly identified.

5. A large scale map of Gavrelle village, hand-draw

however, that Barnett was also under considerable strain during this period: the Division had been in the line, including fighting a major battle, virtually continuously for over three weeks, and they were now defending a precarious, but vital position. Nevertheless, it is hard not to come to a similar conclusion as Macmillan that there was a certain antipathy to Asquith at Brigade Headquarters.

The Battalion moved away from the frontline into billets on 9 June, relieved by the 12th battalion Yorks and Lancs. Asquith informed their CO that he had been providing a digging party nightly of 150 from 8.30pm to 4am, and handed him a copy (and obtained a signed receipt) of the Defence Scheme for the Sector.[48]

Out of the line, the routine of Army life had to continue: baths and haircuts had to be organised; kit renewed and cleaned; men sent away on courses (Shaw Stewart was attached for a short time to a Royal Field Artillery Battery),[49] iron rations had to be brought up to scratch, disciplinary offences needed hearing, and various personnel promotion matters required attention; on 11 June, for example, Asquith recommended Sub Lieutenants Arblaster and Carder for promotion to Lieutenant.[50] Asquith, McCracken, Egerton and Hilton entered the Brigade Horse Show, costing two francs in entrance fees for each event.[51] Working parties and digging teams were still provided while the Battalion was in the rear areas: Asquith's Company Commanders were now Shaw Stewart (A), Barclay (B), Arblaster (C), and Fish (now recovered from the wound to his foot received in the Ancre battle), D

After this trying period, Asquith received some good news from his father:

My dear Oc,

I was very glad to hear from the king yesterday that he has sanctioned a Bar to your D.S.O. in recognition of your fine performance at Gavrelle on April 23rd.[52] He enclosed the terms of the official recommendation which make very good reading. If you have not seen them I will send them to you.[53]

There followed some comments on how glad Asquith Senior was that Plumer had been successful at Messines, as he had 'clung on to that bloody salient at Ypres, & had few chances of real offensive work.'[54]

Arthur had taken the opportunity for a few days' leave in France: he had written to Freyberg asking if he could get away at the same time, closing his note unselfconsciously with 'Love from all, Yrs Oc'.[55] Freyberg could not be spared, and Asquith travelled to Paris with the doctor, McCracken, and eventually arrived at Deauville via Honfleur on 18 June, where he spent two happy days walking and indulging his love of sea bathing. While at the Normandy Hotel he replied to his father's good wishes:

Many thanks for your letter of congratulation. I had just heard from our Division, but have not seen the terms of the recommendation. It came as a complete surprise to me: so few of our officers survived the action. I am very glad that our Battalion Doctor, who impressed the services of a captured German doctor and his 14 Red X men and treated between 100 and 150 of our wounded, many of whom would have been blown to pieces where they lay, has been given the D.S.O.

He is here with me now. Our five days local leave will be spent mostly in the train. On the evening of the 16th we got a lift in a motor to St Pol: and by good fortune secured places in an empty Supply Train thence to Abbeville, – arriving there 3am 17th.

At one point en route we passed a canal. A barge manned by Inland Water Transport was seen by some of the men on our train, and greeted by them with shouts such as 'Do you get many cases of Shellshock down there?'

We reached Paris about 10.30am 17th: lunched luxuriously in great heat at Armenonville: . . . Yesterday . . . we took the only train of the day, at midday, for this place . . . This hotel is almost empty. We bathed in the sea, a few hundred yards away, before breakfast. I could do with a week here, but have to start on the long journey back at 6am – the only train of the day – tomorrow morning . . .

By the time I get back to the Battalion, we shall be beginning a period of ten days training – long overdue. Since our April fighting we have done one spell in the front line trenches, – mud and water six inches above the knee – and all the rest of the time we have been doing digging and fatigues in that same desolate part of the world. I trust we may get out of the destroyed zone for our training.

We all like our new Divisional General Lawrie. I have especial reason to be grateful to him as he has given me a very delightful and well favoured chestnut mare.[56]

When Asquith returned on 21 June, his Battalion was in a tent camp near the small town of Maroeuil, which gave time for recreation and small arms training. His first action on arriving at Battalion headquarters was to request the transfer of Sub Lieutenant Ramwell to Hood from Drake Battalion. He had discovered that Ramwell was the foster-brother of his adjutant, Lieutenant James Hilton.[57] The ensuing exercise programme was of mixed value: one turned out to be a shambles due to confusion over exactly where the limits of the training area were, and lack of liaison between the various Divisions using it: at one stage Hood were about to begin rifle grenade firing only to discover that Hawke Battalion were already engaged in their own bombing practice; having resolved that problem by moving the Hawkes away, Hood's training was interrupted by troops of the 5th Division who made an unannounced attack across the sector allocated to Asquith.[58] A more successful Brigade assault took place in the exercise area on 2 July. On 4 July Hood relieved the 15th Warwicks in the trenches in front of Oppy Wood. Pencil notes in his Field Message Book show that Asquith took into the trenches 466 men; B, C, and D Companies were to man the line, and A Company was held in reserve.[59]

NOTES

1. Green diary, entry for 21 April 1917.
2. Green diary, entry for 22 April 1917. Asquith was concerned about Lewis: he had heard, possibly from Commander Nelson, whom Lewis had relieved, that Lewis was of questionable competence, and a 'dug-out'. As his personal safety, and that of his entire Battalion, depended on Nelson Battalion's performance, his need to ensure that their CO understood exactly what was required is apparent. His concerns were unfounded; Lewis was an excellent officer.
3. Green diary, entry for 22 April 1917.
4. Field Message Book, Army Book 153, used between 23 April and 6 May 1917, AMA notebook No. 14, AMA papers. Message HD1/23 From 'Cushion' to 'Billiards': 'Battalion is in position. 2.30am'.
5. Hood Battalion War Diary, written by AMA in his own hand, and in the first person, for the period 22 to 29 April 1917, PRO WO 95/3115.
6. 'In Memoriam, W.S B., DSO 'A tribute in St Paul's School Magazine.
7. Jerrold, *The Royal Naval Division*, p230.
8. War Diary of the 189th Brigade, PRO WO 95/3112. This document clearly indicates that the GOC of the Brigade, Philips, sent for Sterndale Bennett and gave him the appropriate instructions for his deployment. Jerrold, who conducted extensive research among the survivors of the Division for his History, knew all the principal characters very well, and generally gave credit where it was due, equally clearly asserts that it was the Battalion Commander's decision to adapt his attacking formation.
9. Hood Battalion War Diary, PRO WO 95/3315.
10. Message from AMA to GOC 189th Brigade, AMA Notebook No. 14, p31, entry for 23 April 1917.
11. Hood Battalion War Diary, PRO WO 95/3315, entry by AMA for period covering 9am to 11am.
12. Message from AMA to 'Billiards', Brigade HQ, AMA Notebook No 14, p33, dated 23 April 1917.
13. Letter from Mr James Morrison of Edinburgh to AMA dated 3 November 1918, AMA papers.
14. Hood Battalion War Diary, PRO WO 95/3115, entry by AMA for the period of the forenoon 23 April 1917.
15. Message from AMA to Brigade HQ, AMA Notebook No. 14, pp38 and 40, timed at 5pm, dated 23 April 1917.
16. Message from AMA to Hilton, AMA Notebook No. 14, p42, timed at 5pm.
17. Message from AMA to Hilton, AMA Notebook No. 14, p46, timed at 7.20pm.
18. From *Narrative of Operations against Gavrelle-Oppy line and Gavrelle Village*, a report by Acting Commander W Sterndale Bennett, written in his own hand, dated 27 April 1917, PRO WO 95/3114.
19. Macmillan papers, IWM, p198.
20. Note in Asquith's pocket diary for 25 April 1917, AMA papers. Asquith must

have carried this tiny journal with him in the trenches, for besides routine daily comments, it includes the various codes for SOS actions, and cancelling them.

21. Recommendation for awards from AMA to GOC 189th Brigade, undated, but written either on 24 or 25 April 1917, AMA Notebook No. 14, p52, AMA papers.

22. From a copy of a citation, written in Asquith's hand, dated 27 April 1917, in the McCracken papers, IWM.

23. From Field Message Book covering period 1 May 1917 to 14 May 1917, hereafter referred to as AMA Notebook No. 15, several entries for 1 and 2 May 1917, AMA to 189th Brigade HQ, AMA papers.

24. Note from AMA to GOC 189th Infantry Brigade, dated 25 April 1917, AMA Notebook No. 14, p67, AMA papers.

25. Letter from Patrick Shaw Stewart to AMA, dated 21 September 1916, AMA papers.

26. Macmillan papers, IWM, p199.

27. *The Diaries of Lady Cynthia Asquith*, entry for 21 April 1917.

28. Letter from AMA to HHA, dated 24 April 1917, AMA papers.

29. Letter from HHA to AMA, dated 25 April 1917, AMA papers. Sybil Rocksavage was Philip Sassoon's sister.

30. Message from AMA to 189th Brigade, timed at 4.2Oam dated 6 May 1917, AMA Notebook No. 14, AMA papers.

31. Message from Hood Battalion to HQ 189th Infantry Brigade, dated 5 May 1917, AMA Notebook No. 14, pp122 and 125, AMA papers.

32. The note, written from Asquith to the carpenter, reads 'Prier de donner au porteur de ceci la grande croix que vous avez fait pour nous, et pour laquelle je vous donnai 60 (soixante) francs.' AMA Notebook No. 15 entry for 10 May 1917, AMA papers.

33. A copy of his intended inscription is in AMA Notebook No. 15 10 May 1917, AMA papers.

34. Statement by AB W MacGregor to OC Hood Battalion, dated 17 May 1917. AMA Notebook No. 15, AMA papers. Bailey, 23, from Builth Wells, Breconshire had been promoted from the ranks.

35. Letter, in pencil, from WP Bryan, 4th Platoon, D Company, Hood Battalion, RND, BEF, France, to Mr Olley (no address), dated 2 May 1917, AMA papers.

36. 'Preliminary Instructions for the Capture of Gavrelle and South Gavrelle Trenches', Brigade Memorandum number BM 572, dated 28 May 1917, signed by Captain Barnett, AMA papers.

37. For example, pencil briefing notes in Field Message Book, Army Book 153, in use by Asquith from 1 to 8 June 1917, hereafter referred to as AMA Notebook No 16, either 31 May or 1 June 1917, AMA papers.

38. Draft orders, dated 4 June 1917, in AMA Notebook No. 16, AMA papers.

39. Battalion Memorandum No. BM 643, to OC Hood Battalion from 189th Infantry Brigade, dated 3 June 1917, marked 'Recd. 7.40pm' in Asquith's hand, also marked with instruction in manuscript from Asquith to OC A Company, AMA papers.

40. AMA Notebook No. 16, entry for 4 June 1917, AMA papers.

41. Confidential Battalion Memorandum No. BM 676, to OC Hood Battalion from 189th Infantry Brigade, dated 5 June 1917, AMA papers.

42. Note from OC Commanding Hood Battalion to HQ 189th Infantry Brigade, No. A5, marked Confidential, dated 5 June 1917, timed at 4. 30pm, AMA papers.

43. Macmillan papers, IWM p205.

44. 189th Infantry Brigade Memorandum BM 678, dated 5 June 1917, AMA papers.
45. Macmillan papers, IWM, p206.
46. Manuscript personal letter from Brigadier General Philips to Commander Asquith dated 8 June 1917, AMA papers.
47. Field Message Book, Army Book 153, used by AMA from 8 to 14 June 1917, hereafter referred to as AMA Notebook No. 17: letter from AMA to General Philips, dated 9 June 1917, AMA papers.
48. AMA Notebook No. 17 entry for 10 June 1917, AMA papers.
49. AMA Notebook No. 17, note from AMA to Captain P Shaw Stewart, dated 11 June 1917, AMA papers.
50. AMA Notebook No. 17, Confidential note, ref A 16, from CO Hood Battalion to HQ 189th Infantry Brigade, dated 11 June 1917, AMA papers. One of the great strengths of the Royal Naval Division was that officers were almost invariably found from within their own existing battalions, by promotion from the ranks if necessary. The system was wholly dependent on merit, i.e. by how well the man performed his duties in the peculiar circumstances of trench warfare. A prerequisite was good leadership in battle, and demonstrated physical courage in action.
51. AMA Notebook No. 17, entry for 11 June 1917, AMA papers.
52. Notified by Routine Order No. 2381 dated 10 June 1917, the citation reads: 'Awarded Bar to Distinguished Service Order for conspicuous gallantry and determination in the attack and clearance of a village, when he personally captured ten of the enemy and later organised its defence and by his contempt of danger under heavy fire, contributed greatly to the success of the operation and to the steadiness of all ranks with him' (2nd Supp. *London Gazette*, 18 July 1917).
53. Cynthia Asquith records that she was at a lunch party given by HH Asquith at Cavendish Square, his home now that he was no longer in office, where 'The dear Old Boy was delighted with Oc's awarded clasp to his DSO and his father handed round the King's letter of congratulation all round the table with proud sniffs.' Quoted in *The Diaries of Lady Cynthia Asquith 1915-18*, entry for 12 June 1917.
54. Letter from Herbert Henry Asquith to AMA dated 9 June 1917, AMA papers.
55. Letter from AMA to Brigadier General Freyberg, copy in Field Message Book, Army Book 153, used by AMA from 15 June 1917 to 6 July 1917, hereafter referred to as AMA Notebook No. 18, AMA papers.
56. Letter from AMA to his father from the Normandy Hotel, Deauville, dated 19 June 1917, AMA papers.
57. Note from AMA to HQ 189th Infantry Brigade, numbered A 30, dated 21 June 1917. Ramwell, from Wigan, 19 years old, joined Hood Battalion one week later. He was a gallant and resourceful officer: on Welsh Ridge on 27 December 1917 he won the Military Cross for 'gallantry in the field', *London Gazette*, 4th Supplement, dated 4 March 1918, p2729. He was awarded a Bar to the decoration during the German March offensive when, on 24 March 1918, he showed 'conspicuous gallantry and devotion to duty when the enemy attacked his position after an intense bombardment. By his leadership and good judgment he kept his men well under control and drove back the enemy with heavy losses. Though his flank was exposed he maintained his position intact encouraging his men throughout by his coolness and courage under very heavy fire', *London Gazette*, 4th Supplement, dated 16 August 1918, p9567. During this action Ramwell was taken prisoner. He was

repatriated on 19 December 1918, and demobilised the following February.
58. Message No. A33 from OC Hood Battalion to HQ 189th Infantry Brigade, dated 25 June 1917, AMA Notebook No. 18, AMA papers.
59. AMA Notebook No. 18, AMA papers.

CHAPTER XI

Trench Warfare, July to October 1917

After Gavrelle, although they did not know it at the time, Hood Battalion had entered another period of trench holding duties which was to last until their inevitable involvement in the battles of Third Ypres. Asquith's notebooks of the time contain a very comprehensive record of what life was like for a Battalion commander during a relatively quiet spell in the line.

His first area of responsibility was the line at Oppy, some few hundred yards north of Gavrelle, in the sector allocated to 189th Brigade. The new positions had been taken during an attack by the 31st and 5th Divisions on 28 June. Jerrold points out that the importance of the work of 2nd Royal Marines and HAC in capturing the Windmill on 28 April was now apparent, as holding this high ground effectively prevented an enemy counter-attack from Oppy.[1] At the same time, 188th Brigade of the RND took over the right sector, which included Gavrelle and the Windmill.

Asquith's Battalion inherited the area in front of Oppy Wood: a contemporary photograph of the area in Asquith's papers shows that the wood itself had been very badly damaged in the recent battles, but nevertheless, the trunks of many trees are still in evidence, and there is reference to 'a hedge' in Asquith's field service notebooks written at the time.[2] Thus it seems that the devastation of this sector was not as complete as, for example, that around the Windmill at Gavrelle. The trenches were, however, in a very bad state, and the main task of the Battalions in the front line was to consolidate the defences.

Using techniques first employed in Gallipoli, the trench work took place at night. Covering parties were sent out into no man's land, and digging parties took every precaution to avoid detection. Work invariably included widening and duck-boarding of existing trenches, and digging new ones to consolidate the new front line: a new front line was pushed out over 100 yards in front of the old. Such was the effort expended that, by the last day of this period in the line, Asquith was able to instruct his men to finish fire steps, dig latrines and dumps, and remove salvage and spoil prior to relief by Drake Battalion,[3] and he proposed names for the newly-dug trenches, 'Crow' and 'Killick'.[4] In fact Hood had to remain in the line until the night of the 11th. The work continued under fire, and there were occasional casualties: fortunately twelve to fifteen British shells fired from a position far to the west which fell around Earl Trench, were all duds, otherwise there would have been many more![5]

On the night of 11/12 July Hood were relieved by Sterndale Bennett's Drake Battalion, and took over their billets at Wakefield Camp behind the line. The billeting arrangements had been undertaken by Asquith's second in command, Egerton, who had returned to duty after his wound earlier in the year. He arranged for the men to be served breakfast on arrival at the camp. Asquith carried out an inspection of his lines between 6pm and 8pm. Relief began at about 10pm, and was planned to be completed as soon after midnight as possible. Asquith's orders for the operation emphasise the need to take all their own gear with them, and to obtain signatures for the trench stores left behind. Transport was provided for officers' kit and mess effects, signals equipment, medical stores, and Lewis gun gear only. The officers' chargers were to be available at the battalion dump at 2.30am.[6] Asquith left a note for Sterndale Bennett of the work in hand and proposed in his sub-section, including wiring of the newly dug front line, floor boarding, and removal of some of the traverses of the communications trenches which used to form part of the German defensive system.[7] He took with him from the trenches a German 'listening apparatus' recovered from a blown-in enemy dug out by Sub Lieutenant Skipper of his Battalion. Asquith believed that the find was important, as, from his time attached to Intelligence, he was aware that no such device had fallen into British hands.[8]

Out of the line again, Asquith's thoughts returned to the important things of life, including requesting a Royal Marine Instructor to improve the Battalion band,[9] and the inevitable ritual of bathing, begun by sending twenty-five men per company to the baths at Roclincourt, near Arras.[10] A and B Companies spent a great deal of time on the range improving their musketry skills.[11] His mail included a letter from Betty, who at the time was staying at Hartland Abbey, expressing her enjoyment of the summer surroundings in rural Devon. She remarked 'I feel quite ashamed of sending this country pleasure-loving letter to you out there in such grim surroundings'.[12]

It was only a short rest, however, for on the night of 16/17 July, Hood were back in the trenches, to relieve 7th Royal Fusiliers, one of the Army battalions of the Division. Three Companies would be in the front line, and one in support. This time they were holding a front of about eight hundred yards in the sector opposite Gloster Wood, on the northern outskirts of Gavrelle, in trenches adjacent to those they had just left. The sector was still active and hostile: a trench map of the time shows over fifty reported active battery positions in the German lines opposite Gavrelle.[13] Box respirators were worn by the troops in the 'alert' positions, and the Battalion Orders stressed that 'posts in the front line are to be held at all costs. The loss of any one position will not be regarded as a reason for retirement from any other'.[14] The OC support Company was instructed in the same order to reconnoitre 'all means of access and communication trenches to the Front Line with a view to being able to launch an immediate counter-attack across the open against any part of the Front Line which may fall into the hands of the enemy'. In an addendum to the original order, Asquith emphasises that 'Control of "No man's land" must be obtained and maintained by every means'.[15] The expected enemy attack during this period did not materialise, although one of the battalion snipers lying out between the lines on the 19th reported considerable movement in the enemy front line, Crumpet and Windmill Trenches, which resulted in Asquith issuing more orders in case of an enemy assault.[16] Major improvements to the trench system were made in very rainy conditions under continual enemy bombardment, with new advanced posts, splinter-proof shelters for the officers and men, shelters from the weather for Battalion dumps, improvements to the light railway track and latrines, and the running of a water pipeline.[17] Also on this day before relief, Asquith forwarded to Brigade HQ a proposed programme of work for the battalion relieving him, adding that 'Offensively the most urgent need of the moment is in my opinion a large number of well-camouflaged LTM positions to allow us to deal with enemy activities . . .'[18]

Brigade had other problems on its mind at the time: there were rumours that the Germans might withdraw from their exposed positions occupied since their ejection from the line running through Gavrelle, to a heavily-fortified line about three miles to the east, known as the Drocourt-Quéant switch. Barnett, the Brigade Major, therefore drew up orders to ensure that all his troops were aware of their responsibilities in the eventuality. They are excellent Staff work, clear, comprehensive and unambiguous, and provide a good example of the important part played by key Staff figures, such as Brigade Majors, so often maligned in less well informed commentaries on the war.[19]

Among the routine duties which occupied these few days in the front line, Asquith reported on one of his officers, Sub Lieutenant CN Spencer: this young officer had evidently been removed from active service. Asquith sent him a copy of the report worded thus:

I have today reported to O.C. Special Hospital as follows:
    I certify that Sub Lieut Spencer was not subjected in the course of his duty to exceptional exposure as defined.
    He spent about one month with this Battalion. During this period his work lay from the gun-line forward, and during six days of this time he was with his Platoon in an anxious part of the line, subjected to considerable shelling, without any roof, in very wet weather.
    I am not aware that any of the other officers or men of his Company were affected by this to the same extent as he was. But his company

Commander and I formed the view that his was a 'bona fide' case of overstrained nerves and that he was deserving of pity, not of disciplinary action or blame. Please initial and return this letter.[20]

A further period out of the line began on 23 July, for which, besides the usual training round, Asquith had organised recreation for the men, including cinemas, band concerts by the Royal Marines and the Artists Rifles, now part of the Division, and a 'Follies' which took place on the 25th, the day on which Asquith began a period of leave, delegating command to the highly competent Egerton. Two days later, in the company of Margot and his half-sister Elizabeth, he met Cynthia Asquith in London, who noted that he looked very war-worn.[21] Arthur and Betty Manners spent some time together, and it seems that once more he broached the subject of marriage to her, for she wrote from her home at Avon Tyrrell, 'Your visit gave me fresh food for thought and you were very nice to me and I wish I could say more and the war would end and I would know my own mind'.[22]

His leave lasted from 26 July to 6 August when he rejoined the Battalion in the trenches in the same area he had recently left. Shaw Stewart was requested to provide a batman as Asquith's servant had been sent to hospital: AB Haggis was selected for the post.[23] On relief by 2nd Royal Marines of 188th Brigade, Hood Battalion were allowed to withdraw to positions farther west than usual, but they were required to be at fifteen minutes' readiness to move to man the support lines behind Gavrelle in the event of an enemy attack. Half of the Battalion officers were to be permanently in camp, and those who took leave were ordered to go no farther afield than Arras.[24] Asquith seems to have been in a grumpy mood for this period; for the next few days his notebook contains complaints of various sorts: to Brigade HQ for sending a secret document in a single envelope rather than the double envelope which should have been used,[25] reporting that a water cart sent from Brigade had defective brakes and a leaking body,[26] and suggesting that the current routine of front line, support line, followed by hut camps, was apt to allow the troops to get very stale and that consideration should be given to the Battalion being sent to more inviting places when away from the front, he optimistically suggested Boulogne or Hermin.[27] His Company Commanders also were criticised for unpunctuality in the rendering of returns about iron rations, gas helmets, etc.[28] A draft note probably meant for Brigade refuting suggestions by a Divisional Staff Officer that his Company Commanders were insufficiently caring of their men's welfare may have added to Asquith's unusually short manner.[29] Around this time Thomas Macmillan, clerk of the 189th Brigade, arrived back from leave. He reports a visit to HQ by Asquith in his diary:

When I arrived at Roclincourt the Brigade was out of the line.

I had not been many days in harness when I ran into Commander Asquith. He seemed calm and collected, but there was a look of concern which touched me to the core. I volunteered the information that neither the General nor the Major were about, and asked if I could take a message . . . In gentlemanly fashion he asked me merely to say that he had called and that he would call again soon.

Too often the success in life of a man is due to the fact that he is the son of his father. This could not be said of Commander Asquith. Here was a one who was a master of life's rough and tumble and one who seemed fated to bear more crosses than his own.

Commander Asquith, as he appeared to me, could not by nature do anything underhand, and although I was unable to point the finger at any man or men who were exploiting their brief authority over him, inwardly I now felt convinced that he had enemies behind our lines who gave him more concern than those who wore the dull grey and sought to close with him in battle. Yet, despite the fact of his father's eminence, he seemed to scorn the idea of seeking help from that quarter against those people who were getting him from behind. Perhaps he felt that his father's cross was already enough for an ageing man to bear.[30]

Most of the rest of August was spent out of the line in training and recreation. On the 21st Asquith learned that Hood would be taking over from 2nd Royal Marines in the front line immediately north of Gavrelle on the night of the 24/25th. On 21 August Asquith made a trip to the Marine lines to work out his own dispositions, and to receive a programme of work in hand and stores on demand from the OC of the Battalion in the line.[31]

Meanwhile there were personnel matters to be dealt with. Sub Lieutenant Carnall, recovering with the Divisional reserve at Blandford, had requested to rejoin the Battalion in the rank of Lieutenant. Asquith replied that, while he sympathised with Carnall's claim, there was no vacancy in the Battalion at present. He also criticised the system which at the time was unable to keep battalion commanders informed of the likelihood or otherwise of their officers in England sick or wounded ever being fit again.[32] Other matters dealing with officers included a request by Sub Lieutenant Milton to join the Inland Water Transport organisation;[33] a request that Sub Lieutenant Sanford should rejoin the Battalion (he had been seconded to transport duties since March);[34] Sub Lieutenants Baird and Gibson[35] were gently rebuked for drawing too much cash during this rest period. They had each taken out five hundred francs for the month against an allowance of three payments of one hundred and twenty five. To rectify this they were instructed to draw only two hundred and fifty francs in September.[36] The punishment was not severe, particularly as there would be little opportunity for the young men to spend any money for some weeks! Finally, Asquith resubmitted the recommendation for one of his Company Commanders, Lieutenant Sidney Fish, for the award of a Military Cross for his part in the attack of 13 November on the Ancre: the original citation had been delayed because the two witnesses, Commander Freyberg and Sub Lieutenant Donaldson, were both wounded in the engagement. Asquith was determined that Fish, an officer of whom he thought highly, should not suffer because of the circumstances.[37]

The Battalion went back into the line with three companies numbering fewer than three hundred men in all; C Company was in support. Reinforcements were not due to arrive until the night of the 28/29th.[38] Work was immediately begun to widen and deepen the front line trenches, improve wiring and dug-outs, and collecting and salvaging loose small arms ammunition and grenades in the vicinity.[39] Stand-to was ordered at 4.30am and 8pm,[40] and, as a sign of the changing times, five Lewis guns were detailed for anti-aircraft work.[41]

Throughout August and September, when the Battalion was in the line, raids and reconaissances were carried out on an almost daily basis. At least seven were led by officers; some parties were commanded by NCOs, one by Leading Seaman Sherry, who had been court-martialled for drunkenness in June 1916. On the night of the 27th, a patrol was carried out between the lines by Sub Lieutenant Baird of B Company and five other ranks, east of the Miller's House, i.e. opposite the Windmill position; the party carried 'P' Bombs, large tins containing phosphorus, usually used in the clearance of enemy dug-outs, and the raiders were ordered 'to carry with them no maps, documents or other articles which might be of use to the enemy or facilitate identification.'[42] The Battalion War Diary records at least twenty separate patrols for the months of August and September.[43] They found signs of occupation in a shell hole between the lines, but a party sent out a couple of nights later to ambush the possible inhabitants returned without contact with them.[44]

From the end of August until 10 September, Hood Battalion was employed in the same areas, manning the front line, carrying stores and the usual round of training evolutions and reorganisation. Asquith allowed his Battalion to be sent into the line by companies rather than as a whole, which gave him time to supervise the training and recreation for those in the rear quarters. The administrative tasks included the processing of an application by Sub Lieutenant Baird to join the Royal Naval Air Service. The date of the correspondence indicates that the matter had been in hand for some time and had not arisen as a result of Baird's experience in the raid of 27 August.[45]

At 2.30pm on 10 September the main body of the battalion, numbering about 650 officers and men entrained for the rear area, about twenty miles from the front, this time in the relatively unspoilt Artois villages astride the Arras road a few miles east of St Pol. Only three hours before he was due to leave the front, a dud British shell landed twenty yards from the parapet. Asquith, obviously piqued, sent it and a copy of a note to Brigade HQ, giving the exact place of landing and observing that it 'was apparently fired from a point about due west of the place where it fell'.[46] A detailed training programme for the week was drawn up by Lieutenant Hilton, the Adjutant of the Battalion and submitted to Brigade HQ for approval.[47] There was bathing and recreation every afternoon; the fore-noons were taken up in Battalion route marches (twice), range work, where the officers were instructed in firing their revolvers, and in practice raids and attacks. The final training session was, optimistically, an evolution in open warfare.[48] The break permitted Asquith to return once more to the instruction of the Battalion band, this time by requesting the assistance of a musician in the Artists Rifles, now serving as a battalion in 190th Brigade of the Division.[49]

On 15 September Asquith travelled to Vimy to meet his father and Maurice Bonham Carter at the Headquarters of 1st Army. After this, the Battalion moved back to the Windmill area for the last time, relieving 2nd Royal Marines. Another week of training followed in the Averdoingt area before the Royal Naval Division received the inevitable orders which would involve them in the enormous struggle to the east of Ypres, a series of battles which had been raging since 31 July.

The last week in the training area was one of high activity: the Battalion was inspected by General Philips during a route march on the 30th; Asquith's men sent on bombing and Lewis gun courses in XIII Corps area did not do well and he had to account for their lack of elementary knowledge: 'it is generally true of our NCOs that they are better at practical work in the field rather than at oral expression' is written in his notebook as part of his draft reply. Asquith evidently thought this remark a little too provocative, and crossed it through.[50] There was an oral briefing by Asquith for his officers on some of the lessons learned from earlier stages of the Third Ypres campaign. His pencil notes show that the usual attack formation was expected to be with A and B companies on an attack front of about eight hundred yards, with C for counter-attack, and D in brigade reserve. Great emphasis was placed on the troops' formations: the first waves were to be in line with the second and third in 'blobs'. The importance of reconnaissance was stressed, as was the need to treat all farms and buildings as potential enemy strong points. The limit of the advance in the forthcoming battle would be twelve hundred yards. Arthur pointed out that smoke had proved of great value, and that rifle grenades, fired at point blank range, had been effective against block houses. Precautions against gas were gone through, and the officers reminded of the vital importance of intensive digging to consolidate captured positions.[51] The redoubtable Sherry was in trouble again: this time he and another Petty Officer called Davis were tried by Field General court martial on 2 October. The offence must have concerned one of the locals, as an interpreter was nominated for the trial.[52] For the forthcoming rigours of the trenches, Asquith ordered a new pair of black field boots from Messrs Flack and Smith: they were 'to lace up at the front, with 3 buckles and straps at sides: the foot to be like ski or "Lotus" boots so that the toes are not squashed: designed for comfort and water-tightness in the trenches'.[53] In addition, there was the usual bustle of activity in preparing to vacate the quarters: cleaning and inspection of billets, foot inspections, settling outstanding claims with the locals, and ensuring that the men had all the right kit.

On 3 October, the day when the Divisional sports meeting was planned, Hood Battalion formed up and marched the six miles to the village of Savy where they entrained for the town of Proven a couple of miles north-west of Poperinghe, to begin their preparations for taking part in the final acts of the battles of Third Ypres.[54]

NOTES

1. Jerrold, *The Royal Naval Division*, p245.
2. Report of patrol activity, OC Hood Battalion, night of 9/10 July 1917, entry for 10 July 1917 in AMA Field Message Book, Army Book 153, marked in Asquith's hand 'OPPY Subsection July 4/5th – 11th/12th, 1917', hereafter referred to as AMA Notebook No. 19, AMA papers.
3. Note to COs Companies from CO Hood Battalion, dated 9 July 1917, AMA Notebook No. 19.
4. Note to HQ 189th Infantry Brigade from OC Hood Battalion, ref A6, dated 9 July 1917, AMA Notebook No. 19.
5. Note to Liaison Officer from OC Hood Battalion dated 10 July 1917, AMA Notebook No. 19.
6. 'Orders for Relief', a Note for OCs Companies from OC Hood Battalion, reference A13, dated 11 July 1917 at 1.15pm, AMA Notebook No. 19.
7. Note 'Centre Subsection, Work in hand and proposed' dated 11 July 1917, AMA Notebook No. 19.
8. Note to HQ 189th Infantry Brigade, reference A14, from OC Hood Battalion, dated 11 July 1917, AMA Notebook No. 19.
9. Note to 189th Infantry Brigade, reference A15, from OC Hood Battalion, dated 12 July 1917, AMA Notebook No. 19.
10. Hood Battalion Orders for 15 July 1917, signed by Lieutenant Commander Egerton, AMA papers.
11. Field Message Book, Army Book 153, marked in pencil, '20/7/17 – 14/8/17, AMA', henceforward referred to as AMA Notebook No. 20, message No. A45 to HQ 189th Infantry Brigade, entry for 20 July 1915, AMA papers.
12. Letter from Betty Manners to AMA dated 10 July 1917.
13. Trench Map 'Gloster Wood,' Scale 1:20000, prepared by 1st Field Survey Co, Royal Engineers, No 2445, marked 'Trenches corrected to 6/7/17', AMA papers.
14. Hood Battalion, Orders for Relief, dated 15 July 1917, copy No. 2, signed by Asquith as Battalion Commander, para 9a, AMA papers.

15. Addendum, dated 16 July 1917, to Hood Battalion Orders of 15 July 1917, Copy No. 2, signed by Asquith, AMA papers.
16. Messages A44 to 'OC Castle', and a second to 'E Special Coy R.E.', both dated 20 July 1917, AMA Notebook No. 20.
17. Message, probably to HQ 189th Infantry Brigade (address lost) dated 22/7/17, AMA Notebook No. 20, AMA papers.
18. Message to HQ 189th Infantry Brigade, No. A52, dated 22 July 1917.
19. 189th Infantry Brigade B.M. 1/201, 'Orders in the Event of an Enemy Withdrawal', marked 'Secret', dated 21 July 1917, signed by Captain Barnett, Brigade Major, acknowledged by Asquith 22 July 1917.
20. Note to Sub Lieutenant CN Spencer, RNVR, dated 21 July 1917, AMA Notebook No. 20. Poor Spencer, from Wakefield, 19 at the time, never recovered to rejoin the Battalion: he spent the rest of the war at various hospitals, including Craiglockhart, diagnosed with neurasthenia.
21. Lady Cynthia Asquith, *Diaries 1915-18*, entry for 27 July 1917, p322.
22. Undated (but some time in early August 1917) letter from Betty Manners to AMA from Avon Tyrrell.
23. Note to OC A Company dated 8 August 1917. AMA Notebook No. 20.
24. Note to all Company Commanders, number A65, dated 9 August 1917, AMA Notebook No. 20.
25. Note to HQ 189th Infantry Brigade, number A68, dated 11 August 1917, AMA Notebook No. 20.
26. Note to HQ 189th Infantry Brigade, number A69, dated 11 August 1917, AMA Notebook No. 20.
27. Note to HQ 189th Infantry Brigade, number A74, dated 13 August 1917, AMA Notebook No. 20.
28. Note to all Company Commanders, number A70, dated 11 August 1917, AMA Notebook No. 20.
29. Pencil note (undated) in Asquith's hand at the back of AMA Notebook No. 20, the draft of a letter, on the subject of how the men of the Battalion received their food in unsuitable containers on the night of their relief in the front line on 9 August. Asquith points out that there were only nineteen dixies for his Battalion and that extra containers had been requested in July, but not supplied.
30. Macmillan Papers, pp215-6, IWM.
31. Pencil notes in Asquith's hand in Army Field Message Book, in use from 14-27 August 1917, henceforward referred to as AMA Notebook No. 21, AMA Papers.
32. Note, numbered A 87, to HQ 63rd (RN) Division Reserves, dated 20 August 1917, AMA Notebook No. 21. Carnall, a Tynesider, won the DSM as a Chief Petty Officer in Gallipoli, where, as the senior survivor of the ill-fated Collingwood Battalion, he led them from the line after their gallant but disastrous attack on 4 June 1915. Promoted from the ranks, he was awarded the Military Cross for 'gallantry and devotion to duty' on the Ancre in November 1916 (*London Gazette*, 2nd Supplement, dated 10 January 1917, p456). He was wounded by gunshot in the right leg on 21 January 1917, and was not fit for General Service until 17 September 1917. He never returned to active service in the RND, although pronounced fit on 9 October 18. His record is annotated 'Recommended for promotion by Brigadier General Asquith (RND 8553)'.
33. Note, numbered A 84, to HQ 189th Infantry Brigade dated 18 August 1917, AMA Notebook No. 21. Milton, a fine officer, had been promoted from the ranks in September 1915. He won a Military Cross during the Ancre battle in

November 1916, and a bar for conspicuous gallantry in saving a pilot from a burning aircraft in July 1917. He suffered from back trouble from January 1918 and was demobbed in May 1919.

34. Note, numbered A 85, to HQ 189th Infantry Brigade, undated, but either 18 or 19 August 1917, AMA Notebook No. 21. Sanford finally rejoined the Battalion on 14 October 1917. Note from Lieutenant J C Hilton to HQ 189th Infantry Brigade dated 15 October 1917: Correspondence Book, Army Book 152, in use from 12 October 1917 to 5 November 1917, by both Hilton (Adjutant) and Asquith, hereafter referred to as AMA Notebook No. 25, AMA papers.

35. Gibson, from Sunderland, was a gallant officer. He had joined the Battalion at the end of 1916 at the age of 19. For his work at Gavrelle he was awarded the Military Cross (*London Gazette*, 6th Supplement, of 4 June 1917, p5479). He went on to be Adjutant of the Battalion for a while in 1918, and won a second MC as a Company Commander for his courage and leadership at Niergnies, in the last few weeks of the war (*London Gazette* of 11 January 1919, p 592). He was demobilized as a Temporary Lieutenant on 27 January 1919.

36. Note, marked Confidential, numbered A 93, to Sub Lieutenants Baird and Gibson, dated 24 August 1917, AMA Notebook No. 21.

37. Pencil draft in Asquith's hand, undated, at the back of AMA Notebook No. 20.

38. Note, marked Secret, numbered A 94, to HQ 189th Infantry Brigade, dated 25 August 1917, in reply to BM 1/592, AMA Notebook No. 21.

39. Message to COs Companies dated 25 August 1917, AMA Notebook No. 21.

40. Message to COs of A, B, C and D Companies, dated 25 August 1917, AMA Notebook No. 21.

41. Message to COs Companies, dated 27 August 1917, AMA Notebook No. 21.

42. Message to the COs of A, B and D Companies, dated 27 August 1917, AMA Notebook No. 21.

43. Hood Battalion War Diary, pp219-224, Box ADM 137/3064, PRO Kew.

44. ibid.

45. Letter from AMA to HQ RN Air Department, number A121, dated 4 September 1917, in reply to their AIR/N.2 Appin. 15089, Field Message Book, Army Book 153, in use from 3 September to 11 September 1917, hereafter referred to as AMA Notebook No. 22, AMA papers. Baird, a Scot, was a 21-year-old ex-Petty Officer from the Clyde RNR who had been promoted Temporary Sub Lieutenant in December 1915. He was severely wounded in the left leg on the Ancre on 14 November 1916, and had returned at the end of May 1917. A few days after Asquith's correspondence with the RN Air Dept, Baird was wounded again in the left hand by a gunshot, and evacuated to England. He service in the RND was terminated on 28 October 1917 to allow him to take up his appointment in the RNAS. Information from the *List of Officers of the Royal Naval Division*, held by the RN Historical Branch of the Ministry of Defence.

46. Note from AMA to HQ 189th Infantry Brigade, number A 137, dated 10 September 1917, timed at 11.55am, AMA Notebook No. 22.

47. Hood Battalion Orders by Commander AM Asquith DSO, signed by Lieutenant JC Hilton, dated 10 September 1917, AMA papers.

48. ibid.

49. Note from AMA, numbered A 136, to OC Artists Rifles dated 8 September 1917, AMA Notebook No. 22.

50. Draft reply to Brigade HQ in Asquith's hand, undated, but 28 or 29 September, in reply to BM 1/807, Field Message Book, Army Book 153, in use from

26 September 1917 to 6 October 1917, hereafter referred to as AMA Notebook No. 23, AMA papers.

51. Pencil briefing notes, undated, but either 1 or 2 October 1917, AMA Notebook No. 23.

52. Note from AMA to Lieutenant W Barclay, Sub Lieutenants JS Collins and J Clark (Interpreter), dated 2 October 1917, AMA Notebook No. 23.

53. Letter from AMA to Messrs Flack and Smith, undated, but 28 or 29 September 1917, AMA Notebook No. 23.

54. Note from AMA to Road Traffic Officer, at the town of Proven, dated 3 October 1917.

CHAPTER XII

In Action near Passchendaele

It was but a short journey to the area where Hood expected to begin their training for the next test. They were at first billeted in the vicinity of the small town of Herzeele, about eight miles WNW of Poperinghe, and a short march from their point of disembarkation at Proven. The expectation of the Divisional Commander for the coming battle was that he would be required to fight three battles in turn, each requiring one of his Brigades: 189th Brigade of which Hood was a part were scheduled for the second action, after 188th, with 190th Brigade to be committed in the third. The training period would be about fourteen days, but, on arrival, it was decided that one infantry brigade would be set to work immediately in the forward area. 189th Brigade was selected as it was not due to be in action until after the 188th, and the 190th, with two new and largely untested battalions, was most in need of intensive training.[1] Asquith was not happy about missing out on training, and with considerable misgivings led his Battalion to Dirty Bucket Camp, a couple of miles north-west of Vlamertinghe, and about six miles from the front line, the new Headquarters of 189th Brigade. From there, to be nearer the working zone, Asquith's Battalion moved forward to Reigersburg Camp, on the road midway between Brielen and Ypres, about half a mile west of the Yser Canal which runs north from Ypres to the coast.

The Ypres battles had been in train for over two months by the time the Royal Naval Division arrived for its turn. The final effort was intended to clear the Germans from the ridge on which the small village of Passchendaele stands. On 4 October the line from which the RND was to attack stretched north-west from the cemetery at the village of Wallemollen to the Lekkerbokkerbeek, a stream which had been reduced to a wide morass in the past few weeks of artillery bombardments.

In Asquith's papers is a trench map of the attack zone, prepared by one of his more artistic Company Commanders, the aptly named Lieutenant Fish of D Company. On it Fish has marked the 'wetness' of the various parts of the battlefield: the ground around the parts of the two streams in British hands, the Lekkerbokkerbeek and the Strombeek (which runs just behind the British front), is marked in dark blue, indicating appallingly wet conditions; most of the rest of the attack zone, traversed by another small stream, the Paddebeek, which runs into the Lekkerbokkerbeek, is in a lighter blue. Only the ground well to the north and east of the RND zone is marked as not completely or partially flooded.[2]

The Divisional historian describes eloquently the conditions:

It is safe to say that the Division was never confronted with a task which, on the lines laid down for them, was more impossible of fulfilment. Flanders mud had become proverbial, and even under ordinary conditions exposed the troops in the front system to extraordinary hardships. Front line and communication trenches were non-existent. The forward system consisted of posts isolated from each other by a sea of mud, and the support line of another line of posts, the elements of a trench, or, more probably, of a ruined farmhouse and outbuildings where a company or so could be concentrated. These forward positions were scattered in depth over a wide area, and each was dependent on itself for protection. The enemy posts often lay between our own, and every ration and water party had to be prepared to fight its way forward. Communication with the reserve positions was equally dangerous, if less difficult. All supplies and reinforcements had to be brought up on duckboard tracks, which with every advance stretched further and further forward. Off these tracks progress was impossible, yet the reliance placed on them was an evil necessity; they marked to the enemy, as to ourselves, our line of supply, and, though used only at night, they were a perilous substitute for the old communication trench. From an accurate bombardment of these tracks no party using them could escape. To turn aside by so much as a yard was to plunge waist-deep in a sea of mud, where the bodies of the dead were rotting in the primeval slime.[3]

To add to the general misery, the weather was vile, with frequent heavy rain.

The work of the 189th Brigade, including Hood Battalion, consisted of the back-breaking, but vital task of building roads, railways, and duck board tracks in the area around the small town of St Julien, and the 'Triangle', about half a mile north of it, some of it very close to the front line, and much of it under fire. The working parties drew their equipment from either the Commandant at Reigersberg, or from the Corporal in charge of the XVIII Corps Engineering Dump at Zouave Villa, just east of the canal on the Pilckem road.[4]

Asquith's irritation and concern at not being permitted to train his Battalion led him to write confidentially to General Philips on 9 October:

The importance and urgency of the road making upon which this Battalion is now engaged are fully realised. At the same time, if we are to be used for attack within the next month, I wish to put it on record that we cannot be expected to do ourselves justice in attack unless we are given an opportunity for at least one fortnight's uninterrupted training.

Ten days at the end of March is the longest continuous spell of training which we have had since January, 1917. Meanwhile our personnel have changed very largely, and possibly two-fifths of the Battalion as it is at present have never practised following a barrage, or had one day's training as the Battalion in an attack.

I believe it is intended that we shall soon be relieved from our present work and given an opportunity of training, but my experience is that if one is employed on useful work, one is apt to be kept on it rather longer than was originally intended; while events often move faster and wastage of troops ahead of one is apt to take place quicker than is anticipated, with the result that the training period may be cut short at either end.

It is requested that representations be made to ensure that, subject to the exigencies of the Service, no risk of such curtailment may be run.

Granted proper opportunities of training, I have no anxiety about results.[5]

Poor Philips' patience with his thorny Battalion Commander finally snapped. He wrote back immediately in his own hand in a letter marked 'Private', enclosing Asquith's note:

Dear Asquith

This letter is quite unnecessary – especially as you had already mentioned the subject both to Barnett [the Brigade Major] and myself. I once told you jokingly that we had plenty to read without getting unnecessary correspondence from C.O.s, and now I feel bound to tell you that the Corps & Divl. Commanders and I myself are quite aware of the condition of this Brigade as regards training and that it is not our business to criticize the orders of our superiors, in fact it is a breach of discipline to which I shall not lend myself by making representations on the subject. I have already told you that you are much too apt to criticize the decisions and orders of your superiors. By constantly doing this, you only weaken any possibly strong case you may as C.O. feel justified in submitting to higher authority. I have been called on to make a special report on all my C.O.s and you must not be surprised if I embody some of the above remarks in my report, which will be sent to you to initial.

As I told you the other day, the work on the roads is most important, and I should be sorry to think that there is a danger of the work suffering by the fact that you seem to think that someone else should be doing it. The few men I saw on the road outside St Julien this morning

151

were not working well, in fact they were sitting or standing about with their hands in their pockets, smoking.

I looked for an Officer of the Battn., but could not find anyone supervising the work. Please again impress on all ranks the vital importance of this work, upon which the whole advance depends.

This letter does not require an answer.

Yrs sincerely

L F Philips[6]

Philips' letter, obviously written in haste, and with a fair head of steam, shows the sort of pressure officers of Brigade Commander level were under in the period just prior to a major battle on the Western Front, but Asquith was not a man to accept meekly so serious, and, he felt, unjustified, rebuke. On the following day, on pages torn from one of his Field Message Books he wrote:

Dear General Philips,

You say that your letter dated yesterday, returning mine about the preparedness of this Battalion for attack, requires no answer.

In fairness I submit that it does.

You criticize in it my personal sense of discipline; and you suggest that my officers are not properly supervising the road-making.

As to the former point, there is no criticism of superiors in my letter. In it I offer such counsel as I think it is my duty to offer in a matter of vital importance to this Battalion and to the success of any operations in which it may take part. This counsel may be unnecessary, but I cannot understand how it can be regarded as a breach of discipline for me to offer it.

If in your confidential report on me you state that I am too apt to criticize orders of my superiors, and if the letter of mine above is regarded as an instance of this, I request that a copy of the letter in question may be attached to the report.

As to the latter point, I am unable to inquire into the alleged slackness of the few men you mention unless I know their Platoon and the time at which they were smoking and doing no work. I have not yet found any signs of slackness, or want of supervision among the Officers, of whom one has been killed and two wounded on this work during the last three days.

Yours sincerely

AM Asquith[7]

Thus ended another small trial of strength between Asquith and Philips, but the way of the Service is that the odds are usually heavily weighted in favour of the senior disputant in such cases. There is no evidence that this matter resulted in lasting damage to Asquith, but his Battalion remained on construction duties until relieved on 20 October. Philips, as we shall see, did not remain much longer with the Division.

In the expectation that Hood Battalion would still be required for action in the next few days, Asquith gave constant attention to working out which officers and men he intended to use, and those who would form the Battalion cadre left behind in reserve. Large scale models of the area to be assaulted had been made, not only by 188th and 190th Brigades,[8] but also by the Canadian Corps who were on the right flank of the RND.[9] Asquith asked for visits to be made by his officers and NCOs to view them, and demanded up-to-date intelligence and aerial photographs of the battle zone from Brigade.[10] Among the myriad minor items on the mind of a Battalion Commander expecting to take his men into action on the Western Front, is one ominous word, a pencil reminder on the back of a note, 'crosses'.[11]

On 19 October Divisional Headquarters learned that their battle would begin on the 26th. It was left to General Lawrie, the Divisional Commander, to decide when the troops of the 188th Brigade would move forward into the line. On 20 October Asquith learned that Hood were to be the Counter-Attack Battalion, coming under the orders of General Prentice of the 188th Brigade for the operation. His Battalion was relieved from its working party duties and moved back to billets at Brake Camp, in the relatively safe area just east of Poperinghe. Before leaving, Asquith took four of his officers on an inspection of the line of the imminent Divisional attack.[12] Until the battle began, Asquith sent teams of men from his Battalion to carry out detailed reconnaissances of the battle zone.

Having read 188th Brigade Order No.148, for the coming attack, Asquith proposed some changes. First, he suggested that his Battalion, if it was to be effective in its counter-attack role, needed to be closer to the action; he proposed assembly positions near Albatross Farm, less than 1,000 yards from the start line, rather than at Springfield which not only was too close to an artillery battery and therefore a target for enemy guns, but would involve a further 1,200 yards of movement down a mainly forward slope on a single duckboard track.[13] He also reiterated his concern that his men were untrained and knew none of their objectives by sight.[14] General Prentice accepted Asquith's main point about the positioning of Hood Battalion. Asquith re-emphasised the point about the great difficulties of movement in the forward area after going up again to see for himself, adding that movement off the duckboard tracks was 'almost impossible'.[15] He remained very apprehensive about the lack of training for the forthcoming battle: after speaking to General Philips he drafted a note to HQ 189th Brigade:

I wish to confirm my opinion previously expressed to you verbally today and in writing to the effect that this Battalion is not at present trained for offensive action, and has not had time to properly study the ground. It is not for me to judge the necessity or otherwise of employing untrained troops as counter-attack Battalion for the coming offensive: but I request that this letter be forwarded to the Divl. Cdr. as I feel that the Battalion may be placed in a false position, and may fail to do itself justice.[16]

Setting his concerns aside, Asquith's next entries in his notebook deal with his proposed route to the assembly region via La Brique, just east of the canal, where General Prentice had his Headquarters, in daylight on the 24th, moving up to the area just north of Albatross Farm, as recommended by Asquith to Prentice, at 5pm on 25 October.

Meanwhile, in accordance with the Divisional Plan, 188th Brigade took over the line from units of another fine division, 9th (Scottish), during the night of 24/25 October. The plan was for the attack to be made on a two-battalion front, with Anson on the right and the 1st Royal Marines on the left. When they had taken the first objectives, all the enemy positions west of the Paddebeek except Sourd Farm, Howe and 2nd RMs would push through them, across the Paddebeek, and consolidate on a line running north-west through the formidable defences of Tournant Farm. The distance to the final objective was over 1,200 yards.

The Divisional History notes that 'The 25th October and the night of the 25th/26th were brilliantly fine, but at 3.30am on the 26th the weather suddenly broke and rain was continuous throughout the day. The already heavy going was thereby made considerably worse, and the difficulties of the attack proportionately increased.'[17] At 5.40am, keeping as close to the barrage as they dared and as the appalling conditions permitted, the attack began.

At 6.15, while the battle ahead was in full spate, Asquith ordered his A and C Companies up to the original front line by a note: 'Move to Front Line positions starting not before 6.30 not later than 6.40. Artillery formation.'[18] He kept his Adjutant informed by a similar message which added that one of his officers, Sub Lieutenant Lloyd Evans, had been 'wounded in the chest and gone down'.[19] When the barrage began, he had already sent his Intelligence Officer, Lieutenant Barclay, and two scouts to mark out proposed jumping off points for a possible counter-attack from the German positions to the north-east of the Paddebeek at Middle Copse, and Vat and Veal Cottages, by taping a line which ran roughly north from the Wallemolen Cemetery along the road for a short distance, continuing along the remains of the track, which, in peaceful days ran on to Bray Farm. He pushed forward under heavy shell fire. At 8.30 Barclay sent a handwritten note pinned to a Message Form, i.e., a small section of 1:10000 trench map with a series of pro forma messages on the reverse side: the note, difficult to read in parts because of the rain splashes, informed Asquith:

Proposed jumping off lines are marked in blue on accompanying map. That against Vat cottages is dry road and needs no taping. The other has not yet been taped for the following reasons:

1. Boche is in positon B (in red) [just north of Varlet Farm, and less than one hundred yards from the proposed line to be taped]
2. About a Platoon of our men are sitting doing nothing at A[just behind the tape line]
3. Boche is firing at all movement and one of my own men is hit I reached point marked X [about one hundred yards west of Varlet Farm] reconnoitreing the road as a jumping off line.[20]

Barclay sent his wounded man back with the other of his scouts, and despite being 'deeply wounded himself above the eye by a splinter from his shrapnel helmet, . . . he established liaison between two parties of attacking troops, and showed them how, by their combined action, the enemy trench which had been holding them up might be dealt with. He sent back a valuable report on the situation, remaining on duty for a further 36 hours'.[21]

By the time Barclay's note was written, Asquith had two Companies ready in the old front line east of Inch Houses, which formed his temporary Battalion headquarters; the third, D Company, was about to join them. Their Company Commander, Sub Lieutenant Oldridge, was wounded by a shell soon after.[22] B Company were in reserve. He notified Hilton of this, and commented that Varlet Farm appeared to have fallen to the attacking Ansons. He also reported Sub Lieutenant Clark as wounded.[23] By 9.55am Asquith was calling for stretcher bearers from his MO, McCracken.[24]

The remaining daylight hours were desperate: the advance by 188th Brigade had quickly stalled after a promising start, which meant that the formed Front Line from which the attack had originated was effectively still very close to the battle zone, although the conditions for Hood Battalion were far better than those for the wretched remnants of Howe, Anson and the Royal Marine Battalions clinging to hard-won and exposed positions a few hundred yards farther forward. The enemy shelled British positions heavily and continually throughout the day. Hood Battalion lost the remaining two officers of A Company, Sub Lieutenants Barclay-Brown, and Ramwell, both badly shaken from being buried as a result of shell fire, the former three times: Asquith sent Sub Lieutenant William Bach, from C Company to take charge of A.[25] His notebook contains no further entries until later that evening. By the forenoon of the 27th, seeing that there was nothing more for him to do in the front line, and that information on which posts were in RND hands, and which were still held by the enemy, was practically non-existent, he decided to undertake a reconnaissance. His report, written after the battle, records what happened:

There were now rumours that the enemy were massing for a counter-attack, but very little could be seen from the cemetery as to what was taking place beyond Varlet Farm – a better view could be obtained from the farm itself. A reconnaissance by Lieutenant Gammon (commander of a six-inch battery)[26] plus an officer and man of the Hood, who all succeeded in reaching the plantation surrounding the pill-box and ruins from the south-east. [The driest approach][27]

Asquith neglected to confide to the War Diary that the officer of the Hood Battalion involved was himself. When the three got to the pill-box concerned, they discovered, in Asquith's words, that:

A duel was in progress between the garrison of this pill-box and two enemy groups to the north-east and north-west. The pill-box, knee-deep in water, was being held by Sub Lieutenant Stevenson of Anson Battalion and just 11 survivors of his platoon, with one Lewis gun. They were putting up a good fight and keeping at bay a large number of the enemy, some of whom occupied a pill-box about 100 yards away. Other Germans moved from place to place, sniping from ranges of between 30 and 100 yards. The Ansons were embarrassed by the presence of several wounded, including . . . four Germans. They were running short of small arms ammunition, and it seems probable that they must have lost some direction when attacking.[28]

Asquith's account does not record the outcome of this reconnaissance, which is left to the Divisional historian, Jerrold, not one given to fulsome or undeserved tribute, who noted that, under Asquith's leadership,

the enemy who were closing in on the party were dispersed. Stevenson was promised relief, and Commander Asquith and his party, going on to get in touch with the Howe and Anson on the right, were able to inform them of the position and to establish touch between them and the Canadians. This reconnaissance was a decisive incident in the day's fighting, for it enabled our artillery to safeguard the line won, and prevented any incursions on the flank of the Canadians, who were thus able to make a more appreciable advance. Plain facts are often obscured by technical terms. A reconnaissance on this front meant a two hours' walk in full view of the enemy under heavy fire, and such a prosaic description of the achievement of these officers, with their solitary rifleman, gives a truer idea of the quality of mind and spirit necessary to support it, than do the more hackneyed phrases of the official reports.[29]

Macmillan, seeing the battle from Brigade HQ, noted later that:

The four battalions [Anson, Howe and the two Royal Marines] were getting out of hand when Commander Asquith advanced with his battalion and saved the situation. He placed the 'Hoods' in the most advantageous position to meet any counter-attack which might develop, and in the teeth of heavy artillery and machine gun fire, he passed from end to end of the line we were holding and superintended the consolidation of our gains. In addition, he established connection with the Canadians on our right, thus closing a breach which might have caused them infinite trouble and perhaps been the source of their undoing.[30]

Brigadier General Prentice realised that a further attempt to renew the attack without many more fresh troops was impossible, a decision vindicated at about dusk (5pm), when the Germans counter-attacked in the northern part of the Divisional sector. Sub Lieutenant William Arblaster, commanding C Company of Hood Battalion saw a party of about 120 RND men retreating towards the positions where he was dug in. They apparently were retiring, 'not from any panic, but for want of leadership, ignorance of what was expected of them, and in some cases because of a rumoured order of withdrawal.'[31]

The Divisional War Diary reports that, by about 6pm, Brigadier Prentice was receiving information that his two naval battalions, Anson and Howe, had been suffering heavy casualties from continuous enemy fire and were in a bad state. He decided to use Hood to relieve them both as, in the laconic prose of an official report, they 'had not been employed during the day'![32] The relief was carried out without major incident. Asquith moved all his Battalion up to the line, and instructed Arblaster to send 'an intelligent man to . . . show Howes our 1st Assembly positions'.[33] Howe had been nominated to relieve Hood as the counter-attack battalion. At the same time Hawke took over the positions won and held by the Royal Marines. In the confusion of the relief, however, some hard-won positions were relinquished, as the garrisons of Banff House, Bray Farm, and Berks Houses joined the retirement of the remnants of the other Royal Marines, who earlier in the day had crossed the Paddebeek with great gallantry, being forced to retreat when almost surrounded, and without ammunition or water. Hawke Battalion, under the dynamic and inspired leadership of Commander Ellis,[34] restored the situation, retaking the three evacuated points, and establishing touch with Asquith's Battalion on his right.

Asquith had to take one more walk that evening: patrols from one of Ellis's Companies reported that they were being fired on from a position thought to be held by Sub Lieutenant Stevenson east of Varlet Farm. Again he went forward, in bright moonlight. The Battalion War Diary continued:

He was observed by the enemy, but in spite of the heavy rifle and machine-gun fire directed at him and the awful state of the ground (which made the going very slow), he approached the Farm. Alone, he entered the concrete building and found it occupied by a small British garrison, who were exhausted, mostly wounded, and almost without ammunition. After investigating the ground thoroughly, he returned to the Hood lines and led up three platoons to relieve the garrison, putting one platoon in the building itself and the other two on each flank.[35]

The position was kept in British hands by the gallant conduct of the three platoons, under Sub Lieutenant Norman Roberts.[36]

Hood and Hawke held the line for the rest of the night and the following day. Asquith's Battalion was relieved by Nelson at about 11pm on the 27th. Throughout that time the medical parties of both sides worked ceaselessly to clear the battle zone of casualties. Hood's Surgeon, William McCracken, who had been working in the open at the regimental aid post at Albatross Farm, heard that many wounded were lying in the mud and shell holes in the forward area. Ordering his men to take cover, he advanced through heavy shelling and machine gun fire, carrying a walking stick to which was attached a Red Cross flag. Eventually this was recognised by the Germans: for the whole of the morning he and his team worked on the wounded in a zone which, according to Asquith, would normally have been under short-range enemy rifle fire. As at Gavrelle, McCracken's courageous action saved many who would have died where they lay, or been blown to pieces by the heavy and continual shell-fire.[37]

Back down from the line, Brigadier Prentice wrote to Asquith complimenting him on the performance of Hood Battalion while under the command of 188th Brigade, and passed on his 'warmest thanks for the loyal and thorough way in which you carried out my wishes, and for the personal supervision which you exercised over your dispositions'.[38] No officers had been killed, but seven were wounded; thirty-five ratings were dead or missing, and 114 wounded, a mercifully small toll for such a battle, although Hood had two more officers killed before they went down to rest.

On 30 October Philips was relieved in command of 189th Brigade by Brigadier General Coleridge, and went to be Commandant for the Rouen area.

There were many recommendations for awards as a result of this action. Asquith drafted citations for all his men who had done well.[39] It gave him particular pleasure to write proposing that McCracken should be awarded the Victoria Cross, supported by written notes to support the application by three Hood Officers, Gibson, Bach, and Arblaster, and one Canadian, Raven, attached to the 189th Infantry Brigade, who was with McCracken at Albatross Farm.[40] The citation reads as follows:

Throughout the operations of 26th and 27th October 1917, in the neighbourhood of Wallemolen, this Officer displayed the most conspicuous and devoted bravery in attending the wounded, and in evacuating them from the forward area.

For the first 24 hours he dressed the wounded without intermission in the open at the R.A.P. near Albatross Farm, where enemy shelling was heavy and practically incessant.

The next morning, on learning that many wounded were still lying in the mud and water of the shellholes over which the attack had passed, he led up two Platoons with stretchers to clear this forward area.

This party was being heavily shelled on its way up, Surgeon McCracken ordered them to take cover, and himself advanced through shelling and machine gun fire, bearing a Red Cross flag on his walking stick. Eventually, the enemy recognized and respected this, and Surgeon McCracken was able to bring forward his stretcher squads and to work with them throughout that morning at rescuing wounded from a zone which would normally have been under short range enemy rifle fire. By his determined action he undoubtedly saved many valuable lives.

Throughout these operations, as on former occasion [sic], Surgeon McCracken's gallantry, devotion, and contempt of danger have been of such a rare and positive quality as to inspire all who have come in contact with him to emulate his splendid example.[41]

Macmillan returned to the Brigade Headquarters where he found Barnett

closeted with six officers from the 'Hood' battalion who had come to testify to the outstanding gallantry of Commander Asquith and to plead that he be awarded the Victoria Cross. The Major was joined by the General who, after listening to their story agreed to recommend Asquith for the highest honour, and this is the report I was given to type:

'Near Poelcappelle during the operation of October 26/27, 1917, Commander Asquith displayed the greatest bravery, initiative and splendid leadership, and by his reconnaissance of the Front Line, made under heavy fire, contributed much valuable information which made the successful continuance of the operations possible.

During the morning of the 26th, when no news was forthcoming of the position of the attacking troops, Commander Asquith went forward through heavy fire, round the front line, and heedless of personal danger, found out our positions, got into touch with the troops on our right and returned after some hours with most valuable information. On the night of the same day he went forward alone in bright moonlight and explored the ground in the vicinity of Varlet Farm, where the situation was not clear. He was observed by the enemy but in spite of heavy rifle and machine gun fire directed at him, and the fact that the going was necessarily slow owing to the awful state of the ground, he approached Varlet farm, then reported to be in the hands of the enemy.

Entering a concrete building alone he found it occupied by a small British garrison who were exhausted and almost without ammunition and most of them wounded. After investigating the ground thoroughly, he returned and led up three platoons of a company of his battalion and relieved the garrison. He superintended the disposal of the troops, putting one platoon in the building as garrison and placing the other two platoons on each flank.

A very important position was therefore kept entirely in our hands owing to the magnificent bravery, leadership and utter disregard of his own safety. This example of bravery and cool courage displayed throughout the operations by Commander Asquith encouraged his men to greater efforts and kept up their morale. His valuable reconnaissance, the manner in which he led his men and his determination to hold the ground gained, contributed largely to the success of the operations.'[42]

One of the trench maps of the area in Asquith's papers is almost certainly that which he took with him on this reconnaissance: It is daubed with mud, and has pencil notes which indicate his assessment of the sizes of the enemy garrisons holding various points. It is apparent from this map that his walk took him as far as Tournant Farm, over one thousand yards from the most forward of the recently captured British positions. He noted that the Farm was held by two Platoons.[43]

Macmillan continued:

I had prepared many recommendations for awards, but none gave me greater pleasure than this one, and I therefore longed to see the outcome of it. 'Surely,' I thought, 'this claim will go through.' But it was not to be: Asquith was again ploughed, and was merely awarded a second bar to his DSO.

I doubt if the Commander knew that he had been recommended for the Victoria Cross; but whether or not, the witholding of it from him was, in my opinion, one of the gravest injustices ever perpetrated on a citizen soldier of the King. If his father had still been Prime Minister, the haughty backwoodsmen who barred the way would have been falling over themselves to do him honour.[44]

Macmillan was certain that the award had been withheld from spite, and he rails against the 'caprice of soulless Brass Hats and exalted grafters'. In fact, he was wrong that Asquith was unaware that he had been recommended for the highest honour. In writing Arthur's obituary in *The Times*, Bernard Freyberg noted:

At the finish of these operations [Passchendaele] Asquith recommended Surgeon McCracken for a well-earned Victoria Cross. He was asked however to alter his recommendation to a bar to McCracken's DSO.

It then became apparent that Asquith himself had been recommended for the VC and that if both names were sent forward from the same battalion neither would get it. Asquith's reply was characteristic of him: 'McCracken's name must go forward'. They both got bars to their DSOs.[45]

On 30 October 190th Brigade launched the second of the attacks on this front and, despite great dash and bravery, made very small gains and suffered large casualties.[46] Nevertheless, it was decided to attempt to achieve the intended objectives across the Paddebeek, and this time it was the turn of 189th Brigade, of which Hood was a part, and who took over the line on the night of 31October. Nelson and Hawke Battalions were on the right and left respectively; Drake were in support and Hood in reserve. All were to be involved in the series of operations that took place in the next four days, which were to result in the attainment of practically all the objectives at a very small cost. To understand the reason for this transformation in fortune it is necessary to go back to Asquith's report on the actions of 26/27 October in the Hood Battalion War Diary.

On completion of drafting the narrative, Asquith added a list of his own recommendations to the report. The draft for this list is contained in his own hand in the Field Message Book of the period: these include the need for the duckboard tracks to be pushed as far forward as possible, and for the troops engaged to have a good knowledge of the country and terrain; he suggests that forty-eight hours is the limit of useful employment of troops in the conditions, that one officer per Company should not participate in the inital assault, and that rifles must be in cases and sandbags to avoid clogging with mud. He also recommends that rum should be carried, but that hand grenades are useless in the conditions, and points out that it is impossible to mount a counter-attack in daylight across the sodden ground without a barrage. Finally, Asquith proposes that pill-boxes should be knocked off one by one. This last point formed the key difference in tactics between the first two actions and the third. In the comments at the end of the Battalion War Diary Report of Operations, these points were consolidated. In summary, additional points were:

i.   The objectives were too ambitious for the state of the ground

161

ii. Well trained, fresh, and lightly equipped troops with good knowledge of the ground could take enemy strong points piecemeal. Some might need preliminary bombardment: some, if surrounded at night, would cave in.

iii. A counter attack battalion is useless in the conditions

iv It is a mistake always to 'attack at dawn'[47]

Jerrold, who had access to all Divisional records, and was able to interview hundreds of RND personnel in compiling the History, reports that Asquith, having seen the disastrous attack of the 188th Brigade on 26 October, and after seeing and experiencing himself the conditions, his conclusion was definite. 'Absolute mobility, prior reconnaissance, surprise and personal leading by senior officers were, he was convinced (and so suggested in his official report), the indispensable elements of success against the enemy's new system.'[48] Later Douglas Jerrold, writing to Betty after Arthur's death, states that 'the influence he had by that time won for himself with the staff of the Division enabled him to force a change of tactics which not only led to success when others had failed, but saved hundreds of lives.'[49]

In the dreadful conditions, it was not possible to follow closely a creeping barrage. In any case artillery fire was less effective because of the very soft ground. Thus, infantry attacking in daylight were easy targets for machine gunners in concrete emplacements, which enjoyed virtual invulnerability. Asquith realised that night attack could produce a solution: the individual pill-boxes would be on their own, and not mutually supporting as by day; they would have fewer targets, and would be vulnerable to surprise attack. The first requisite for the tactics to work was expert reconnaissance. Sterndale Bennett, CO of Drake, and Asquith undertook just such a walk, leaving their horses at St Julien, and together reconnoitreing the whole area after dark on 1 November.[50]

The new tactics had their first trial on the night of 1/2 November. Just after 8pm a party from Nelson Battalion of eleven ratings led by Sub Lieutenant Brearley rushed a formidable concrete fortress on the southern side of the Paddebeek, capturing one under officer, eleven other ranks, and a machine gun. Two Germans were killed. Brearley had no casualties. At the same time, Hawke Battalion were carrying out a similar operation against a line of hostile posts just north of Bray Farm. Of the garrison of twelve men, eleven were captured or killed; later in the night an enemy party arrived at the post with rations, and were killed or taken prisoner. The following night, Hood relieved Nelson, and Drake took over the left of the line from Hawke; on the night of the 3rd, Drake repeated the performance, and captured Sourd Farm, which left only the complex around Tournant Farm as the final objective. Asquith, accompanied by Lieutenant Harris, OC of B Company of Drake Battalion, attached to Hood

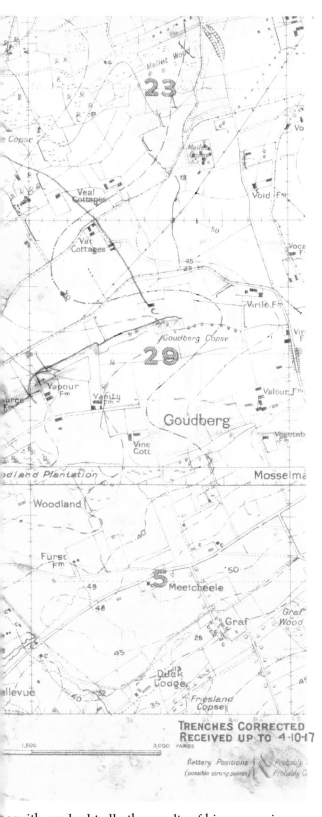

TRENCHES CORRECTED
RECEIVED UP TO 4-10-17

1,500   2,000 YARDS

Battery Positions { Probably
(possible strong points) { Probably C

squith, undoubtedly the results of his reconnaissances. His assess-
proached them. The brown stains are mud from the original map.
DSO.

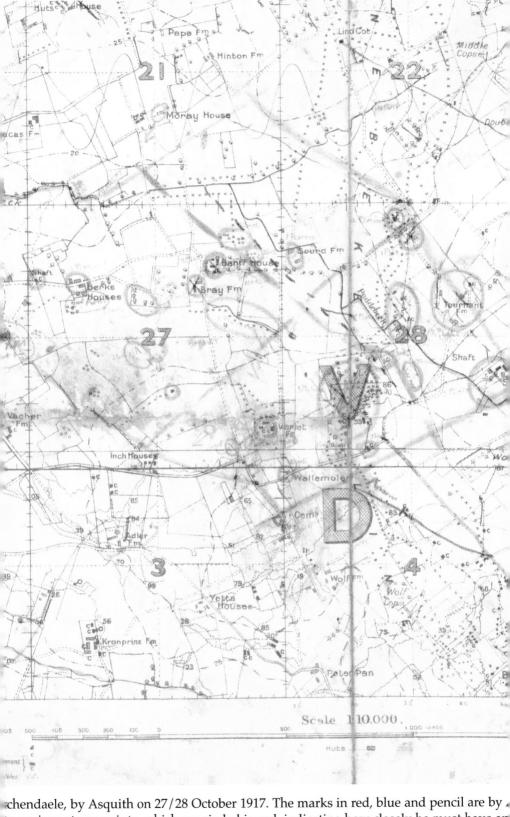

Scale 1:10,000.

chendaele, by Asquith on 27/28 October 1917. The marks in red, blue and pencil are by
he various strongpoints, which are circled in red, indicating how closely he must have ap
was recommended for the Victoria Cross for this action. He received a second bar to his

6. Part of a trench map carried in action near Poelcappelle, near Pas
ments of the strength of enemy garrisons can be seen in pencil by
Asquit

for the operation,[51] carried out a detailed night reconnaissance of the area. Tournant Farm was a problem of a different order from the previous attacks on isolated outposts: the position consisted of a 'nest of mutually supporting concrete structures, with a screen of shell hole posts well in front of them. Tournant Farm was supported by a concrete structure to the North of it'.[52] The whole position was dominated by two other strong points. On the strength of the report by Asquith and Harris, it was wisely decided not to try to rush the complex unless surprise could be guaranteed. Nevertheless, Hood and Drake pushed forward to advanced positions which would threaten Tournant Farm. The German artillery was very active at this time, and during the late afternoon of the 4th, Sterndale Bennett was mortally wounded by a shell while visiting his Battalion's forward posts. He died of his wounds on 7 November at the 61st Casualty Clearing Station, and was buried with full military honours in Dozinghem Cemetery. General Lawrie and the Battalion Commanders of the 189th Brigade were among those attending. His death was a severe loss.

Hood and Drake Battalions were relieved during the night of 5/6 November, and marched back to Irish Farm; on the 6th they were bussed to the Road Camp, out of the battle area a couple of miles west of Poperinghe, on the road to Houtkerque, and their involvement in the Third Battle of Ypres was at an end.

NOTES

1. The battalions concerned were the Artists Rifles and the 1/4 King's Shropshire Light Infantry. The former had replaced the 1st Honourable Artillery Company on 2 July 1917, who went to the Guards Division, while the latter took the place in the order of battle of the 10th Royal Dublin Fusiliers on 20 July 1917, which was transferred to the 16th(Irish) Division.
2. Trench Map 'Spriet', Edition 1, Trenches corrected to 4 October 1917, signed 'S H Fish', with various colourations and markings. Fish had also noted that the opposing German force was the 2nd Bavarian Reserve, a first class unit.
3. Jerrold, *The Royal Naval Division*, pp250 and 251.
4. Several requests for materials, including duck boards, picks, helves, trench floor boarding, and revetting canvas are in Army Field Message Book, Army Book 153, in use by Asquith from 6 to 21 October 1917, hereafter referred to as AMA Notebook No. 24, AMA papers.
5. Letter from AMA to Headquarters 189th Infantry Brigade, marked 'Confidential', Hood Battalion No. 1071, dated 9 October 1917, AMA papers.
6. Letter from Brigadier General Philips, GOC 189th Brigade to Asquith, in his own hand, marked 'Private', dated 10 October 1917, AMA papers.
7. Note from AMA to General Philips, in his own hand, dated 11 October 1917, AMA papers. These pages were almost certainly removed from AMA Notebook No. 24, where, in the middle of several entries for 10 October 1917, a wad of eight pages has been torn out. This would indicate that Asquith's reply to Philips was drafted on the 10th, and sent the next day. In fact, Asquith lost two officers killed during this period, both Sub Lieutenants: S G James, 28 years old, killed in action 9 October 1917; his father's address is

given as the Royal Sandwich Golf Club; and F J Newell, 27, from Keynsham, near Bristol, killed on 12 October 1917. Newell's effects are listed in Asquith's hand on a page of Army Book 152, Correspondence Book, in use by both the Adjutant, Hilton, and Asquith himself in the period 12 October to 5 November 1917. They included £122 in cash, a great deal of money for the time, and, ironically, a piece of lucky white heather in his wallet. Both officers had only recently joined the battalion direct from initial training at Blandford on 7 September 1917.

8. From the War Diary of the 63rd(RN) Division, 'Report on the Operations of the 63rd (RN) Division East of Ypres during Period 24 October to 5th November [1917]', marked 'Secret', G. 855/28, para 6. PRO Kew, Box WO 095/3095.

9. Note from AMA to COs Companies dated 22 October 1917, AMA Notebook No. 24.

10. Note from Asquith to Barnett (Brigade Major), dated 10 October 1917, asking for intelligence about 'present and pending operations . . . beyond scraps of Press gossip'. Also note number A14/X, from AMA to HQ 189th Infantry Brigade dated 13 October 1917. Both from AMA Notebook No. 24.

11. AMA Notebook No. 24.

12. One from each Company: Sub Lieutenants Oldridge, Clark, Bolton and Bishop: note from AMA to Lieutenant Barclay and OCs Companies dated 20 October 1917, AMA Notebook No. 24.

13. From notes in AMA Notebook No. 24, in his own hand, undated, but between entries for 20 and 21 October 1917.

14. ibid.

15. Note from AMA to HQ 189th Infantry Brigade, no A 20/X, marked 'urgent', dated 21 October 1917.

16. Pencil draft, in Asquith's hand, of a letter to General Philips, undated, but probably written on 21 or 22 October 1917, AMA Notebook No 24, between entries for 21 and 22 October 1917. I have no evidence that this letter was actually sent.

17. War Diary of the 63rd(RN) Division, 'Operations of 26th October', p 6 para 25, PRO Kew, WO 95/ 3095.

18. Note from AMA to OCs A and C Companies, timed at 6.15am, dated 26 October 1917. Field Message Book, Army Book 153 in use from 25 October to 15 December 1917, hereafter referred to as AMA Notebook No. 26, AMA papers.

19. AMA to Adjutant Hood, timed at 6.50am, 26 October 1917, AMA Notebook No. 26. Lloyd-Evans, 25, of South Shields, was sent home with a gunshot wound in the chest. He never regained fitness for service, and was invalided in May 1918.

20. Map with pinned note, timed at 8.35am, dated 26 October 1917, signed by Sub Lieutenant Warren Barclay, AMA papers. Barclay, from Sydenham, Kent, did well under very trying circumstances. He was wounded during the course of the day. Gassed in March 1918, he was awarded the Military Cross for 'Conspicuous gallantry and devotion to duty', a medal presented to him by the King at Aldershot. He was demobilised in June 1919.

21. From The War Diary of Hood Battalion, PRO Kew ADM 137/3064. The Diary was written by Asquith after he had called for inputs from all his Officers, requested in a note from AMA to Company Commanders, undated, but before an entry for 31 October 1917, AMA Notebook No. 26.

22. Sub Lt B H Oldridge, 27, from Surrey, promoted from Leading Seaman, was

wounded in the legs and head. After recovery, he transferred to the Army.

23. Note from AMA to Adjutant Hood Battalion, timed at 8.37am, dated 26 October 1917, AMA Notebook No. 26. Joseph Clark, 32, from Aberdeen, had been promoted from the ranks. He had previously won the MC for his conduct in action in operations north of the Ancre earlier in the year. When he recovered, he transferred to the Gordon Highlanders.

24. Note from AMA to MO Hood Bn, timed at 9.55am, dated 26 October 1917. AMA Notebook No. 26.

25. Sub Lt Barclay-Brown, from Putney, was badly wounded in the left arm and leg, and did not return to the Division in France. Sub Lt William Bach, of Aston, Birmingham, served with the Battalion until his luck ran out in September 1918, when he was wounded in the buttock by a bullet. Although his injury was initially assessed as 'mild' he was invalided in April 1919.

26. Jerrold, p255, records the Officer as Garnham R.F.A. (forward observation officer).

27. Hood Battalion War Diary for 26 October 1917, PRO Kew, ADM 137/3064.

28. ibid.

29. Jerrold, p255.

30. Macmillan papers, p234, IWM, Department of Documents.

31. Hood Battalion War Diary for 26 October 1917, PRO Kew, ADM 137/3064.

32. War Diary of the 63rd(RN) Division, 'Operations of the 26th October 1917', p7 para 31, PRO Kew, WO 095/3095.

33. Note to CO C Company from AMA, undated, but written on 26 October 1917, AMA Notebook No. 26.

34. Commander Bernard Ellis, a very fine, even brilliant, officer, was promoted from Chief Petty Officer in Benbow Battalion. A Londoner from West Hampstead, he won the DSO on the Ancre in 1916 with Anson Battalion, and took over as Commanding Officer Hawke after Gavrelle. He was severely wounded in the neck during the German offensive of March 1918, and died four weeks later.

35. Hood Battalion War Diary for 26 October 1917, PRO Kew, ADM 137/3064. Sub Lt Stevenson, 24, from Manchester, was awarded the MC for 'conspicuous gallantry and devotion to duty', on Asquith's recommendation; he was invalided home with stomach problems in July 1918.

36. Roberts was, as were so many good RND officers, promoted from the ranks, where he had already won the DSM. For his conduct in this battle, he was awarded the MC for conspicuous gallantry and devotion to duty. He died of wounds the day after being wounded on Welsh Ridge on 30 December 1917.

37. Hood Battalion War Diary for 27 October 1917, PRO Kew, ADM 137/3064.

38. Letter from Brigadier General Prentice, Commanding 188th Brigade, to AMA, dated 1 November 1917, AMA papers.

39. He recommended Arblaster, Barclay, Roberts, and Barclay Brown for the MC, and Harris, of Drake Battalion, who had accompanied him on his reconnaissance, for the DSO. He also put forward five NCOs and one OR for the DCM, and sixteen for the MM. Many of the recommendations were for stretcher bearing duties or rescuing wounded.

40. Hood Battalion War Diary, PRO Kew, ADM 137/3064, pp288-291.

41. Citation, dated 7 November 1917, by Asquith for McCracken in Hood Battalion War Diary pp286 and 287, PRO Kew, ADM 137/3064.

42. Macmillan Papers, p239, IWM Department of Documents. The citation is also to be found in an Annex to Hood Battalion War Diary, pp285-6, dated 3 November 1917, headed 'For Immediate Award, Victoria Cross', PRO Kew, ADM 137/3064.

43. Trench Map 'Spriet', Edition 1, 1:10000 inscribed 'Trenches corrected from information received up to 4-10-17', marked 'C.O.', AMA papers.
44. Macmillan Papers p 240, IWM Department of Documents.
45. *The Times*, 29 August 1939, newspaper cutting in the papers of Surgeon McCracken, IWM Department of Documents. The award of Asquith's second Bar to his DSO was announced in Divisional Routine Order 3299 of 30 October 1917, and in the 4th Supplement to the *London Gazette* dated 18 January 1918, p953.
46. Jerrold notes that the two advances of 26 and 30 October cost the Division thirty-two Officers and 954 men killed or missing, and eighty-three Officers and 2,057 men wounded, Jerrold, p258.
47. Hood Battalion War Diary, PRO Kew, ADM 137/3064 p282.
48. Jerrold, p259.
49. Letter from Douglas Jerrold to Betty Asquith dated 27 August 1937, AMA papers.
50. Note, undated, but written on 1 November 1917 from AMA to Commander Sterndale Bennett, AMA Notebook No. 26.
51. Harris was a most gallant officer. An Australian from Newcastle NSW, he had already won the MC and Bar for operations north of the Ancre at the age of 27. For this action, he received a second Bar to the decoration on Asquith's recommendation. As a Lieutenant, he was awarded the DSO, for 'most conspicuous gallantry' on Welsh Ridge at the end of December 1917, when he was wounded.
52. War Diary of the 189th Brigade, Narrative of Events: 31 October – 3 November, p8, File WO 095/3112, PRO Kew.

CHAPTER XIII
Promoted, Badly Wounded, and Married

In early November 1917 Hood Battalion found themselves in the area around Roubrouck and Ledezeele, west of Cassel, and only about ten miles from the Channel coast: the Brigade had had only ten days' rest since 21 January. On 13 November Asquith took some leave in England. He left Patrick Shaw Stewart in command of the Battalion, celebrated by the latter in typical style in a letter to his sister:

> Meanwhile, Oc. Asquith has gone on leave and left me in command, by Jove! No nonsense from the junior officers, I can tell you. My first action was to put in for immediate promotion to Lieutenant-Commander, sound, don't you think? My second, to place a man who has just arrived from spending three years in England, more or less, and who is senior, not only to all my company commanders, but to myself, handsomely – to place him, I say, second in command of a company.[1]

Before he went on leave, Asquith learned that he was to be given a Brigade. A telegram was received at Divisional HQ from the Military Secretary at the War Office that he was 'required to command a Brigade'.[2] Coleridge, who had relieved Brigadier-General Philips in command of 189th Brigade made the following recommendation dated 8 November 1917 to General Plumer, commanding Second Army:

> This officer's military experience commenced with the present War; but, during that time, he has developed military qualities of a high order. Possessed of great personal courage, he inspires confidence in his men, and leads them successfully in action: he possesses decision, driving power, and energy, & has a good capacity for organisation. His tactical knowledge is limited by the length of his service, but his natural intelligence, backed by a good knowledge of the world gained previous to the War as a Government Official, and 3 years war experience, combined with the military qualifications enumerated above, should enable him to overcome rapidly any defects due to his short service.

The Divisional Commander, General Lawrie, added:

> I concur. An exceptional leader of men, would make an excellent Brigade Commander, and I should very much like to have him, a Commodore, in command of the 189th Infantry Brigade, in which he has so brilliantly distinguished himself.[3]

During this leave period, which was extended from 28 November to 12 December, Betty finally came to believe that she was in love with Arthur, and that he was the right man for her. Cynthia Asquith reported in her diary a conversation with Freyberg in London:

> He told me all was well with Oc as far as Betty was concerned – she had confided in him [Freyberg] walking home from a dinner in Leeds the night before. He had been extolling Oc and she said, 'I am very, very fond of him,' which was a cue easily taken, so he said, '*How* fond?' and the tale was told. She said, 'I know people think I have treated him abominably, but I couldn't help it – I didn't love him before.' I suppose if Oc hadn't been recalled [he returned to France on the 12th], all would now be settled and the Old Boy [Cynthia's affectionate term for her father-in-law] would have had to stomach a lowering of the average of beauty amongst his daughters-in-law.[4]

Then, before his extended leave expired, Asquith was called back urgently to France, disrupting plans for him and Betty to spend some time at Clovelly with Aunt Christine. Betty wrote on 11 December:

> I felt stunned when you went off so hastily . . . now I don't dare to hope and think the war brings fresh vistas of danger and loss. I wish I could shut my eyes and wake up, to find you safe in three months and everything over. I am trying to hear why you were sent for so urgently.[5]

Meanwhile, the Cambrai offensive and the German counter had taken place, which resulted in a vulnerable salient around Flesquières, to the south west of Cambrai itself. The Royal Naval Division, about to return to the Ypres area, was quickly sent to take over the line which ran along Welsh Ridge, a total frontage of nearly seven thousand yards, which meant that all three Brigades were required to be in line. On 6 December the RND received their orders to move, and by the 13th, by train and marching, they arrived at the town of Metz en Couture, west of Cambrai, and took over the lines on Welsh Ridge beginning on the night of 14/15 December. The position, recently captured, in Jerrold's words, 'formed a very sharp salient which, in the event of a serious attack, could hardly have been held'.[6] The salient, in front of Flesquières, poked impudently right through the defences of the Hindenburg Line.

Asquith, recalled early from leave, was surprised to rejoin the Division on the 9th and find that he was still the CO of Hood Battalion. Betty, in fine ignorance of the workings of the Army promotion system, expressed her annoyance: 'How too annoying about your really being able to have stayed. Was it that stupid Brigadier? Do Stellenbosch him quickly and be one yourself I feel it's a bit safer. I hear every general is being sacked right and left so there will be lots of vacancies!'[7] Arthur wrote to his father telling of the cold weather and complaining that: 'a bibulous ancestry, the Sudan, and three weeks at Cav Square [Cavendish Square was the private London home of Herbert Asquith] have quite unfitted me for the rigours of a winter campaign'. He ended: 'I have not seen the Divisional Commander yet, so know nothing more about the proposed promotion'.[8]

Arthur did not have long to wait. A memorandum from 63rd (RN) Division to Headquarters 189th Infantry Brigade appointed Coleridge to relieve Prentice in command of 188th Brigade, while Asquith took over from the former in command of 189th Brigade in the rank of Temporary Brigadier General whilst so employed. Asquith relieved Coleridge in accordance with his orders at 10am on 16 December 1917.[9] The very final entry as a Battalion Commander in his field message books is one to the HQ of his Brigade requesting instructions on the allocation of reinforcements who had just turned up at his Battalion HQ.[10]

The positions of 189th Brigade were very exposed: the situation was not so bad where the new British line was able to incorporate parts of the captured Hindenburg positions into their defences, but for the remainder it was a case of establishing new trenches and dug-outs. In a secret message from Division to Brigades on 15 December, General Lawrie stressed that 'the Front Line is the main line of resistance', if incursions were made by the enemy they were to be driven out 'by immediate counter-attack . . . The most important work to be undertaken is the construction of a complete Front Line trench system'. Lawrie left the details of the work to his Brigade Commanders: 'After reconnaissance and co-ordination by Brigadiers, the new trenches will be sited, and the work pushed on as soon as possible'.[11] The order, which with hindsight contained an ominous warning for Asquith, continues: 'The positions of both Brigade Headquarters in the Forward area are considered to be too advanced. Brigadiers concerned will please reconnoitre new positions for these and forward locations of the sites . . . for Division Officer's approval (by 20 December).'[12] Lawrie was undoubtedly correct: Asquith's Brigade HQ was sited in the old German defences behind the newly gained, and as yet ill-defended, salient. The closest enemy were less than 1,000 yards from his Headquarters. The new Brigade HQ selected was in a far more appropriate position, more than 1,000 yards farther back from the front line, just east of the hamlet of Beaucamp on the road to Villers Plouich. The 189th Brigade staff were due to move to the safer location in the rear at 4 pm on 20 December 1917.[13] At about 1.20 that afternoon, Asquith was wounded for the fourth time.[14]

It had been foggy for some while: The Divisional Intelligence Summary for the period 10am on the 19th to the same time on 20 December says: 'possibly enemy is taking advantage of the foggy weather', and 'the weather has been too thick for observation'.[15] The Summary for the next twenty-four-hour period notes that 'Fog made distant observation impossible, except at intervals'.[16]

Less than forty-eight hours after the event, in a letter to his father, Asquith recounted what happened in his own words:

> I had climbed out of a trench thinking there was enough mist to conceal me while I cast an eye over the lie of the land. A Bosche sniper, who had also, I suppose, taken advantage of the mist to advance his position, had three shots at me, one penetrating and, I fear, smashing up the left ankle joint: one kicking up the snow: and one grazing my right leg.[17]

After emergency treatment, he was driven out of the area in a private motor car, in great pain, and after initial treatment, spent

> 13 long hours in the train [and] came to rest early this morning here under the shade of Lady Murray's benign and matronly presence.
> Except when they are dressing my foot, I have more discomfort from the small of my back and stomach than I do from it – this from being forced to be always in the same position.[18]

He concluded with a typical comment: 'The alternatives before one would appear to be one's own stiff ankle, or a nicely articulated ankle and foot bought in a shop.'[19]

Hit and unable to walk, Asquith had managed to roll himself across the snow to reach the safety of his own trench, and was taken quickly to the Casualty Clearing Station after first aid by McCracken.

On admission to 10th General Hospital at Le Treport, on the coast south of Abbeville, on 22 December, the diagnosis was: 'GSW Left ankle, fractured, severe'.[20] On 31 December he was assessed as 'progressing satisfactorily, not known when he will be evacuated to England'.[21]

McCracken wrote to Asquith in hospital on 23 December. Having treated him, he knew the full extent of the injuries and the pain associated with them. McCracken had obtained information that the theatre team were quite pleased with the initial operation, and added:

I trust it is now much less painful, for it was simply hellish. That awful journey in the Ford car was only justified by the fact that you were being speedily evacuated. I really think that it is the most unkindest cut the Battalion has ever had. However, nothing matters so long as the recovery is complete. I am afraid it will take longer than any of your previous wounds.[22]

In fact, the healing was not going as well as had been hoped, and even Asquith's normally buoyant character shows the occasional sign of depression. He confided to his father that he had 'not been feeling inclined to see friends or acquaintances. I have had some uncomfortable days and nights'.[23] In spite of this he was optimistic of being able to keep his leg. Inspection of his clothing on arrival in hospital revealed that, despite the seriousness of his injury, things could have been much worse. At the end of the same letter he wrote:

Did I tell you how lucky I was? Either the same or another bullet went thro' my right boot and made a shallow grazing wound just forward of the right inner ankle – this wound is utterly insignificant. My right gaiter was also penetrated and a small harmless scar made about 1/3 of the way up the outside of my right leg. So I really got off lightly, but it's going to be a long business.[24]

On the last day of the year McCracken again wrote to Asquith to tell him of the circumstances of the death of Patrick Shaw Stewart, who had taken command of Hood after Arthur's promotion:

I'm quite heartbroken. Poor Pat was killed yesterday morning. Things remained uncannily quiet after you left except for hostile air activity. At 7 am (about) yesterday the Boche put down a terrific barrage – really the worst I have ever struck, and pounded us for half-an-hour & cut all communications. About 7.30 he came over in great style, white overalls etc, and got right down to the RAP [Regimental Aid Post] trench . . . There was no panic. The old 'Steadies' [the nickname for Hood Battalion, taken from their motto] shut their teeth & B Coy Officers' cook tackled 3 Hun Officers – killed one, smashed another's leg & took the third prisoner. Our fellows simply knocked hell out of them . . . . Patrick was round the line when the show started & was hit early on by a piece of shell & lived only a few minutes.

After further reporting the brave conduct of the Hoods who had fought in the action, he concluded with some advice:

Unless there is a preponderance of good professional opinion in favour of amputation I would be in favour of leaving it as it is. The amputation could be performed later if absolutely necessary.[25]

All who knew Shaw Stewart were deeply saddened by his death. Having heard the news, Asquith wrote to Diana Cooper on 6 January:

The last I saw of him was Dec 20th – the day I was wounded. He met my stretcher in the trench going down, and was full of 'petit soins' for me, gave me cigarettes and helped the stretcher bearers in places where it was difficult going. He and our Doctor bore me company to the Dressing Station 2 miles away and saw me into the ambulance car.

Shaw Stewart had shared Oc's HQ after returning from leave in London, a place described by Asquith as a 'lean-to corrugated iron, all cracks and draughts, no floor, and a rather fitful brazier. Here, poor Patsy, fresh from . . . Mayfair, had to stretch himself on our table . . . You can imagine what a joy and source of laughter and fun his company has been to me since May'. He continued:

I may keep my leg, but I fear it will be a stiff and ungainly object . . . I am asking Violet to see if she can arrange for me to go to Lady Ridley's where they specialize in legs, and I think one would be nearer to having a room to myself than in your hospital. The point is that I'd sooner be slightly wounded in your delicious hospital, but bed-ridden elsewhere.[26]

Unfortunately, Arthur's leg had turned septic, and in the middle of January it was finally decided that the leg was never going to heal properly, and it was amputated below the left knee. The fact was reported in the papers and, among the letters of commiseration he received were from General Gough, commanding Fifth Army south of the Somme, and Major General Malcolm, who had just taken over 66th Division. Both commented on what they saw as the continuing campaign by the Northcliffe press to undermine the Army in France. Malcolm concluded: 'A power which poses as the voice of the people but is really only the voice of a few men has its dangers!'[27] Gough ended by saying: 'All will be well if the vile campagn now being conducted by Northcliffe & his Press does not undermine the confidence & the discipline of the Army. But with the example of Russia before us, we would be fools if we shut our eyes to the great dangers to which he is exposing us'.[28]

Shortly afterwards, Asquith wrote to his friend, McCracken, on 7 February congratulating him on his recent marriage, adding: 'It is a nice point whether by marrying without the previous consent or approval of any of the Commanders or Ex-Commanders of the Steadies you have not committed a breach of etiquette which may invalidate the bond! . . .'[29] Asquith revealed little of his medical condition in his letters of the time other than to Betty, his father, and McCracken himself, and he continued:

> About my leg . . . For about a month I had a good deal of pain while they thought they could patch it up. Then they realised that the ankle was smashed as well as the two other bones and they took it off below the knee about 3 weeks ago. My temperature has been normal and I've had practically no pain for the last fortnight. Healing is retarded by the fact that the leg was septic at the time of amputation. But it is going well, and I shall probably be in England in about a week . . . I believe they make wonderful artificial limbs nowadays and I still hope that they may be able to fix me up so that I may rejoin the Divn. but I suppose its very doubtful. Best love, and take care of yourself.[30]

When he was fit enough to travel, on 23 February, Asquith was transferred to the King Edward VII Hospital in Grosvenor Gardens, in the Hospital Ship *Warilda*. A few days later, on 28 February 1918, he was visited by the King, who invested him at his bedside with his DSO and two Bars.[31]

His recovery was fairly swift thereafter, and he was soon able to get about on crutches while the doctors arranged an artificial leg. Following a Medical Board at Caxton Hall on 21 March, he was declared 'fit for Home Service Only';[32] he and Betty decided to wait no longer and on 27 March their engagement to be married on 30 April 1918 was announced in the Press, the cutting from the *Daily Sketch* embarrassingly titled 'A Hero's Engagement'! There was universal approbation in the families: in particular, Aunt Chris wrote that:

> I have always been so <u>very</u> fond of you dear Arthur since the very first time you came here (as a boy from Winchester) with Violet – who was then a little girl – and you have never been anything but most courteous and charming to me all these many years. As I say if you make Betty happy what more can a childless old Aunt want?[33]

Other congratulations came from General Sir Ian Hamilton: after the warmest tributes to the couple he ended with a prescient note about the conduct of the war, only six days after the massive German attacks on Fifth Army, at a time when it seemed possible that the BEF might disintegrate. His conclusion was:

> We are at an anxious moment but to myself this attack by the Germans in the West seems the most providential happening. As I have said . . . the West is unbreakable by either side. Had the Germans sat tight

behind their successive lines in the West nothing we could have done would have prevented them from overwhelming at their leisure Italy, Salonika, the Caspian districts, Persia and India. Now they have staked all on a desperate stake & the Lord has delivered them into our hands.[34]

In order to ensure that he would be fit for the occasion, Asquith booked in to the Hotel Bristol in Brighton, a place to convalesce; his leg still had not fully healed. He wrote in reassurance to his father of his likely financial situation after marriage: Betty would receive a lump sum from her parents; in addition, Arthur's income, half pay as a Brigadier, plus Directorship of Government and General Investment Company, together with the quarter salary he was still receiving from his old employer Franklin and Herrera, would total about £930. His investments included £1,500 in the latter company, assessed as 'of doubtful value', plus a piece of land purchased for £500 in the Grand Chaco, South America and two other very small interests. There was light at the end of the tunnel, however: Winston Churchill had offered Asquith the job of Controller of Trench Warfare Research at the Munitions Office to relieve Major General Tom Bridges, who had also lost a leg in action earlier in the war.[35] If he accepted the post, for which Bridges was paid £1,500, Asquith wrote that he would receive either that sum, or at least the full pay for his rank, £1,000 per annum. Arthur had replied to Churchill that he was unsure whether he would be fit enough to take up the post before June. He concluded to his father in typical style:

He [Lord Manners] made no mention of subvention from you: and naturally I do not expect one, as I expect you have your hands full with K [Katherine], Beb, V, and Cys: and that Bet and I shall be as well or better off than they, without subvention.

But let it not be supposed by our rich friends that we are a rich young couple to whom cheques are not agreeable wedding presents! . . . Mrs Hamlyn's requirements in a husband for a Twin [it will be remembered that Betty had a twin sister, Angela] were moderate Churchman, moderate Tory, moderate means. In all respects I fear my moderation is excessive.[36]

Asquith Senior replied confirming that: 'while I shall always be ready to give any help I can am afraid that I cannot – with all the others more or less dependent – enter into any legal covenant. I think that between you you should be fairly comfortable.'[37] He also volunteered to write to Churchill asking him to keep the job open. As it happened, Asquith joined the Ministry of Munitions on 18 April 1918. A note in his record states 'not entitled to emoluments from Naval Funds from 18 April 1918 onwards.'[38]

Asquith wrote to Freyberg in France, then commanding 88th Infantry

Brigade of the famous 29th Division, inviting him to be his best man, but by this time, the British Army was fighting a desperate rearguard action to contain the German offensive which had begun on 21 March. Freyberg replied requesting details of the wedding and ended: 'If I fly over, (and it seems my only chance) I will arrive on the day. You understand that I want to come and help, but we may not be able to, as the situation here will sooner or later involve us, we are waiting and may go into battle any day. You know how much I wish you happiness'.[39] By the 24th it was obvious that Freyberg was not going to be available, the situation was still critical, and his 29th Division had already been in action, and would continue to be. He explained: 'I can't tell you how sorry I am not to be able to hold you up on the 30th, and I am damned grateful to you for asking me to be your best man please remember that . . . but we are involved and will be in a big battle (our second) any day now.'[40] In fact, few of Asquith's RND friends were able to be at the ceremony: the military situation in France was just too desperate. Arblaster of Hood Battalion also reluctantly had to turn down the invitation to be his best man; Petty Officer Fairburn, his former batman, was, however, able to attend; he was serving in the Division's Reserve at Aldershot, in the Brigade Bombing School.[41]

On 29 April, the day before his wedding, Asquith was again seen by the Medical Board at Caxton Hall, and was pronounced 'Permanently Unfit General Service. Fit for Sedentary Employment only.'[42] Arthur and Betty were married at All Saints Church, Thorney Hill, Christchurch, near the Manners' home at Avon Tyrrell: Anthony Asquith, Arthur's half-brother, who later became a very well known film director, was the best man, and the service was conducted by the Reverend J Bramston, formerly chaplain of Winchester College. After the ceremony, as Asquith hopped down the path on crutches in his uniform, the guard of honour was formed by New Zealand officers from Lord Manners' convalescent hospital. The honeymoon was spent at Manor House, Cranborne, the Dorset seat of the Marquess of Salisbury, and at Clovelly Court, lent by Betty's Aunt Christine. Among their many wedding presents was a magnificent silver punch bowl inscribed: 'From the old Officers of the Hood Battalion R.N.D. to their adored Commander Brigadier General AM Asquith D.S.O.' His old friend, Surgeon McCracken, had organised the gift.

A belated wedding present arrived from the Admiralty in September 1918: their Lordships wrote granting compensation for the injuries Asquith had suffered on active service. In wonderfully archaic language he was informed that:

I am commanded by My Lords Commissioners of the Admiralty to acquaint you that they have been pleased to award you the following sums: £34.2.6 for the injury received on 6th May 1915 [shot through the knee]; £63.14.0 for the injury sustained on 21st October 1916 [buried by a *Minenwerfer*, eardrums burst]; and £42.14.0 for the injury sustained on 5th February 1917 [shot in the left arm]; making a total of £140.10.6.

I am to add that the question of compensation for the injury sustained by you on 22nd December 1917 [resulting in the loss of his left foot] is under consideration.[43]

He later learned that, for this last and most serious wound, he would receive £950, plus £350 a year for life.[44]

Asquith worked as the Controller of the Trench Warfare Research Department at the Ministry of Munitions for the rest of the war. When it became clear that the Armistice of 11 November 1918 was going to hold, the thoughts of the Lloyd George government turned to the massive problem of demobilisation. It had become apparent in his short time at Munitions that Asquith was a highly competent administrator, and he accepted a job in January 1919 at the Ministry of Labour as Controller of the Appointments Department and a member of the Council, retaining his rank.[45] This caused much amusement in the family: Betty wrote: 'Aunt Chris and I laughed over your working for L-G's Government, "that beastly little man"'.[46]

Asquith brought his customary ability and diligence to his new job, which involved the re-training of demobilised officers and men to enable them to rejoin their broken careers. Training grants were awarded to over 20,000 applicants, totalling over two million pounds Sterling at 1920 prices. RC Nesbit, writing from Switzerland after seeing Asquith's obituary in *The Times*, and who worked with him from the outset on this project, wrote:

> . . . without the steady judgment and the sympathetic handling of the scheme by Arthur Asquith, the results obtained would have been far different [worse]. Little has been said or heard of this valuable piece of post-War reconstruction work in which Brigadier General Asquith, working as a civil servant, took so large a part, and he would himself say nothing. It deserved well of the nation; its results are still visible, and I feel it should not be lost sight of.[47]

He still kept in touch with his old friends: Cardy Montagu and he attended Mark Egerton's wedding, after which Montagu wrote to McCracken with Asquith's address, concluding, 'he works like a slave at the Ministry of Labour on demobilisation'.[48] He stayed in this post until March 1920; Asquith himself was demobilised on 25 May 1920, and allowed to keep the rank of Brigadier General. He had been a sailor in khaki for five and a half years, risen from Temporary Sub Lieutenant to Brigadier in just over three years, and was 34 on promotion. Now a married man with one leg, and still only 37, he had to decide on his future direction.

NOTES

1. Letter from Patrick Shaw Stewart, dated 13 November, quoted in Ronald Knox, p203.
2. Note in AMA's personal record, ref RND/93 19, dated 28 November 1917.
3. Transcript of remarks from a file, not in Asquith's hand, headed A/Commander A M Asquith DSO. Recommendations to 2nd Army, dated 8 November 1917. Someone in the Brigade Office appears to have copied out these recommendations and given the copy to Asquith, AMA papers.
4. *Lady Cynthia Asquith, Diaries 1915-1918*, entry for Saturday 15 December 1917, p380.
5. Letter from Betty Manners to AMA dated 11 December 1917, AMA papers.
6. Jerrold, *The Royal Naval Division*, p266.
7. Letter from Betty Manners to AMA dated 15 December 1917, AMA papers.
8. Letter from AMA to his father dated 11 December 1917, AMA papers.
9. Confidential Memorandum from 63rd (RN) Division No. 1334/71/2/A, to Headquarters 1 80th Infantry Brigade, dated 15 December 1917, and memo from 189th Brigade to AMA, no. BM 2/477, of same date, AMA papers.
10. Note from OC Hood Battalion to HQ 189th Infantry Brigade, dated 15 December 1917, at 7.45pm. AMA Notebook No. 26, AMA papers.
11. Secret Order No. G1001/3 from HQ 63rd Division to 188th, 189th, and 190th Infantry Brigades, dated 15 December 1917, PRO Kew, Box WO 095/3095, Appendix 34 to 63rd Division War Diary.
12. ibid, para 6.
13. War Diary of the 189th Brigade entry for 20 December 1917, PRO Kew, Box WO 095/3112.
14. ibid.
15. Intelligence Summary No. 4, marked 'Secret', from 10am 19 December to 10am 20 December 1917, Appendix to the War Diary of the 63rd (RN) Division, PRO Kew, WO 095/3095.
16. As for Note 12 above, but Summary No. 5 from 10am 20 December to 10am 21 December 1917, PRO Kew, WO 095/3095.
17. Letter from AMA to his father, from Lady Murray's Hospital, No. 10 B.R.C., Le Treport, France, dated 22 December 1917, AMA papers.
18. ibid.
19. ibid.
20. Govt Despatch No 237, dated 23 December 1917, from Asquith's Record of Service.
21. Asquith's Record of Service note: 'Tel GHQ', dated 31 December 1917.
22. Letter from Surgeon W McCracken to AMA dated 23 December 1917, AMA papers.
23. Letter from AMA to his father, from Lady Murray's Hospital, dated 30 December 1917, AMA papers.
24. ibid.
25. Letter from Surgeon McCracken to AMA dated 31 December 1917, AMA papers. Lieutenant Commander Alan Campbell, son of the actress, Mrs Patrick Campbell, was also among the many killed in this action; he and Commander West DSO, commanding Howe Battalion, were killed by the same shell which burst outside their Battalion HQ.
26. Letter from AMA to Diana Cooper dated 6 January 1918, AD MSS 70704.
27. Letter from General Neill Malcolm to AMA dated 25 January 1918, AMA papers.

28. Letter from General Gough to AMA dated 25 January 1918, AMA papers.
29. Letter from AMA to Surgeon McCracken dated 7 February 1918, McCracken papers, IWM, Department of Documents.
30. ibid.
31. Asquith's Record of Service, manuscript entry dated 28 February 1918, authority C.W.2051 1.8/20.
32. ibid.
33. Letter from Mrs Christine Hamlyn to AMA dated 27 April 1918, AMA papers.
34. Letter from General Sir Ian Hamilton to AMA, dated 27 March 1918, AMA papers.
35. Letter from Winston Churchill to AMA dated 27 March 1918, AMA papers. Churchill, despite his disagreements with Herbert Asquith Snr, had a high regard for Arthur, and was careful to point out that the post would be kept for him until he achieved full fitness. He added that the Prime Minister, Lloyd George, 'expressed great pleasure . . . [on] the proposed appointment'.
36. Letter from AMA to his father, incorrectly dated 30 May 1918, it was written on 30 March, in the possession of Mrs Susan Boothby, one of Asquith's four daughters. The reference to the twins is about Aunt Christine's concern for her two nieces, Betty and Angela. Betty was the elder by a short time.
37. Letter from HH Asquith to AMA dated 1 April 1918, AMA papers.
38. Manuscript note in Asquith's Service Record.
39. Letter from Bernard Freyberg to AMA dated 31 March 1918, AMA papers.
40. Letter from Bernard Freyberg to AMA dated 24 April 1918, AMA papers.
41. Letter from Petty Officer W Fairburn to AMA undated, postmarked 28 April 1918, AMA papers.
42. Note in Asquith's Record of Service ref RND/10055.
43. Letter from The Admiralty, ref CW dated 5 September 1918, signed by Charles Walker, AMA papers.
44. From Asquith's Record of Service, Naval Historical Branch, Ministry of Defence.
45. Asquith's Record of Service, ref CW 369971, '1/19 Allowed to take up appt under Ministry of Labour'. Also ref RND/9852.
46. Letter from Betty Asquith to AMA, undated, AMA papers.
47. Letter to *The Times*, from R C Nesbit, from Grindelwald, dated 1 September 1939, entitled 'A Further Tribute'.
48. Letter from the Hon. L Montagu to Dr McCracken, McCracken Papers, Department of Documents at the IWM.

CHAPTER XIV
Back to Civilian Life

Asquith was among those who attended the ceremony on Horse Guards Parade to mark the disbandment of the Royal Naval Division on 6 June 1919. The Prince of Wales inspected the troops and gave the valedictory address. In a special reference to Freyberg and Asquith, the Prince mentioned that:

> There are few here today of those to whom the King bade farewell in February 1915. Some who were then Lieutenants have risen to be Generals and have gained the highest honours for actions of valour and skill.[1]

Alongside Asquith near the saluting point were Lord Fisher, Lord Beresford, Mr and Mrs Churchill, Sir Arthur Wilson, and Members of the Army Council. The four remaining Naval Battalions on parade were Hood, commanded by Commander H B Pollock DSO, who also commanded the Parade; Drake, Commander Beak VC DSO; Hawke, Commander Shelton DSO; and Anson under Commander Buckle DSO.[2]

In spite of their official disbandment, the RND continued in spirit for many years after. There were the usual reunions, notably the annual dinners organised by the Royal Naval Division Officers Association. At the first occasion, in January 1920, held at the Hotel Great Central, Major General Sir David Mercer, formerly a Brigade Commander in Gallipoli, presided. Winston Churchill was the speaker. In 1928 Arthur Asquith was himself the Chairman. The dinners took place until 1976 every year except for those of the Second World War: speeches were of a high order; A P Herbert often attended and treated the company to his 'incomparable wit and oratory'.[3] Brigadier Basil Rackham chaired the last ten functions: on the last occasion only eight former members of the Division were able to attend.[4]

Immediately after the war the survivors and relatives of the Division set in hand the raising of money to erect a memorial to their dead: it is not well known that over forty per cent of the total Royal Navy casualties in the First World War were suffered not at sea, but on the battlefields of Gallipoli, Salonika, France, and Belgium by the Royal Naval Division. Total casualties of the Division, including those from their Army units, totalled nearly 45,000. More Royal Navy personnel were killed and wounded in action in the RND than in the sea-going arm of the Service. Sir Edwin Lutyens was commissioned to design a magnificent memorial at a cost of about £3,000: the outcome was an elegant obelisk mounted on a plinth on which are engraved the badges of the units which served in the Division, and where they fought. Towards the base of the obelisk is a circular lead-lined dish which forms a reservoir for streams of water from the four lions' mouths mounted above, so that water cascades over the lip of the dish forming a glittering cylinder, which catches the light in a scintillating way. A quotation from Rupert Brooke, 'Blow out ye bugles . . . ,' on one of the memorial sides, reminds the passer-by of the loss of one of England's most brilliant poets, and at the same time calls attention to the sacrifice of thousands of his lesser-known comrades. On the tenth anniversary of the Gallipoli landings, 25 April 1925, the RND Memorial was unveiled by Sir Archibald Paris, the first Divisional Commander. The Division's creator, Winston Churchill, gave the address, replete with the phrases of ringing oratory which were his trademark. The Memorial stood as part of the balustrade at the south-west corner of the Old Admiralty Building overlooking Horseguards Parade until 1939, when it was decided to dismantle it so that the Citadel could be built, and the RND Memorial was put into storage for the duration. After the Second War, the monument was re-erected within the grounds of the Royal Naval College at Greenwich, and accepted into the care of the Royal Navy by the then Second Sea Lord, Sir Alec Madden, at the unveiling ceremony in 1951. This location proved ideal for the various reunions and commemorative services of the Royal Naval Division, organised by the RND Association, despite the fact that its situation, in a secluded backwater of the College, did not meet the intentions of those who commissioned it, that it should be in a very prominent and public place. The last gathering of the survivors of the RND took place at the Royal Naval College in 1981.

Recently, however, the Navy Board has decided to vacate Christopher Wren's historic site, and Greenwich has passed out of naval control. Under these circumstances, many consider that the memorial should be restored to a place as near its original site as possible, so that it might again be enjoyed by the public as the fine work of art that it is, and as a reminder of the sacrifice of those it commemorates. The maintenance of the RND Memorial in London, and one in France, erected by the generous support of Lord Rothermere, whose son, Vere Harmsworth, was killed in action on 13 November 1916, was taken care of by a trust fund, of which Arthur Asquith was the first Chairman. The Trust is still in existence, in the safe hands of the Commandant General Royal Marines, although the income is now so small to be sufficient only for the provision of wreaths for services, and for basic repairs to the obelisk at Beaucourt, where Freyberg won his VC.

As a further step to ensure that the memory of the Division was not allowed to die, the journalist and author Douglas Jerrold was 'asked and entrusted [by Asquith] with the task of writing the Naval Division's history' as soon as the war was over. Jerrold was a popular member of Hawke Battalion: he had been severely wounded during the action north of the Ancre in November 1916, losing an arm. *The Royal Naval Division* was published in 1923: Jerrold not only had extensive access to all unit records, but, in the course of his research, interviewed and corresponded with hundreds of those who had served. Asquith read the 'whole of the typescript and spared himself neither the time nor the truth in improving it out of all recognition'.[6] There is no vainglory or triumphalism in the work: the people about whom Jerrold writes are not supermen, but a cross section of British society who were thrown together in a mighty and lethal enterprise. In the course of my research, I have found remarkably few errors of fact, and even fewer cases of the exaggerations that can sometimes understandably be found in other similar works. There is but one serious omission: the case of Sub Lieutenant Edwin Dyett of the Division, who was shot by firing squad having been convicted of cowardice by a court martial after the 1916 action on the Ancre. This story is sympathetically and movingly told by Sellers.[7] 1923 was too soon after the event for the wounds to be re-opened, nor were the relevant documents available even if the historians had been minded to tell the tale.

Part of Asquith's contribution was to draft for Winston Churchill the Introduction. A copy is in Arthur Asquith's papers at Clovelly, written in his customary precise and elegant style, and would serve as an excellent piece of work in its own right. However, Churchill's final offering, more flowery and evocative, stands out as a masterpiece of prose and acts as a perfect foil to the laconic understatement of Jerrold's text.

Asquith began to make a new life for himself as a businessman. Any ambition he may have harboured as a young man to 'get to the top' of the Establishment had largely been dissipated by his experiences in the war. All his post-war efforts were devoted to making a financially sound base for himself and his family. He seemed to realise that he had been through, and survived (just) an experience whose memory would never leave him, and that the days of taking personal risks were over, particularly in view of his increasing reponsibilities. In time he became a Director of the Westminster Bank, and several other financial institutions in the UK and abroad. In addition he maintained business interests in South America and the Sudan.[8] He spent much time travelling abroad on business. Following Herbert Asquith's shattering defeat in the 1924 election, which saw him unseated from his Paisley constituency by a Labour candidate, and the Liberal Party reduced to forty members led by Lloyd George, Arthur invited his father to accompany him on a visit to the Sudan via the Nile Valley.

Asquith, Betty and their four daughters lived in reasonable comfort, first in Upper Berkeley Street, and then in Sussex Square, London, although they spent as much of their free time as possible with Aunt Chris at Clovelly, or at Rottingdean, where the family rented the home of Roderick Jones, then the Head of Reuters. It was a source of amusement to Betty that Arthur, whose wartime exploits included reconnaissances in the most barren and featureless terrain, often in pitch dark, and bad visibility, had great difficulty finding his way around London. She joked with the girls that he 'couldn't find his way out of Sussex Square!'

In November 1936 the formidable Christine Hamlyn died at the age of 80. She had been widowed for over thirty years. Her husband, Frederick Gosling, had taken her name on marriage, and the couple had spent their combined wealth on restoring the village. They were childless, and, in her will, Christine Hamlyn left Clovelly Court, and the village of Clovelly, to her eldest niece, Betty, who inherited by virtue of being marginally older than her twin, Angela. The Asquith family continued to spend term time in London, and the holidays in the house they had always loved. Life carried on at Clovelly much as it had under Aunt Chris's regime, with large parties of mixed old and young during the summer. There was a thriving social life in the area, a legacy of the close circle of long-term friendships of Christine Hamlyn. The summers before WW2 were particularly notable for the plays, organised by Mary, the eldest daughter, and produced by Betty Stucley, whose family lived nearby at Hartland Abbey; these were large productions involving Mary's friends and people from the village.

Asquith rarely spoke of his wartime experiences, even to his closest family. However, he kept very close touch with his wartime companions. He was also in constant demand for references from his former sailors. One of his daughters recounts the tale of Able Seaman Smith, who had been with Asquith when he received his wound at Welsh Ridge: Smith was also severely wounded and lost his arm, and returned to the north-east to live. Many years later, he wrote to Asquith asking if he knew of any employment. Arthur wrote back offering him a job at Clovelly, and Smith and his family made the trip south. Even though he was guaranteed employment by Asquith, he initially took employment at a gravel pit, to show that he was determined to find a worthwhile job. He soon moved to the Estate, where he and his family settled.

James Hilton, MC and Bar, Asquith's former Adjutant in Hood battalion and assistant at the Ministry of Munitions, wrote enquiring after a job. He was very quickly recruited to be the Agent on the Estate, a job which he discharged with distinction for thirty years until his death in 1963. His grave in Clovelly bears the understated epitaph 'worthy of remembrance'.

The Asquith family friendship with the Freybergs was particularly warm and enduring. Bernard Freyberg was godfather to Asquith's eldest daughter, Mary, and Asquith was the godfather of Freyberg's son, Paul. Other family friends included the Jones, of Reuters, Oliver Lyttleton, L P Hartley, and the Frasers. They also kept in touch with the Churchills, and there is a story that, at a dinner party with them during one of the pre-war crises, Winston was speaking on the need 'to guarantee Polish territorial integrity by military means, if necessary'. Asquith's quiet and sceptical interjection reputedly made the great man ponder, so much so that Churchill invited Asquith to be one of his close advisers if he ever came into a position of power again. Unfortunately, Asquith was to die before this hypothesis could be tested.

Asquith's company interests continued to require him to travel frequently to South America and the Sudan, and his letters to Betty reveal that, while he enjoyed the experience of visiting new places, he seemed to miss his family more and more and his health deteriorated; from the last of his trips, in the spring of 1939, he returned unwell, and was too tired even to go with the girls to the cinema, which he loved. He had known for some time that he had cancer, although even his closest friends were unaware. He was diagnosed as having Hodgkin's disease, which is more common in younger people: nowadays sufferers have an excellent chance of being cured. Despite his illness, manifested by a slightly grey complexion, he was still well enough in July to swim and play tennis. In early August he suddenly relapsed, and was taken into the Middlesex Hospital for radium treatment. His daughter, Susan Boothby, recalls that she was shocked when she learned from Aunt Angela that her father's illness might be fatal this time. Even then, Asquith's natural optimism remained. Writing to Violet on the 10th, he expresses annoyance at being kept in hospital because of 'this infernal temperature. For the past days, regular as clockwork, it has been subnormal at 8 a.m., normal at tea-time, and 101 or 102 at 10 p.m. Then I take a Veganin or Phensic'. He bemoans the fact that he has to take a week away from Clovelly, and looks forward to seeing Violet and her family there in September.[9] Asquith was only in the Middlesex for about ten days. Shortly before his death, Susan visited him and noticed that he had cut himself slightly while shaving, and that the wound had not healed. It was then that she finally realised that her father had not long to live.

Arthur Asquith died early in the morning of 25 August 1939, and was buried at his beloved Clovelly. A plaque on the wall of the churchyard reads, 'Remember Arthur Asquith who loved and cared for Clovelly'. His grave is a bare patch of earth marked only by a blank wooden cross, and there is a memorial tablet in the church itself. A small building near Brownsham on the estate bears his initials and the date '1936'.

His step-mother, in a contribution to *The Times* obituary wrote: '. . . it was his high purpose, singleness of mind, freedom from self, and the example which he unconsciously set to everyone with whom he was acquainted which will be missed . . . I shall always be grateful that I was privileged to spend so many years of my life with someone of such a noble nature and rare understanding'.[10]

Two years before Asquith died, Douglas Jerrold wrote:

Arthur Asquith was the finest of all our amateur soldiers, and the most respected. He was from Winchester and New College but he had long ago escaped into the world and had no illusions about old school ties. His dominating gift was a quiet, patient and inquiring mind inspired by a profound humility to go on learning. Having known men and cities he had learnt a lot, but he came to us [the RND] with a mind still open to impressions. In the first two years of the war he had learnt more than some generals learn in a long professional career. His promotion to Brigadier in the autumn of 1917 was a generous admission of a professional competence which was certainly unrivalled among all the great civilian soldiers of the Great War. He had inherited, evidently, his father's gift of seeing through to the heart of a problem with a ruthless, if detached, logic, and unlike Lord Oxford, he came to the war with a body and mind still fresh and vigorous. He had a rigid economy of manner and expression and a genius for inspiring confidence, as much among the regular officers as ourselves. He had no need to advertise. He never employed a 'gesture'. He was irresistibly convincing – a born leader who was allowed to lead – the rarest event in war.[11]

A few days after Asquith died, and war had been declared against Germany, Violet wrote to her friend, Desmond MacCarthy, former editor of the *New Statesman*:

. . . Watching beloved Oc dying through those last 3 weeks and knowing oneself quite powerless to help or save him pain was unspeakable. I was thankful to be with him to the very end . . . I think he was one of the most perfectly and unselfconsciously <u>good</u> people I have ever known. His courage was cold courage. He <u>hated</u> fighting and never – even when he joined up – romanticized the War. I remember a talk with him and Rupert [Brooke] at Downing St one evening before they left – when Rupert said he had been born for this hour – to go and free Constantinople from the Turks etc – and Oc said very prosaically through his teeth that he just considered the whole thing 'a beastly duty'. But he made it more than that by his humanity – which gave him his great powers of leadership.[12]

In the *Daily Telegraph* and *Morning Post* of 29 May 1961, in an article about Rupert Brooke's burial, Lieutenant General Lord Freyberg VC DSO described the party of friends who had been at Skyros on that day. He included the following:

Arthur Asquith, third son of Mr Asquith (later Lord Oxford and Asquith) survived the War, but never fully recovered from his severe wounds and died on the eve of the Second World War. He was the bravest man I ever knew, and his war record was second to none.[13]

But perhaps the final word should go to Tom Braund, who, as a young man, helped Arthur to swim at Clovelly, taking him to the beach, and assisting him in and out of the water. To Tom, Asquith was 'a perfect gentleman'.[14]

NOTES

1. Cutting from *The Times* of 7 June 1919, in AMA papers.
2. This was a very high-calibre group of battalion commanders indeed: each of them was either mentioned in despatches, or given a more tangible award, practically every time he went into action.

   – D M W Beak was a truly heroic figure. A native of Salisbury he was promoted from Ordinary Seaman in May 1915, commissioned into Drake Battalion. He received the MC for gallantry during the battle of 13 November 1916, and a Bar at Gavrelle. As Commanding Officer of Drake, his courage and leadership of desperate rearguard actions during the early days of the retreat before the massive German onslaughts of March 1918 earned him the DSO. He was awarded the Victoria Cross for his brilliant work and valour over an extended period during the advance to victory in the last weeks of the war.

   – Commander H B Pollock, a Dubliner born in October 1883, joined Drake Battalion in October 1914. Before the RND saw action in a major engagement in France, he was wounded in the shoulder (July 1916) and was unable to return to the BEF until October 1917. He won the DSO with Hawke Battalion for conspicuous gallantry on Welsh Ridge at the end of that year. After taking command of Drake Battalion, he was severely gassed during the preliminary German bombardment before their March 1918 offensive, a misfortune which allowed Commander Beak's promotion. Pollock recovered by September 1918 to take command of Hood Battalion, winning a Bar to his DSO at the village of Niergnies, near Cambrai, the last major action of the RND in the war: he personally destroyed an enemy tank by using a captured enemy field gun.

   – Commander Robert Shelton, of Notting Hill, born in September 1882, was promoted from acting Leading Seaman in the London RNVR in October 1914. He was awarded the DSO for gallantry as a Lieutenant Commander in Hawke Battalion in the action north of the Ancre in early 1917. He was severely gassed at Ypres in November, but returned by the end of the war to command first Anson, then Hawke Battalion.

   The last Battalion Commander, Commander Archibald Walter Buckle, was an amazing man. As were so many RND heroes, he was promoted from the ranks: another former member of the London RNVR, his career was good rather than exceptional until he took over Anson Battalion at Welsh Ridge in December 1917. In a period of just over nine months from then, he won the DSO and three Bars, one for each time his Battalion was in major action. His final DSO, at Niergnies, was gained when he personally put out of action a German tank with a captured anti-tank rifle. During this battle he was shot in the shoulder. All four officers were demobilised in June 1919. Beak went on to rise to the rank of Major General in the Second World War.

3. Letter from Brigadier B B Rackham CBE MC, the last Chairman of the Royal Naval Division Officers Association, in a letter entitled 'Recapitulation' sent to all remaining members, dated May 1979. Letter in file C551591/10, in the archives of the Royal Naval College, Greenwich.

4. Rackham was another fascinating character: promoted from Able Seaman early in the war, he was wounded twice, and on both occasions remained at duty. He was awarded the MC early in 1917 for conspicuous gallantry and devotion to duty. Later, during the great German attack, he earned a Bar to his decoration for gallantry and great bravery, although gassed: in this latter instance he had to be ordered to hospital after his Battalion had held up the enemy advance. He finished the War as Adjutant to Hawke Battalion. Demobilised in 1919, he rose to the rank of Brigadier in WW2.

5. Letter from Douglas Jerrold to Betty Asquith, 27 August 1939, AMA papers.

6. ibid.

7. *For God's Sake, Shoot Straight*, by Len Sellers, Leo Cooper, 1996.

8. Besides the Westminster Bank, Asquith's business interests included:
Membership of the Sudan Plantation Syndicate
Chairman of the Kassala Cotton Company
Chairman of the Parana Pine Plantations
The Rio de Janiero Improvements Company
Sao Paulo (Brazil) Railway Company
The Government and General Investment Group
The Underground Electric Railway of London
The Ocean Accident and Guarantee Corporation, and
The National Discount Group.

9. Letter from AMA to Violet Bonham Carter, 10 August 1939, VBC MSS 0034/021.

10. Part of the obituary in *The Times*, dated 26 August 1939.

11. *Georgian Adventure*, by Douglas Jerrold, pp201 and 202, Wm Collins, 1937.

12. Letter from Violet Bonham Carter to Desmond MacCarthy, 8 September 1939, quoted in *Champion Redoubtable*.

13 From *The Daily Telegraph* and *Morning Post*, 21 May 1961.

14. Discussion with the author, 16 April 1998.

Bibliography

I. UNPUBLISHED SOURCES

1. The Private Papers of Brigadier General AM Asquith DSO, and Mrs Elizabeth Asquith. The Private Papers of Lady Asquith of Yambury, formerly Violet Bonham Carter
2. Public Record Office
    WO 95/3112, 95/3114,95/3115, 95/3117,95/3119
    ADM 137/3064, 137/3088A
3. Imperial War Museum
    Macmillan Papers
    Archibald Paris Papers
4. Liddle Collection at Leeds University
    Bentham Papers
5. The Private Papers of Bernard Freyberg

II. PRINTED BOOKS

Asquith, Cynthia, *Haply I May Remember* (James Barrie, 1950), and *The Diaries of Lady Cynthia Asquith 1915-1918* (Hutchinson, 1968).

Asquith, Violet, *Churchill As I Knew Him* (Wm Collins, 1965).

Balfour-Paul, Glen, *The End of Empire in the Middle East* (CUP, 1991).

Bonham Carter, Mark, ed *The Autobiography of Margot Asquith* (Methuen, 1985).

Bonham Carter, Mark and Pottle, Mark, eds, *Lantern Slides, The Diaries and Letters of Violet Bonham Carter 1904-1914* (Weidenfeld & Nicolson, 1996), and *Champion Redoubtable, The Diaries and Letters of Violet Bonham Carter 1915-1945* (Weidenfeld & Nicolson, 1998).

Brock, Michael and Eleanor, eds, *Asquith's Letters to Venetia Stanley* (Oxford University Press, 1985).

Cornwallis West, G. *Edwardian Hey-Days* (Putnam, 1930).

Farrar-Hockley, Anthony, *Goughie* (Hart-Davis and MacGibbon, 1975).

Foster, Rev H.C., *At Antwerp and the Dardanelles* (Mills and Boon, 1918).

Freyberg, Paul, *Bernard Freyberg VC – Soldier of Two Nations* (Hodder & Stoughton 1991).

Gillon, Stair, *The Story of the 29th Division* (Nelson, 1925).

Hassall, Christopher, *Edward Marsh, A Biography* (Longmans, 1959).

Herbert, A.P., *A.P.H. – His Life and Times* (Heinemann, 1970).

Jenkins, Roy, *Asquith* (Wm Collins, paperback edition, 1988).

Jerrold, Douglas, *The Royal Naval Division* (Hutchinson, 1923), *The Hawke Battalion, Some Personal Records of Four Years 1914-1918* (Benn, 1925), and *Georgian Adventure* (Wm Collins, 1937).

Jolliffe, John, *Raymond Asquith Life and Letters* (Wm Collins, 1980).

Kingsmill, Hugh, *I was Captured at Beaucourt*, from the series, *Great War Adventures* (World's Work (1913) Ltd, 1932).

Knox, Ronald, *Patrick Shaw Stewart* (Collins, 1920).

Lambert, Angela, *The Unquiet Souls* (Macmillan, 1984).

Lloyd-Baker, Lieutenant Colonel A.B., *A Gloucestershire Diarist*, (Thornhill Press 1993).

Macdonald, Lyn, *1914* (Michael Joseph, 1987).

MacKenzie, Jeanne, *The Children of the Souls* (Chatto and Windus, 1986).

Macmillan, Thomas, and Fry, James. W. *The Complete History of the Royal Naval Division* (Alnwick, 1919).

Marsh, Edward, *A Number of People* (Heinemann and Hamilton, 1939).

Murray, Joseph, *Gallipoli As I Saw It* (Wm Kimber, 1965), and *Call to Arms: from Gallipoli to the Western Front* (Wm Kimber, 1980).

Nicholls, Jonathan, *Cheerful Sacrifice, The Battle of Arras* (Leo Cooper, 1990).

Ribblesdale, Lord, *Charles Lister – Letters and Recollections* (T. Fisher Unwin; 1917).

Roskill, Stephen, *Hankey: Man of Secrets* (Wm Collins, 1970).

Sellers, Leonard, *Hood Battalion* (Leo Cooper, 1992) and *For God's Sake, Shoot Straight* (Leo Cooper, 1995).

Spender J.A. and Asquith, Cyril., *The Life of Herbert Henry Asquith, Lord Oxford and Asquith* (2 vols. Hutchinson, 1932).

Steel, Nigel and Hart, Peter, *Defeat at Gallipoli* (Macmillan, 1994).

Verses, Letters, and Remembrances of Arthur Walderne St. Clair Tisdall V.C. (Sidgwick & Jackson, 1916).

Index